LOVING YOUR WAY TO ENLIGHTENMENT

Loving Your Way to *Enlightenment*

DR. MARC GAFNI

Collected by Chahat Corten

VENWOUDE ● *press*

© 2014 Chahat Corten
Venwoude Press, Lage Vuursche, The Netherlands

US V3: september 2014

Editorial work: Giselle Gouverne
Author photo cover: Jock Fistick
Production: Erik Kunst, MultiLibris, The Netherlands

ISBN: 978 15023 0514 5 (paperback US)
ISBN: 978 94 919460 6 6 (ebook)

The editor and publisher have made an effort to produce a reliable
publication. However, they cannot accept responsibility for any
inaccuracies.

Contents

Introduction by Chahat Corten – *7*

About Dr. Marc Gafni – *11*

About this book – *13*

Enlightenment – who cares?! – *15*

Introduction to the Five Awakenings – *45*

The First Awakening, to separate self – *49*

The Second Awakening, into True Self – *57*

The Third Awakening, to the Personal Face of God – *75*

The Awakening to the Beloved – *81*

The Awakening to the Mother – *97*

Turning back to the Mother – *115*

The Fourth Awakening, to Unique Self – *125*

The Fifth Awakening, awakening to Evolutionary Intimacy – *147*

Introduction to the Six Christmas Meditations − 173
First Christmas Meditation: The Path is the Goal − 175
Second Christmas Meditation: 'Here I Am' − 185
Third Christmas Meditation: God's Yearning for You − 195
Fourth Christmas Meditation: Stages of Evolution − 207
Fifth Christmas Meditation: A conversation with God − 223
Sixth Christmas Meditation: Being Love − 239

Loving Your Way to Enlightenment,
    an invitation to a new spiritual path − 255
Loving Outrageously − 263
Prayer and Communion − 277
The Secret of the Kiss − 285
A Prayer for Haiti − 305
Being a Home, Receiving a Home − 315
Love Before and after Creation − 333
The World is a Waiting Lover − 353
Writing Outrageous Love Letters − 397

Chahat about Venwoude and its founder Ted Wilson − 407
About Venwoude − 411
About the Center for Integral Wisdom − 413
Acknowledgement − 415

Introduction by Chahat Corten

When Dr Marc Gafni first visited Venwoude in 2011, he immediately acknowledged the depth and sacred nature of the place, infused by years of intentional community spiritual work. This marked the beginning of an ongoing love affair between a remarkable American teacher and a remarkable intentional community in The Netherlands. As is the case in true love affairs, both partners felt deeply inspired by each other's soul, while at the same time feeling deeply appreciated for who they are - hence allowing for a synergy that enriches both.

I remember Marc saying about Venwoude, at his first visit: "There are few places in the world where sacred teachings are held. I don't know many places where people have dedicated themselves in such depth, and especially over such a long time, to heart-based community living, personal growth, relationships, sexuality and intimacy, encouraging and inviting large groups of people to get in touch with the greatness of who they truly are."

I believe that those who know Venwoude in any depth are likely to agree with him wholeheartedly.

Had they been able to meet on this plane, Dr. Marc Gafni and Ted Wilson, the founder of Venwoude, would certainly have enjoyed, challenged and admired each other's scope of vision, wisdom, brilliant minds, charisma, total commitment, sense of humor and big heart. Both share the capacity to invite you to step over many thresholds and no one is ever left untouched by their lively presence.

Meeting Dr. Marc Gafni

When I met Marc Gafni in November 2011 at Venwoude a new layer of love opened up within me.
It was while receiving his first teaching/transmission that I experienced how, his dharma, vision and heart matched the depth of my own practice, experience and heart, and how they were of the same substance. Through my tears there was only one joyful word welling up from my heart: YES!!

What I soon came to realize, was that Marc Gafni is a postmodern teacher of ancient wisdom, whose devotion, wisdom, love, humor, brilliance and unique intimate way of transmitting wisdom from ancient sacred texts allows for a most uncommon accessibility of the deep wisdom embedded in these texts. For me, as a living, breathing western soul, these revelations are already in my knowing, in my roots and DNA, only awaiting to be expressed. It is hard to describe the ecstatic joy and recognition that bursts from me when Marc teaches

His transmission allowed me to access a realization of Truth that had been unfolding and deepening in me for years, in a new, most tender and intimate way. As one of Marc's teachers would say… 'embodied in my toenails'.

Soon after, we decided to start having monthly Skype sessions with The Circle of Venwoude', a group of dedicated practitioners, as an experiment. Little did we know about the deep ways in which the Dharma would unfold… Many of these gatherings allowed for pure Grace to pour down on us!

'Loving your way to Enlightenment' are the edited transcripts of the first two years of teaching. Marc Gafni is still deepening and unfolding this Dharma on Loving your Way to Enlightenment as a new Spiritual Path in many ways!

I am deeply appreciative of the ways in which Dr. Marc Gafni and his inspiring teachings on Evolutionary Love, Unique Self, Outrageous Love and Outrageous Pain, have also brought Venwoude to a new phase of unfolding, in full alignment with Venwoude's tradition of renewal, allowing for this great experiment to remain alive and kicking.

I have a profound gratitude for existence's wondrous unfoldings, that have once more brought such a gift to Venwoude in the person of Marc Gafni. Through him, I was offered again the great gift of commitment to a teacher, a true friend and an inspiring and passionate collaborator.

I also want to express my deep appreciation to each and every member of the Circle, for the deep and audacious ways in which they have opened to Love and to fully receiving Marcs' teaching ,allowing for all of us to support and hold the beautiful unfolding of this Dharma.

May Marc's teachings open your mind, body and heart as deep and profound as I know they can!

OLATT,
(*Outrageous Love all the time*)

Chahat Corten,
Venwoude, spring 2014

About Dr. Marc Gafni

*D*r. *Marc Gafni* is considered by many to be one of the great spiritual teachers of our postmodern generation. His teachings on Unique Self, World Spirituality, the democratization of Enlightenment, conscious Eros, outrageous love, a politics of love and much more, are awakening hearts and minds all over the world. Marc is known as an audacious, brilliant, funny, deeply caring, radically loving and very human being.

He is the co-initiator (with Ken Wilber) and leading teacher of the Center for Integral Wisdom, which he founded with Mariana Caplan and Sally Kempton. Since 2011, he is closely connected to Venwoude, Holland, which he regularly visits as our World Spirituality teacher-in-residence.

About this book

*P*art I of this book was mostly taken from Dr. Marc Gafni's opening and closing speeches at the online Enlightenment Conference 2012, by way of an introduction into the three main themes of this book: Integral Enlightenment, Enlightenment as an expanding of one's Love Circle, and the emergence of Unique Self.

Part II and III consist of edited transcripts of a series of teachings and guided meditations, in 2011-2012 given in the form of Skype conversations to 'The Circle', an ongoing Venwoude study group initiated by Ted Wilson and now led by Chahat Corten.

Enlightenment – who cares?!

Why talk about Enlightenment? *Who cares?* That is the first question, really. Don't we have something a little more interesting, pressing, compelling and relevant to talk about? This is the 21ˢᵗ century and there are major issues facing the world. We are pressed by rogue nuclear activity, world hunger, homelessness, any number of tragic regional conflicts, the environment. We struggle with climate change and try to understand how to chart the next stage of the Earth's future, such that we will have the resources to survive there.

And although we only can survive if we start cooperating, we're part of a world in which about 70% of the population still lives in an ethnocentric context, under an exclusive, ethnocentric spiritual view, which says: "My God is right and your God is wrong. I'm superior to you. I don't owe you the same level of human affection, love and rights that I owe my own people."

These are all serious issues, so why speak of Enlightenment?

When I talked to a potential publisher about my book 'Your Unique Self: The Radical Path to Personal Enlightenment', I was told: "Okay, the term 'Unique Self' is great. People like to talk about their unique selves. However, don't put 'Enlightenment' in the title, that will lose you 3/4 of your readership. Enlightenment is just a fringe issue for fringe people. In the *real* world — corporate, consulting, education, psychology, politics — nobody talks about Enlightenment. It's just not relevant. It's kind of weird."

Enlightenment is sanity

So let's have a look at how weird Enlightenment really is. Enlightenment basically means that I realize that the essence of who I am is not a separate self, but a 'True Self'. The True Self of the All that lives in me and through me. There is no part of me that is separate from others, I am not separate from Nature, I am not separate from Source. Separation is an illusion, and if I can pierce the veil of that illusion and realize my oneness with All-that-is, I will have achieved enlightened consciousness. I will have realized my True Nature. This is basic Enlightenment teaching.

Now if I tell you that I am Bill instead of Marc, at first you may well think I'm being funny. If I insist that I'm really Bill, not Marc, you will conclude that I am insane, since I do not know who I am. However, the Belief That I Am Bill is just a minor epistemological mistake compared to the mistake of believing that I am merely a separate self, not an intrinsic part of the seamless coat of the Universe, of All-that-is, living and breathing in me, as me. That mistake, the belief that I am a skin-encapsulated ego, merely a separate self, is utterly, totally and radically insane, much more so than this minor confusion of me thinking that I am Bill.

Normal consciousness, ego consciousness, is the real insanity. How many children went unnourished today? About 20 million; that is how many died last year. Is there food available in the world to feed every single one of those 20 million children? Absolutely. The food thrown out in the Western world could feed an entire underprivileged one. Is that not insanity? Normal consciousness is that I am I, you are you, and we are all separate. That is utterly insane. Normal consciousness produces what Buddhists call 'dukkha', suffering. We live in a world of outrageous suffering, a world of intense brutality and pain, unimaginable, unbearable pain. And so, normal consciousness is insane, it is not knowing your true nature. Enlightenment is knowing your True Nature, and is sanity.

If I achieve Enlightened consciousness, if I realize that we are all part of the One, of True Self, and that the total number of True Selves of the world is One, then I'm not going to be grasping for what is yours anymore, I'm not going to hurt Joe, because he is me, I am him and we are part of the same True Self. So, in other words, I have compassion, I have love, I care for others and for the environment. With enlightened consciousness, the whole game changes, because I can access love and compassion for the All, the All is part of me and I am part of the All. That is a very big deal. So, again, why does no one care?

Enlightenment — eternal or evolving?

The first question was whether Enlightenment is relevant to the 21st century. A second question is: Is Enlightenment a timeless, eternal category, or is it something that is evolving, like everything else? Is there something emergent in the world of Enlightenment? Is the nature of Enlightenment itself changing? I think it is. I think it is changing in two important ways, and I will come back to that, but first, let's explore Enlightenment a little further.

Enlightenment as falling in love

Enlightenment as a widening of our sense of identity

What is Enlightenment in practice? In one word, Enlightenment is a self-realization — I realize something, in a felt, embodied, heart, cognitive sense, in my consciousness. Your actual consciousness shifts — you actually *experience* that you are no longer identified by a separate self. I am no longer only my personal identity, I am not only Marc Gafni. I am *also* Marc Gafni — that is true, that is my personal identity — but I have evolved beyond that limitation. I actually experience myself as being part of a larger context, not merely as a concept, but as a felt-sense experience. That is a radical shift, a self-shift in identity in which I am no longer merely a skin-encapsulated ego, but actually part of a larger context of identity. That is powerful.

To try and understand what that means, imagine the experience of falling in love. What is that? It is precisely the experience of, "Wow! A week ago, I didn't know this person, and now I know this person, and now my whole sense of being alive has shifted, because my sense of identity has expanded to include this new person." That's a big deal.

Now, tragically, we have exiled 'falling in love' to a particular, narrow, romantic-sexual context. So people fall in love, then they fall out of love, and their experience is, "Wow, this didn't work," and they leave the context. They fall in love again, they fall out of love again, and lots of people spend their entire life trying to fall in love and to stay in love. There's a lot to be said about love relationships, but for now, let's expand love. Because love is not just about falling in love with one person, at one particular moment, and then trying to maintain that initial experience forever.

Love as perception, the ability to *see* the other

Love is a perception of the nature of reality, the inner fabric of the Cosmos. In the inter-subjective context, between people, love is a perception, not an emotion. Love is a perception that *creates* an emotion. Love is the ability to see. That's why we call dating 'seeing someone'. If we expand it beyond dating, it is about seeing someone in the broadest sense. When the great traditions talk of 'Love your neighbor as yourself,' they don't say, "Love your girlfriend as yourself." They never actually talk about loving your significant other, girlfriend or boyfriend, or mother or father. Love is about a perception in which I realize the infinite gorgeousness and beauty of the other, in which I realize that we are not separate, that together we are part of a larger context. Then we become inseparable.

Enlightenment as In-love-ment

When you fall in love with someone, you feel as if you have always known them and couldn't live without them. Now imagine expanding that experience beyond the one special relationship, which is really an egoistic fixation, and actually being able to fall in love in this much larger, bigger, deeper way, with the many, many people you meet, without engaging with them romantically or sexually. Let's split love from the romantic/sexual context. Falling in love means realizing that I am not separate from you, that we are both not merely apart and separate, but part of a larger, shared context. For me to hurt you, is to hurt myself. There is actually no distinction between the two. I am actually in love with you — when you are hurt, I am devastated.

Imagine a world in which love actually became the awakened, evolutionary Eros that it truly is. I fall in love with the people in my personal circle, the people I work with, the people I meet. I begin to fall in love with everyone, and then we begin to actually experience ourselves as interpenetrated, intermixed, inter-textured. First it's love between me and you, then I expand my love to include family and friends, next, it's 'my people' in a larger, ethnocentric context, then I expand my love to include all human beings on the planet in a world-centric context, and finally I expand it to include all sentient beings that ever were or will be, taking an awakened, evolutionary perspective in a Cosmos-centric context.

That is the expansion of my circle of love, which is the expansion of my Enlightenment. Love always implies a shift in perception, a shift in self-perception in relationship to others.

Enlightenment is like love, it's an expression of love, it's falling in love with reality. In the great traditions, the concepts of love and light are too often used interchangeably, because they possess the same quality. At their core, En-lighten-ment and In-love-ment really are the same thing. It really is about loving your way to En-lightenment. Instead of working harder to meditate better, it is a shift in love, which is a shift in my identity, in my essential self-perception, and that shifts my relationship to others — to Nature, to the Divine, to everything. Being in love, living as love, is the one change that changes everything. Enlightenment is the awakening to love, to being part of a larger context, not separate from others. And that changes my entire experience of being alive.

My Enlightenment moves and expands and evolves from my own waking up into awakening as God's eyes, letting God see through my eyes. To love God means to let God see through your eyes; it's a shift in perspective. And it is precisely this shift in perspective that makes Enlightenment so important, even critical, for human life on Earth today. Because all of the world issues – our economic, social, psychological, military and environmental issues — completely shift when we approach them from an enlightened perspective.

The democratization of Enlightenment

When Enlightenment becomes a genuine, common experience, beyond the elite, beyond the back streets of Jerusalem or the caves of the Himalayas, and is seen as an actual property of consciousness, an emergent meme of consciousness, part of the serious, mainstream conversation, what William James called 'a genuine option', then we can begin to talk about true democratization. Not just the democratization of political power, which was the new meme in the 18th century, but the democratization of greatness, or the democratization of Enlightenment. The democratization of Enlightenment means that everyone in their own way awakens to the true nature of their reality, and experiences themselves genuinely as part of the larger context, which keeps expanding.

We begin to reach a tipping point in society when we begin to understand the necessity of the democratization of Enlightenment. When Enlightenment begins to become a genuine option in the discourse, there is a shift in the way every one of our issues is approached. That is what Einstein meant when he said: "Problems that are created at one level of consciousness can only be solved at a higher level of consciousness." The problems that we have created by an un-enlightened, narcissistic, narrow-minded, hypersensitive, small-self-involved, contracted, en-coiled sense of being, can only be uncoiled, solved, re-solved and evolved at a higher level of consciousness.

When we awaken to love, when we let ourselves be lived as the living, loving Love — Intelligence and Love-Beauty that is awake in us, then our perception and experience of life itself shift. Then we have a gorgeous, living, felt sense of being part of the larger context and get the passion to heal ourselves and the world, and to celebrate life.

That's why Enlightenment matters so much, why it is so critical. The whole impulse towards Enlightenment is motivated by a deeper, higher vocation and calling that is part of the answer to all of our issues. It is the unfinished dream of humanity that we are trying to evolve and play and co-create together at this moment in history.

The problem with classical Enlightenment

Why is Enlightenment still a fringe concept?

The Enlightenment teaching is the best perennial understanding of the interior face of the Cosmos, of the nature of inner reality, which has been arrived at by repeated spiritual experimentation all across the world. We have gathered the results of all those experiments in the last 50-60 years, harvesting thousands of years of human spiritual insight, coming from the deepest understanding of the greatest and most subtle, open-hearted minds of all the great thinkers and spiritual traditions throughout the ages.

Their basic, shared understanding used to be called the perennial philosophy. The perennial philosophers were beyond interfaith in their thinking, beyond 'let's all just respect each other'; the perennial philosophy said: 'Let's have a shared framework of meaning', which is just what we need so direly today. The only problem with the perennial philosophy is that this shared framework comes from all the great religions, and the great religions were all formed before 1700, give or take, in pre-modernity; in a world that was xenophobic, ethnocentric, homophobic, anti-feminine, anti-sexuality, etcetera, so their realizations are all filtered through those prisms.

Still, if the Enlightenment teaching reflects the best perennial understanding of the interior face of the Cosmos, not just as a casual, passing fancy or poetic flight, but as the deepest result of our most rigorous spiritual experiments, conducted independently in double-blind conditions for thousands of years by the leading spiritual practitioners and experts around the world, then why don't people care about it more? Do we have bad marketing? Maybe the enlightened people don't know how to use social media well? Maybe if they got a Twitter account it would work better? If this is the change that changes everything and we can market things like bubble gum, then why can't we share this incredibly compelling, important, critical insight that we all need to understand and make part of our lives in order to change the whole game? What's the problem? Why is the concept of Enlightenment still so fringe? Why is it so periphery to contemporary mainstream consciousness?

Here we need to understand that the concept of Enlightenment itself needs to be evolved. The reason that Enlightenment hasn't entered mainstream consciousness is not merely because the ego is very clever. Our spiritual teachers have told us that Enlightenment takes enormous effort, and that people don't want to die to their separate self. Those things are true, but those things blame the world.

There is some deep, inherent problem in the classical understanding of Enlightenment itself, which, especially in our contemporary Western world, prevents people from engaging in Enlightenment with the passion, seriousness and depth that it deserves. We need to look at the flaws in our understanding of Enlightenment, and to evolve and correct them, and then we can bring Enlightenment back into the conversation and let it have the transformative effect that we desperately need it to have, and that it will have.

The problem with impersonal Enlightenment & impersonal evolutionary spirituality

The problem with the classical understanding of Enlightenment is that most teachers teach that it is about a movement from the personal self to the impersonal self. The personal self is understood as personality, ego, separate self; the words 'personal' and 'separate' are used as synonyms. The goal of Enlightenment is understood to evolve beyond ego, beyond separate self, beyond the personality and the personal, in order to be able to identify with the impersonal.

And the impersonal is understood to be one of two things:

1   In classical Eastern Advaita and some Western mystical Enlightenment teachings, the impersonal is understood to be the eternal Ground of Being: Sunyata, the Essence, the Ground that lies beneath it all, your original face before your mother and father were born. In Buddhism, it is Nirvana, emptiness; in Hinduism it is the Atman, Brahman, 'Tat Tvam Asi' or 'Thou

Art That'; in Kabbalah it is the Ayin. In this understanding of the move from personal to impersonal, you are no longer this separate self, this 'you', you are part of this timeless time, this placeless place, unchanging and eternal, in which you can rest.

2   According to Western, evolutionary spirituality, influenced by philosophers like Fichte, Schelling and Hegel, you are part of the impersonal, evolutionary, historic, cosmic process, and to the extent that you serve this great unfolding and impersonal process, you are valuable. To the extent that you don't, you are obviously much less valuable, if at all. So you need to move beyond playing this small, personal, separate-self game, and play in this larger context of this great evolutionary process.

That is the basic, classical understanding of Enlightenment and of evolutionary spirituality: the move from personal to impersonal, with the two understandings of impersonal just outlined.

'What about *me*?'

Now let's track down the problem, which is huge. If you are listening to your body right now, your body is screaming out the problem, your heart is crying it out, even before your mind can actually articulate it. What is it? The problem is: What about *me*? Hello?! I'm kind of enjoying being myself, I'm enjoying being John, or Mary, or Marc. Okay, there are some problems involved, I've got some issues, I've got my therapist trying to work it through, I'm studying Spiral Dynamics, I'm doing my coaching, I'm leading the World Spirituality movement. But I *like* being me. If I'm not me, then who am I? Being part of an impersonal, evolutionary process is great — it's a larger context and a larger game — but where did *I* disappear to? It's great to be part of the Ground of Being, that's beautiful and comforting, but what about *me*?

This deep, felt sense of 'what about me?' is interpreted by most Enlightenment teachers to be that hysterical craving of the ego, the small self, which you're supposed to somehow get rid of. Your small self, your ego, is personal; it wants to hold on to itself, it doesn't want to let go. So it desperately clings to its small-self-identity and refuses to let go. But if you, as the Zen masters say, 'die on the cushion', you will evolve into this higher level of consciousness, into an identification with the impersonal, with the eternal Ground of Being, or with the impersonal, evolutionary process.

That's how the classical Enlightenment teachers explain our clinging to our ego. Are they right? Of course they are! But only partially so. Our good friend Ken Wilber has this saying which I love: "No one is smart enough to be entirely wrong." Meaning, of course, that it's true, but only partially. And in its claiming to be the whole story, instead of just a part of it, the entire Enlightenment concept gets erased and becomes irrelevant for mainstream consciousness and culture. Let me explain why.

People have an intuitive, core and correct sense that their personal self is not irrelevant. Yes, we need to evolve to play a larger game. Yes, I understand that I am part of, and not apart from, the larger whole and the larger context. Yes, I want to awaken as love and be lived as love, *but I don't want to disappear into the impersonal.* So I'm told to sit on the meditation cushion, work with my ego, and get over it. In one way or the other, the summation of all these teachings on your relationship to the personal is: "Get over it." And that's not right. Because our very essence cries out and says, "No! No, no, no! I feel I'm special, I'm unique." Then we open 'A Course In Miracles', an example of classical Enlightenment teaching, and we read: "You're not special." That's a major theme in 'A Course In Miracles': if you think you are special, that's a function of ego. So then we get confused again. "What do you mean? I guess I'm not special after all."

Special versus unique; ego versus Unique Self

In classical Enlightenment teaching, there is a complete failure to make a distinction between unique and special at the level of ego on the one hand, and a higher uniqueness, a higher sense of the personal on the other. When you enter enlightened consciousness, through meditation and deep realization, through heart and mind analytics — heart math and mind math – then you realize in your holy, sacred, higher calculus that the personal is not just the narrow, contracted sense of egoic, separate self. That's one place where the personal appears, but the personal is also a quality of Essence itself. Your sense of being unique and special is not wrong. It is completely, utterly and absolutely correct.

The new, Integral Enlightenment of Unique Self

The old, classical Enlightenment: From personal to impersonal

If you map consciousness at a deeper level, what you realize is that at Level 1, you move from the pre-personal to the personal. That's your healthy individuation of the egoic, separate self, where you create your boundaries. Your natural first identity as a separate self, with your name, is established.

Then you awaken to Level 2, beyond separate self to the impersonal, to the Ground of Being that lives in you and as you. You realize that you are much larger. You have to play a larger game, you are living in a larger context — awakened as love. You are part of the eternal Ground of Being, of All-that-is — you are 'Being' itself. When you remove your name, personality, ego, property, possessions, all the externalities of your life, you are still there. You can access that as an awakened, first-person experience, enchanted in meditation. That is correct and deep. That is the second great awakening, which is classically termed 'Enlightenment.'

So the first level we call 'separate self' and the second level we call 'True Self.' True Self is impersonal beyond the merely personal. That's gorgeous, and necessary. You feel all of the power, all of the love, all of the All flowing through you, living in you and as you, and the total number of True Selves is one.

The first shift: Unique Self as part & feature of the Universe

Then, when you awaken even more deeply, you realize that you're not merely a True Self. You're also, and more deeply, a Unique Self. A Unique Self means that you realize that your True Self, which is part of the One, always sees through a unique set of eyes. Your True Self is utterly unique – unlike anyone else's True Self in the world, even though we are all part of the same True Self. You realize that you are part of the seamless coat of the universe, which is the impersonal True Self. Yet though the coat of the Universe may be seamless, it is not featureless. The features are Unique Selves – unique expressions of Essence that are absolutely special and personal.

It is that personal quality that you're aware of when you get together with someone, and you feel like it wasn't such a good meeting. You say to your friend, "That was kind of impersonal. I wanted to have a more personal encounter." That wasn't your ego talking. That was you, yearning for contact, for intimacy, between essences. This takes place as Unique Self, which is the unique expression of the True Self, which is God having a 'you' experience.

God awakens in you, as you and through you

When I wake up in the morning, the Divine wants to have 'a Marc experience'. And if the Divine wants to have a Marc experience, and Marc is trying to emulate Brett, then Divinity says, "This sucks." When God is trying to have a Ken Wilber experience and runs into Marc Gafni, that's called 'the exile of Divinity' in Kabbalah; that's how the Sufis understand it.

That's beautiful, because God awakens in you, as you and through you uniquely. You are a unique expression of All That Is. You have a unique perspective, and that perspective sees the world, understands the world, as an irreducible expression of Essence, unlike any other.

You've realized what the Buddhists call 'emptiness,' or the Kabbalists call 'the fullness of Ayin' — the fullness of no-thing-ness. So you have awakened to the larger context that lives in you, as you and through you (level 2) and then you awaken again (level 3) to the complete, personal expression of that *as you.* That personalness is not the personal of level 1, before the impersonal; it is the personal of level 3, which transcends and includes the impersonal. (Trance-ending: 'ending the trance of' — we end the trance of the impersonal.) So the personal comes back online as the unique expression of Being, in our Unique Self.

The second shift: from Unique Being to Unique Becoming

As in the Big Bang, what emerges out of being is becoming, as Whitehead pointed out in his famous distinction. Being becomes becoming; being begins to emerge and evolve. I realize that I awaken not only as being, which is True Self, but also as becoming, which is Unique Self.

As for being, I awaken as part of the All, not separate from the All, and the All lives fully in me. But then 'becoming' means that the All is evolving, it's moving someplace, it's going somewhere, it has a purpose, a direction, a trajectory, a telos. We're on a journey! This is the realization that there's some place to go, that there's something to do, that the awakened being needs to embrace a sacred activism, to give our unique gifts, which completely changes the Enlightenment game.

Your Unique Gifts

As a function, an expression, of your irreducible Essence, you have unique gifts to give. Those unique gifts can be given by no one else in the world other than you. Those gifts are not a function of your Enneagram typology or your Meyers-Briggs typology, which are ego typologies of level 1, separate self, and are important at that level. Your Unique Self is so much more than that. It is Essence speaking through you, after you have clarified, uncoiled, the contraction of your separate self.

Those unique gifts are not only your external talents, not only what you do in a talent show in summer camp. It's the very unique way that you love and live and laugh and sing. It's the poem only you can write, the song only you can sing. It's the way of loving, living, laughing and being-becoming that is yours, singularly and alone in the most gorgeous, splendid sense. Those are your unique gifts.

Authenticity is living your Unique Self, versus depression from a sense of replace-ability

To be authentic, to live your authenticity, is to live precisely your Unique Self, which is not impersonal. That is the key. Unique

Self is not an awakened, impersonal function, but an awakened, infinitely personal function of your irreducible Uniqueness, the ground of your rights, dignity, beauty, and your sense of being utterly necessary in the world. Utterly necessary — you're not replaceable.

Depression, at its core, is replace-ability. Depression is the sense of being an 'extra' on the set. Depression is the sense that if I weren't here, someone else would do it. Maybe it would be done a little differently, but basically it would get done. No, it wouldn't get done. Because there is something you can do, and there is a way you can do it, that no one else alive, and no one that ever was, is or will be can do, other than you.

Unique Self: the joyful obligation of sharing your unique gifts

Your Unique Self derives, #1, from your Unique being and becoming, which expresses itself, #2, as your unique perspective, which creates in its wake, #3, your unique gifts which, #4, creates your unique obligation. When you hear the word 'obligation', you might cringe at first. "Obligation? Didn't we work to get over that? Didn't my parents go into therapy to move beyond externally imposed obligations? Didn't I work on getting out of these obligations and becoming free?" Yet the greatest freedom is to meet your obligations.

In the original Hebrew, obligation and love are the same word. Obligation means the unique expression of love-intelligence and love-beauty that lives in you, as you and through you, which is your awakened purpose in this lifetime that no one else can fulfill but you. Your sense of joy is coupled with your sense of response-ability, which is your ability to respond, as love, to the corners of your world that are in un-love and can only be addressed by you. That's what obligation means.

Love & Obligation: meeting authentic needs that only you can meet

In the Unique Self teaching, we've developed a fivefold theory of love-obligation. Simply put:

1) There is a need in the world that has to be met.
2) You recognize the need.
3) It's an authentic need.
4) You have the ability to meet that need.
5) No one in the world but you can meet that need.

Wow. That's unbelievable. That is an experience of an awakened Unique Self. I actually see a need; it's a legitimate need; I can meet the need; no one can meet it but me. That's the truth of our experience in the world: there are no extras on the set.

Our worst nightmare: having no purpose

Our worst nightmare is to feel that we are without purpose. Not purpose in the narrow sense, that tomorrow I have to start a Little League team. This may be true — starting a Little League team is awesome; it could be an awesome expression of purpose. But purpose is in the very fabric of my being. I am very purposeful. There is a reason that I am here. By me living the fullness of my Unique Self in the fullness of my interactions with my circle and my expanding sense of love, I will be the vehicle for the love-intelligence and love-beauty to evolve consciousness one step further.

I am the personal face of the Process. Yes, level 2 is the impersonal Process to which I contribute and in which I participate, but at level 3, the Process comes alive, and I realize the Process is me personally. The split between the impersonal Process and the personal 'me' is an illusion of lower consciousness. But when my consciousness awakens, I realize the Process is purely personal, living in me, as me and through me.

An analogy: There was a movie called 'The Truman Show', about a guy on an island. He doesn't realize that he is on an island and that everyone on the island has a part in the movie. The guy, Truman, is the star, but he thinks he is just living his life. The entire world is watching his life, and every move in his life is significant and matters.

That is an very accurate description of reality, with only one catch, which is that each of us is at the center of our own Truman Show. And all of us are supporting actors, co-stars, guest stars, in each other's plays. Each of us needs to have that sense of evolutionary joy, responsibility and intimacy with the Cosmos when we realize that the next step depends on us, because we are irreducible Unique Selves. That's what is changing in the world of Enlightenment, and it's an evolution of Enlightenment itself.

Unique Self as the higher embrace of
Western & Eastern Enlightenment

We are now understanding that Enlightenment doesn't only mean to move from level 1 to level 2, or from a personal, separate self to an impersonal, True Self. The reason Enlightenment has been largely rejected in the Western world is that the Western world has a strongly awakened sense of individuality. Western consciousness borrowed the word 'Enlightenment' to mean 'the awakening to my sense of rights and dignity as a separate self.' Isn't that interesting? The very word, Enlightenment, which is used by mysticism in the East to mean 'the awakening from a separate self to an impersonal True Self', was used in the West in the 18th century by the intellectual elite to mean 'the awakening as a separate, individual self'.

So there is a huge contradiction in the very fabric of consciousness and culture of the East and the West, but that contradiction now yields and melts into a higher, integral embrace when I realize Unique Self. When I realize Unique Self, I realize I am utterly unique, and my infinite dignity stems from my uniqueness. I am a special expression of consciousness. That is absolutely true — but not as separate self. My human dignity is not rooted in my being a separate-self individual, as classical Western materialist or atheist thinking would have it. No, my human rights and my dignity, in the Western sense, stem from my being a Unique Self. The Unique Self is beyond separate self, it's a unique perspective of my True Self and therefore irreducibly unique. Wow! That changes the whole game.

Western Enlightenment: individuation beyond ego

So we can realize the core intuition of Western Enlightenment, which is that sense of individuation, but it is an individuation beyond ego, it is self beyond ego. It's individuation, if you will, at the level of Enlightenment, not at the level-1 consciousness of ego, personality, personality type or separate self. It's individuation beyond ego, individuation *as* Enlightenment: I am enlightened as an awakened Unique Self, which is the personal expression of Essence that lives in me, as me and through me.

I can realize and integrate all of the profound intuitions of Western Enlightenment and thinking, and at the same time, realize and integrate and incarnate the great intuition and understanding of the most subtle and speculative mystical minds that are often identified as Eastern Enlightenment. However, the realization that I am not merely a separate self and that I need to evolve beyond ego, is not only an Eastern but also a Western insight, and Unique Self transcends and includes both. That is the new chapter in Integral Theory that we are unfolding.

So Unique Self is the higher integral embrace in which both True Self and separate self-yield their differences and reveal themselves to be glimmerings of the same higher unity, which is the Unique Self. Unique Self is the irreducible individual dignity of the utter participation in, and indivisibility from, the seamless coat of the Universe, which expresses itself individually as Unique Selves.

With Unique Self, Western resistance
to Enlightenment melts away

So the whole game changes, for in Unique Self, all the resistance to Enlightenment that comes from the individualized Western mind melts away. Uniqueness is no longer dismissed as a hysterical craving of the ego, as Timothy Leary once described it, or as the ego cleverly refusing to die, or as the narcissistic sense of being special. What is ego if not contraction?

We can now move beyond the separate self, beyond the narcissism of specialness, self-contraction and self-involvement, without losing our precious individuality. We awaken as the infinite expression of love-intelligence and love-beauty which is the Unique Self, and we incorporate and integrate the deepest intuition and understanding of Eastern mystical consciousness on the one hand and Western rational consciousness on the other, and evolve the very nature of Enlightenment itself into Integral Enlightenment.

Integral Enlightenment as
sacred activism in the world

Integral or World Spirituality: the perennial
philosophy in a modern, evolutionary context

Even if Enlightenment teaching is the best perennial understanding of the interior face of the Cosmos, where Enlightenment is taken to mean the move from separate self to True Self and to which we now have added Unique Self Enlightenment, is this teaching enough to offer us a new framework of meaning, a new picture of reality? Our picture of reality should always reflect the best, most evolved realization in all the levels and lines of development that are available in a particular moment of time. It is the most evolved take, so in our time you can't be truly enlightened if, for example, psychologically you are not doing your shadow work.

What is the new framework of meaning we can all agree on, gathering the best certainties we have in all of the lines of knowledge, weaving them together into a new picture of reality while fully holding the mystery and uncertainty, the fact that we are evolving, fully hoping this looks different 500 years from now?

A true World Spirituality is the evolving perennial philosophy, a synthesis of the best pre-modern, great traditions, the best of modernity with its science, psychology, etcetera, and the best of post-modernity. We now understand that history matters and that context matters, and now we are trying to go post-post-modernity.

Enlightenment not as a retreat from the world, but plunging fully into it

So Enlightenment is no longer the province of the elite in Nepal, Tibet, India or the backstreets of Jerusalem. In the old Enlightenment, it was about 'how do I get beyond the vagaries of life and root myself in the eternal?' In the new, Integral, evolutionary Enlightenment of Unique Self, I actually place myself directly in life.

It's not about getting out of life, it's about what I want to give to life. I enter life directly as Unique Self, I recognize the evolving nature of Enlightenment, and I see myself at the center of that evolution, even as I co-create that center in an evolutionary We-space, in radical love, within the larger community of evolutionary intimacy.

Selfless, yet filled with Self — that's where we need to go. We need to move from an Enlightenment of Emptiness to an Enlightenment of Fullness. We need to move to a place where we're celebrating a radical celebration of our unique gifts and our unique response-ability: our ability to respond and to place ourselves front and center, in full humility and in full audacity.

We need a Unique-Self revolution. We need to be dancing in the ecstasy of our uniqueness, in full humility, prostrating and bowing before the evolutionary context that produced this unique manifestation that's us. And we need to step up, because that is desperately needed by All-that-is. That's the vision, which invites us into the future with enormous delight, with enormous awe, with trepidation, gravitas, responsibility and joy.

The democratization of Integral Enlightenment

With Integral Enlightenment, we open the door to the potential democratization of Enlightenment. Not that everyone will be enlightened in the same way — of course not. Enlightenment is unique, that's the whole point. Enlightenment has a perspective — your own unique perspective. But we open the door to the democratization of Enlightenment in the sense that Enlightenment becomes a genuine option in a post-individual world in which individuality is front and center.

It's not about dismissing individuality, but about amplifying and evolving individuality beyond separate self to the only true individuality, which is mature individuality, which is individuality in the context of union. I realize that I am God's eyes, God's hands, God's verbs, God's dangling modifiers, and that God lives in me, as me and through me, and that to love God is to let God see through my eyes. It is to act in a sacred activism, as an expression of the evolutionary Force itself. Contact with 'other' is created, and arises as evolutionary intimacy as Unique Selves make contact with each other in the world of relationships.

If we apply the Unique Self insight to every area of life — love, shadow work, parenting, therapy, sexuality, business, psychology, education — it turns out to be a kind of psychoactive substance. As Steve Jobs said in his autobiography about the awakening that came to him through LSD and ayahuasca, we could say that the awakening to our Unique Self can come from ingesting an idea that changes our whole perspective. In that sense, the concept of Unique Self is psychoactive. You ingest it and it changes your perspective on everything.

So Unique Self is desperately needed in our time. We need to reclaim Enlightenment as part of the mainstream conversation of our times, in its evolved form of Integral Enlightenment, which includes our Unique Selves.

The Center for Integral Wisdom

What we are doing now in the Center for Integral Wisdom, together with Ken Wilber who is a leading voice, with Warren Farrell, Eben Pagan, Sally Kempton, Mariana Caplan at the helm and a long list of other people, is that we are engaging every area of culture and applying the core insights of Unique Self to that area, so that we can begin to understand what it means to be an awakened, alive being answering the unique call of my life.

Forgive my wild excitement about this: it is such a gift to people. Our worst nightmare as human beings is that we are somehow extra or irrelevant. The realization that I am profoundly needed by All-that-is, that I have gifts to give that no one else can give, doesn't actually reify my narcissistic sense of egoic, separate self, but reminds me that I am a good child of the Universe, that I'm ultimately needed, that my deed is the Universe's need at the deepest level. It reminds me of my innate and essential goodness and of the purposefulness of my Essence in my life, which is the truth and basis of self-love, altruism and intelligence, and all that is good in human beings.

Introduction to the Five Awakenings

The need for a map in the spiritual world

*E*nlightenment is often called 'awakening', but usually, we're not really sure what we're talking about. So first, we need to know what awakening means. I'm going to suggest that the word awakening in itself has no meaning at all, but I do want to try and outline a new map of consciousness discerning five levels of awakening, in which you can locate your life. I think a map like this is important, because we're very confused in the spiritual world. We're not quite sure where we're going, so when we see a map, we can step out of the details, the trees, and actually see the forest. Then we can step back into our personal, physical, emotional, sexual self and locate where we are in the big picture.

We've lost the big picture in spirituality

We've lost the big picture. We're doing individual exercises, individual relationships, but we've lost big pictures. Why is that?

There is a kind of anti-big-picture feel in the world, we're anti the Grand Era, and it is why the New-Age movement never succeeded: it never developed a big picture. The big picture of post-modernity is that there IS no big picture; it's all relative, and if anyone tries to provide a big picture, it's suspect. Ken Wilber has been attacked mostly for trying to provide a big picture; in America, Ken is very unpopular in most of the spiritual world.

Most of Western spirituality in the alternative world is based on Buddhism, and Buddhism is about deconstructing the big picture. They see it as just a concept and that's good, that's important. So if you sit with my friend JunPo, he'll deconstruct any context that is a concept, just to be in the present. And it's good. The deconstructive movement in literature says, just like Buddhism, that there's no big picture, there's nothing you can hold on to, it's all based on your context, your sociology, your personal history. There's nothing you can hold onto, everything is deconstructed. Now that's half right and half wrong.

All big pictures are evolving

All big pictures are changing, they are evolving. No big picture is ever fixed, a still shot, it is always a movie, moving, unfolding. At the same time, in this moving and unfolding and evolving, you can take a snapshot of our evolution, which gives you a big picture, a broad world view, a map that we can live, find and locate ourselves in. If I don't have a map, ultimately I will either get lost, or the movement gets lost — the Human Potential movement, the New-Age movement, the Venwoude movement, the Integral

World Spirituality movement. I need to locate myself, to see where I am going, what I am trying to do. I need to be able to articulate it, to speak it.

It's not just about: "Is my relationship, my sexuality, my career going well, is my family okay, is my spirituality okay?" Those are ultimately questions about 'me and my life', all really important, but the beginning of awakening is to step beyond 'me and my life' and to begin to live in service of the All, where I participate in a larger context.

A descriptive, not prescriptive map of the larger context

I'm trying to provide a map that can actually locate me, and give me directions within a larger context. Now why does that matter? It matters for two reasons. The first is that, otherwise; you can never find your way, even if later you change the map, even if the map is evolving. The second is that if we don't provide maps, fundamental religion will seize the day, because it is all about maps. They tell you the way it is, step one to six, and if you go left, you go to hell. Some of those maps are pretty smart and we kind of delight in them, but we need to provide alternative maps that are not prescriptive, such as in fundamental religion, but descriptive, more like framework maps.

I met Charles Taylor, who wrote a book of about 600 pages called 'Sources of Self', which I think is the best book on the self for the last 100 years; it was written in Harvard, and I know it is required reading here at Venwoude. Its first sentence is: "We live in inescapable frameworks," meaning that everybody is living within a framework, everybody has a map. You can pretend you don't have anything guiding you, but you do, consciously or unconsciously. If you don't adopt a conscious map, a conscious framework, you are going to be swept away by your inescapable unconscious map or framework. So part of becoming a good human is to make your map conscious, to make it alive. It's actually seeing the stages in your life you are trying to go through.

Awakening as an ongoing process

So 'awakening' always means awakening to the next level, the next stage. Of course, no one ever becomes for always awakened or enlightened; awakening is a process, it's a verb, so we're always awakening or enlightening.

Still, the basic end of evolution for the human being is Enlightenment, just as a piece of coal put under intense pressure becomes a diamond. As a plant that evolves into a flower, the natural trajectory of development and growth for a human being is attaining Enlightenment.

This insight makes it possible to talk about the democratization of Enlightenment, the reclaiming of Enlightenment as a genuine option for every human being. Not Enlightenment as the end of the story, not Enlightenment as perfection, but Enlightenment as a commitment to be awake, alive and aware.

Introducing the Five Awakenings experientially

I would like to take you on a journey through what I call the Five Awakenings: the awakening 1) to separate self; 2) to True Self; 3) to the Beloved, or God, in the second person; 4) to Unique Self; and 5) to the evolutionary context of Evolutionary Intimacy. And I call it a journey, because I want to give you an experiential taste of these Awakenings, rather than just explain them theoretically.

The First Awakening, to separate self

The First Awakening in individuals

When I'm awake, I'm not asleep, right? So the first awakening from being asleep is a new form of being conscious. Good morning, Vietnam, I'm awake! I see something with my eyes open that I couldn't see when I was asleep — I realize something about myself, something new emerges. So the first awakening is the powerful awakening to ego consciousness, the awakening to separate self.

I'm seeing it very powerfully these days in my little son Zion, who is now 13 months old, my new spiritual teacher. For the first five or six months, he basically was not separated in any way from Mariana, his mother. He was just part of her, no separation, and then, very gradually, he began to awaken and to act separately from Mariana. When you give him food now, he takes the food and throws it on the floor. Why? Because he's asserting his will, he's saying actually: "I like that you've given me food, I totally love you, mummy and daddy, but, I get to do what I want." He's not thinking that consciously — as best we know from modern research, in early childhood it is not a thought process — but what is emerging is his sense of being a separate self. Now that is emerging only gradually, it won't emerge fully until he gets to be older, when his separate self and his separate personality will come online.

That process takes place both in ontology and in phylogeny, which is a fancy way to say: both in the life of the individual and in the life of humanity. So both the human being and humanity are immersed in what Joseph Campbell called 'the Great Mother': the baby is part of the mother, and the human being is immersed in Mother Nature, in Earth. And it takes tens of thousands of years for the human being to emerge as a self, so it is a very gradual emergence.

In the human being, like in Zion, the process of emergence may start at 13 months, and this will intensify when he gets to be three or four. If he's Jewish, he has a Bar Mitzvah at 13, which usually means a lot of bars; if he's Catholic, he has Confirmation but reaches puberty in a secular ritual. When he hits adolescence, he rebels against his mother and father, and by 18 he's a fully independent, legally recognized individual. In all of these stages, he emerges in terms of motive development; then in terms of cognitive development; and finally in terms of independence, a sense of self where he no longer locates himself in the family.

One of my students said to me that she's having a hard time with her daughter, who said: "I hate you, you are a bitcheous human being, I never want to see you or this family again." That was the expression of her emergence: she is no longer locating herself in the family system. The Mother is not just a physical mother;

the Mother is also the family system, the school, the religion, the Church, the neighborhood — all those are expressions of the Mother, and the self slowly emerges from the physical mother, the physical father, the religion, the neighborhood, the school and the guardianship of the parents, until the individual is 18 and at least technically, legally an individual.

Now of course they may take much more time to be spiritually and psychologically fully 'hatched', as Margaret Mahler called it: your psychological hatching is 'your rebirth in your rebirth'. Still, that is basically the process of emergence, an awakening into what Lawrence Kohlberg at Harvard called 'an autonomous, separate self' that is capable of ethical reasoning inside and acting independently in the world.

The First Awakening in humanity as a whole

In individuals, we recognize that process of emergence or awakening into a separate self, but in terms of humanity, the same thing happens. The word 'self' doesn't actually appear in the dictionary until the Renaissance; isn't that wild? It just didn't exist, because until the Renaissance, the self never existed independently of the Mother, who might originally be the Earth. For example, in what researchers have called typhonic times, you have images of human beings that are half animal, half tree and half human. Why? Because in the magical, Neolithic era, human beings still emerged in the Earth. Jean Gerber talks about this extensively.

So within humanity, the human being first emerged into a tribal world, which then moved from hunting-gathering to farming, but you were still part of your community, or part of the Empire, the Mother Church, or Mother Russia; you always belonged to something. It is only with the Renaissance, called 'the Enlightenment' in Western history that the human being awakens as a separate, autonomous self.

Every single person hearing this or reading this, without exception, is defined by this first awakening. We take this awakening for granted, we were born into this awakening, and so we almost don't view it as an awakening. But to become a fully independent, autonomous self is the ongoing job of the human being. For, although we were born into this awakening, most of our psychology is about strengthening our ego, strengthening our character structure, including doing shadow work, in order to make us independent and enable us to make good and proper decisions in life. Most of our schools of psychology deal with this realm — the awakening of the separate self — and they intend to help you move from pre-personal to personal consciousness, which is considered to be the hallmark of a healthy human being. And that's a big deal.

Group exploration: positive aspects of separate self

Now let's write three positive and three negative things about being a separate self. We start with the positives.

P1: This is my body and I have a right to protect its boundaries.

Right, I have a right to protect my boundaries, which sometimes creates a war, but that's just the way it is, because no one has the right to violate my boundaries. For example, in the realm of sexuality, one of the great contributions of feminism was new laws in America and Europe against sexual harassment. You can't violate my boundaries, because to violate my boundaries is to violate the Goddess or the God, so that's very powerful, beautiful and important. Hegel talked about boundaries in the sense of human rights, which began to emerge in the Renaissance: the affirmation of the rights of the individual, respecting the individual's place in the larger context, which is a very big deal.

P2: My creativity comes from within and I can express myself.

Beautiful. All Church art was to glorify the Church, there wasn't room for individual expression, but the Renaissance creates an explosion of new forms of art in sculpture, in painting, in dance, etcetera, that come from the liberation of the separate self. But not only in terms of art, also in the realm of thought new and creative ways of thinking are emerging, like the concept of democracy and the development of scientific research, leading to the Industrial Revolution and new technologies, and later the labor movement and feminism. All this unleashing of creativity comes from the emerging of a separate self from under the burden of the Church and from the affirmation of the dignity of the individual self, respecting his or her own perspective and creativity. We are going to see creativity on much higher levels than that, but that's absolutely the beginning of creativity as the affirmation of the dignity of the separate self, which emerges into the world at the time of the Renaissance. That's a very big deal and it's fantastic.

P3: I have my own opinion and it's a different one from yours.

Right. Part of the spiritual journey is to know what you actually know, know what you believe that no one else believes, because it's really *you* talking. That doesn't end with the separate self, as we will see, but it does begin with the separate self.

Koan: "Anyone who says something in the name of the person that said it, brings redemption to the world."

This reminds me of a beautiful saying in a 3rd century Hebrew text, "Anyone who says something in the name of the person that said it, brings redemption to the world." This is a koan, a 3rd century koan. So what does that mean? Let's say that someone said some wise thing to me, and I'm teaching the next day and I say: "This is what my friend said." That's a nice thing to do, but why does that bring liberation into the world?

P: You make room for the other person.

Okay, I'm breaking out of egocentricity, I'm tempted to steal his wisdom, but instead of stealing his wisdom to pump up my ego, I'm actually bracketing my ego and giving him voice, and that limiting of my ego to make room for the other creates liberation. Nice view.

This is really powerful, and it doesn't matter whether you're in a community with progressive or fundamental opinions, because everybody thinks that the opinions of their community are the right ones — that's why we join a community. The question is:

who is my separate self? I ask you to find the visceral expression of those opinions, which I can actually locate in my body, just like I can locate them in my mind, in my heart, in me. If I can't locate my opinion in my heart, mind and body, then I'm asleep. Anything I say, I will be able to locate in my heart, mind and body. Otherwise it's really bad, simply uncool at every level.

You've got to really feel that in a deep way; that's the way of being separate self. Anyone who says something in the name of the person who said it, brings liberation to the world *because they have this awareness.* They are able to distinguish between 'what Marc said' and 'what Marc said that I decided to receive, and which I can locate in my heart, mind and body.' Of course I listen, of course I receive transmission; but when I do, I need to locate it in my own heart, mind and body. And if I can't locate it there, it is not mine. That's what we call mystic idolatry, or 'worship through the stranger', but it's not *my* worship, *my* service; it's the service through the stranger in me.

Negative aspects of separate self: loneliness

So, recapitulating the positive side of the separate self, we have that sense of individual expression and creativity, of thinking for yourself, and a sense of boundaries. Now let's see some of the negative or shadow qualities of the separate self.

P3: *Loneliness*

Oh my God, loneliness, right. On the one hand there is the loneliness of being unable to share my separate self with another. We have Pink Floyd's 'The Wall', where I'm behind this wall of alienation and I can't get out from behind it. But also, we have the collapse of social communities, as Robert Putnam described 10 years ago in his important sociological book 'Bowling Alone'. Heidegger said that the greatest tragedy of the human being is the inability to traverse loneliness, because I'm locked in my separation. Heidegger wasn't completely right, only partially, because there are ways to move beyond separation, but loneliness certainly is part of being a separate self.

There is another book, 'The Discarded Image' by C.S. Lewis, where he talks about what it was like to live as a medieval person. He says that it's enormously tragic, there is disease and death and you are under the Church, but at the same time, you kind of know your place in the world. If the world has an order, you know where you are, and you are moving to the Renaissance, to this emergence of the individual, but at the same time you're moving into alienation: I'm alienated, I'm desiccated, I'm separate from the rest when I'm alone. I'm no longer held by the Church, the king, the state, there is no obvious order or purpose to my existence. So there is a loneliness, an alienation to the separate self, absolutely.

Remember Billy Joel? Some 25 years ago, he sang about the stranger 'who hits me right between the eyes'. George Steiner said: "Strangers are we, errands at the gates of our own psyche," the stranger being the person who's not me, but acts as me. Albert Camus wrote a novel called 'The Stranger'.

So the awakening to separate self is the first step of awakening, which you cannot skip, and which has to take a whole lifetime.

The Second Awakening, into True Self

Accessing True Self through chanting

What does it mean to awaken to your True Self, the classical Enlightenment? And let's remember that Enlightenment, or Awakening, is a process, it's a verb, so we're always enlightening, always awakening. We want to get a taste of this, so we'll be accessing the direct One Taste, the direct True Self.

To open up the space, following the tradition of the Sufis, of Rumi, Shams and the Levites in the Holy Temple of Jerusalem, I'm first going to chant. I'm going to chant to you as a transmission, and I ask you to engage with me in this dance, I ask you to open your heart to receive the love of the Cosmos, which lives in the chant and which is mediated directly to you, into your heart. If anywhere I'm in the way, I ask you, as always, to please forgive me. If you've got a fine ear and you notice that I don't have a great voice, I ask you to let that go and to receive the transmission of the chant, which is the Universe bathing you in love.

We say that love is hard to find, that it's difficult to achieve, but that's actually not true — love is impossible to avoid. The Universe, the Cosmos, is drenching you in love in every single second. It's the reality of Essence. In Hinduism, we call it Sat-Chit-Ananda. Sat is Being, and the inside of Being is Chit, or consciousness, and the inside of consciousness is Ananda, which is blessed love. So when you use the faculty of your perception, which is the eye of Spirit or the eye of the heart, it reveals the interior face of the Cosmos; just as science reveals the exterior or outside face of the Cosmos. The eye of the heart, of the Spirit, through its own experiment, by its own scientific method, reveals to you that you are the inner face of the Cosmos, and the inner face, the inner feeling of the Cosmos is love. Not to know that is to be alienated, not just from your friends or your beloved, but from reality itself, for you belong to gentle love.

I will give you this transmission from the lineage of the great masters of the love of the Cosmos through this chant. Chanting, like studying sacred texts, is not to get somewhere, there's no place to go, it's right here, right now. Chanting is like making love: hopefully we do it more than once, even though we seem to be doing the same thing over and over. My only request, and it is a huge request and I'll be gratified and humbled and grateful if you will grant it to me, is to open your heart and completely receive the love, which, as you know, is not at all that easy.

Group discussion of Zen koan: What do you do when you've climbed to the end of a 100 foot flagpole?

Now I'm going to ask you a question, which is a Zen koan. Every tradition has its own tools. You don't answer a koan logically, it is not a mind question; you have to answer from your full heart, body, mind and spirit. In this koan, we are going to talk about the Second Awakening, the awakening to classical Enlightenment.

The koan is: What do you do when you climb to the end of a 100 foot flagpole?

Participants answering:

P1: *I am thrilled, I feel like I'm a child, taking its*
      first step. I am sitting on top of the world.
P2: *It's so new. It's like there are just*
      possibilities, the world is open.
P3: *I should yell very loud.*
P4: *I will let myself go with the wind and with*
      the flag, I am just part of the pole.
P5: *I feel as if I'm in front of everyone else. And*
      by the way, I just realized that if I would get a
      new name, it would be 'Hee Nay Nee'.
P6: *I would enjoy the view for a while and then*
      jump down and enjoy the free fall.

Following the flow of the holy moment to Hee Nay Nee

Thank you. Now let's work with the koan. And whenever you work with a koan, you're working with whatever is in the space, because if you are truly in the Holy of Holies, if you are really on the inside, then the space has everything it needs, it's always right there, always. In the words that come up in this space lies the answer, it just presents itself. Now watch, as you are in the Holy of Holies, on the inside: what happened just now when we did the koan? It didn't belong in this space, it wasn't part of the flow, and yet it happened.

Let's go really deep here. When you are in a mystical space, in a genuine transmission conversation, what happens is that you step out of your small self. You make yourself available to the Universe and the space itself, the moment itself, provides you with the opening that takes you where you need to go. So we were doing the koan together and you saw it happen right here, I'm not making it up. The Universe was showing us a direction, it was right in front of you, no one missed it. Six people offered responses to the koan, and one thing happened that wasn't part of the flow. Now we are going to go deeper and try to understand the koan as an Enlightenment teaching, but you can't do it hanging out or as when you watch a movie - you have to step inside. This is not wisdom entertainment. You've got to go dive in deeply, you've got to fall in, and when you fall in, it's all right there.

When one of these six people came up to answer the koan, she added something and said: "Oh, and if I had to get a new name, it would be 'Hee Nai Nee'." Now that actually had nothing to do with our flow, it wasn't part of the koan, it was something extra, something that just popped up in response to an earlier conversation between me and her. Now if something like that happens, holy brothers and sisters, if you are in the inside of the inside, in the deepest of the deep, you pay attention. Because something happened that was a surprise, and that surprise comes from the inside. I didn't send an email telling her to do this, this wasn't prepared before, it happened; it was right there in the moment.

Shem/sham and Jehovah: being here now, not over there, not getting somewhere

So let's unwrap our surprise gift together. Hee Nay Nee means 'here I am'. Let's go in deeper, we are talking about a name, and I'm going to take you to the inside of mysticism, we are now living mystics. We are just playing here, a play with no end; we are not looking for anything specific. The name of something refers to its essence. Now in the original, mystical Hebrew, a word always has its basic meaning, and it will also always mean the opposite, in a hidden way.

Let me give you an example. Essence, as my good friend Ram Dass likes to say, is 'being here now'. According to every great tradition, Essence is the eternity of the Now. In Hebrew, the name of God is Jehovah. 'Je' is the future, and the future is specified as 'hovah', 'which lives in and out'. That's the name of God: the eternal future and past are available and live right here and in the now. So if I am in my name, then I live in my Essence, my Unique Self, which is the essential expression of the Divine that lives in me, as me and through me. My name is the symbol, the outward, visible expression of my internal, invisible Unique Self.

So 'shem' means name, but in Hebrew it is also 'sham', which means 'over there'. So there are two meanings: name or essence, meaning 'I'm right here, I am in my name', and also 'I'm over there', because the opposite of essence is to always try to get 'there', I'm never here, because I am always trying to get there.

So can I reach Enlightenment? If you say: "I have finally gotten there," then where are you now? Or: "I've got to go there again," then I'm there, I'm never here. Hee Nay Nee is here, 'here I am'. As long as I am trying to get there, I'm never here. If I'm never here, I am never present, and then the gifts that live in the moment are lost. Because 'here' is what the masters call 'secret'. The moment contains within it the healing for any pain, any challenge that lives in the moment. The healing, fixing, evolution of that pain, the band aid and the medicine for that pain lives where? In that same moment. But if you are going 'there', you can't find it, because you are 'over there', you are not 'here I am', Hee Nay Nee.

'Here I am' means that I'm doing things 'just because'. Why am I doing it? Just because; I am not trying to get there, I'm doing it just because. 'Here I am.' In mysticism, the highest reason for doing something is called ´lishmah shem', meaning 'I do it for the sake of the name', meaning I do it for its own sake, not to get some place.

Holy sexing is not to get somewhere

I will give you a wild, crazy example, okay? All cultures, and they are probably wrong, but all cultures used to get very angry at the prostitute. A prostitute is someone who sells sex for money, but you've probably never heard of that here.

Ch: No, we only live 30 miles from Amsterdam, so... ☺

I'm sure there is nothing like that in Amsterdam. Now we think that culture gets upset about prostitution because culture is anti-sex, but that's actually not the reason. Sex is awesome, nor do I have any particular problem with prostitution — bless everybody that makes a good living. But why get people, why get culture so upset? This is so deep, my friends. It is because sex is the one place in the world where everybody had at least one experience of doing something for its own sake. I'm not doing it to get somewhere, I'm not doing it to get over there, I'm doing it just to be right here, right? That's the holiness of sex, that I'm doing it just to be right here.

And so culture said: "When someone takes sex and does it to get 'there', wow, that's very heavy, that's a big deal." We are talking about that one thing here that we know is holding Enlightenment that we do for its own sake. I'm not even doing it for the orgasm; even the orgasm is like trying to get money at the end. I'm doing it just to be here with you, fully, open, alive, awake in the divine pleasure of God. Wow, that blows your mind and heart open.

Awakening means to awaken to the place where I'm not trying to get over there, because I'm right here. And what models that Enlightenment is holy union, holy sexing. The reason that holy sexing is so wildly alive and sacred, the reason that Yab-yum is at the center of the temples in Southern India, is because it models the place where I'm not trying to get, because 'Hee Nay Nee', here I am.

Now we all know a secret, just between us. Today, most people when they're making love, they're still trying to get over there, right? There are all sorts of ways to be a whore, all sorts of ways to be sexing in exchange for something else and not to actually be right here. There are all sorts of ways to basically step out of 'right here' and try to get 'over there'.

Meditation is what Buddhists do

Some people came to Zen master Dogen and said to him: "You're already enlightened, and you still meditate?" And he said, "Of course." "But why do you still meditate? Meditation is to reach Enlightenment." And Dogen said: "No, you meditate because that's what Buddhists do."

You make love, because that's what an open heart and what loving beings do. You just do it, there is no answer to the flagpole. When you get to the end of the flagpole, you keep climbing, but we all think that when you get there, that's it — I look at the view, I'm ecstatic, it's beautiful. But actually, you keep meditating, because that's what Buddhists do. You keep making love, because that's what open-hearted, enlightened, awakened beings do. That's what we do, that is the awakening to name, or shem.

My name is my essence, so when I'm in my name, in my essence, there's no place to go; it's my story. If I'm trying to live your story, I'm trying to get 'over there', I want to be in your story. And my story will have ups and downs, it can have disappointments, betrayal, success, joy. But as long as it's my story, it's my path, it's my unique essence, it's my Unique Self, it's the unique signature of God that God wrote all over me in love. I just keep doing it, because that's what Buddhists do. And I do it with radical joy and radical awakeness, I do it as a full lover, because — and here's the teaching of the Zohar, the teachings of the mystics — you can fuck any moment open to God, you can make love to any moment and love it open to God.

And you might say: Why didn't you just say "You can love it open to God," why do you have to be so dramatic and say fuck him? And the answer is: They're not quite the same thing, are they? When I say 'fuck the moment open to God', it means that I engage in the full depth of that moment, I want what that moment has to give and I'm going to penetrate that moment, I'm going to receive that moment, and I'm going to merge and explode it to the fullness of that moment, and that moment is Hee Nay Nee, here! Here I am!

The practice of falling into the hole

I will give you a wild practice, it's the deepest practice of this kind I know in the world, and I'm going to call it 'the Practice of the Hole'.

What do you do when you fall into the hole? Now, there's no one person that I've met who hasn't fallen into the hole. Anyone who tells me that they're always in bliss, in deep serenity, they're lying.

Any teacher who says they are always holding the full presence of God and complete serenity, being unattached, they're lying. That's not the way it works. If a person is always in serenity, they're probably psychotic. That's the truth. The nature of our life is that we go in and out.

The key is, when I fall into the hole, I've got to know two things. One is that I'm not the hole; I've fallen into the hole, but I'm not the hole, I've just fallen into it. And you've got to know something else as well, and that is how to get out. So all the teachers say: "You're not the hole, you're the Eternal Witness, so now you're witnessing the hole." Well, thanks a lot, so I'm sitting in the hole and witnessing it, great.

Right, so what do I do, how do I get out?

P: I learn to enjoy it.

Okay, you could learn to enjoy it. That's probably even more massively depressing than the hole itself, but you could. "I love this depression, I'd love to commit suicide, I'd like to rip my guts out, that's so fun." You could, and I understand the wisdom of what you're saying, bless it. But there is a way through, and here is the way through. It's completely counter-intuitive, against your intuition.

No avoidance – no dancing around the void

The only way to get through the hole is not to avoid the hole. What we do, is avoidance, we do 'a void dance', I dance around the void, I refuse to enter. And I can do anything, I can do drugs, I do a little sex, have a little more food, work hard, watch TV and listen to music, as long as I can do 'avoidance', dance around the void. But the only way to get out of the hole, is to sit in it. Just step in, sit down and say: "Here I am, I'm in the hole." Drop right into the void, let all resistance to the void go and feel anything the void has to give you. But don't run your mind, just sit in the void in your room at night for 15 minutes, just sit in the void.

Now I can give you an absolute promise. Sit in it for 15 minutes and as you stay in it, breathe in it, the void will begin to fill up. It will always fill up, it will fill up with your personal essence, with Hee Nay Nee, 'Here I am.' You just sit right in the void, and you just let all the shit come up, you do not run from it, do not deny it, do not explain it, do not hide it; you just stay in it. When you stay in it, the void always dissipates, and what wells up in you is the unique presence of *you*. You can actually feel that 'here I am.' That's what meditation is, what we call 'shikantaza': just sit. You can teach Zen your whole life — and I have lots of good friends, beautiful people, who teach Zen their whole life — and never get *here*. Just sitting in it, because the magic is *here* and we all try to get *there* - "here I am."

It is all happening right here, not over there

You climb to the end of a 100-foot flag pole and you keep climbing. "Here I am." You keep meditating, because that is what Buddhists do, and Enlightenment means that the taste of the bark of the tree and the taste of the fruit of the tree are exactly the same. There is no means and there is no end, there is no place to go; it is all happening right here. You cannot be late, it is happening right now; right here, right now.

"When is this talk over?" That's 'over there'. "Why don't we do something new? Are we doing another chant? Are we going to meditate? Are we going to do that practice?" That's over there. "Why don't you get your hair cut, your hair has grown too long." That is over there, all over there. "Why doesn't he talk slower?

Enlightened people talk slowly." Here is the holy secret: the only thing you know about people who talk slowly, is that they talk slowly.

We are always 'over there', right? It's all right here, right now. Hee Nay Nee, Here I Am, isn't that awesome? We're sitting here, we are together, committed to Enlightenment, doing Enlightenment teaching, our bodies are functioning, we can feel the air, the breath moving through us, our mind receiving thoughts, bringing it back to center, feel our heart pumping, feel our presence in this space. Here I Am, it's awesome, it is totally awesome; it's ecstatic, there is nothing else to do, Here I Am.

Chanting is being right here

That is why we chant. We chant because in the chant, I can fall into Here I Am, for when I am chanting, I am just chanting, I am not trying to get to the end of a song. With a song, you are trying to get to the end, you perform, it's got to be good, it's got to be in tune, you've got to have a good voice. Chant is right here: Here I Am, let's chant. Why? Just because. Let's make love. Why? Just because. Now, if a guy uses that as a 'come on' line, don't listen to him. But you hear the depth in it, right? It's a big deal.

Enlightenment looks like being a baby, but isn't

A lot of the Enlightenment teachers say that when you are enlightened, you are like a baby. Before this session, I was with my son Zion, who was playing. Why does he play? Just because. What is he trying to get done? Nothing. Is he thinking about what is going to happen in an hour? No. What is he doing? He's right here, right now. "Oh, I look at these people, great. Now I am going with my mom, fantastic. Let's get some breast, mmm, delicious. Let's take a walk in the park, great. I do not like this, aargh." This morning when I came to hang out with Zion, he was pointing to the shutters in the house; there are about eight of them. He goes to each shutter, reaches for it and pulls open the shutter, he looks outside and he goes 'wow'. He has this new word, 'wow', I wonder where he got that from? And literally he opens all eight shutters, one by one, and looks out and says 'wow'. That is why the teachers said: "Enlightenment is like being a baby," but actually, the teachers were wrong, or at least half wrong.

A baby isn't really enlightened; a baby models something that looks like Enlightenment, but is not. Why? Because a baby is pre-personal, the baby hasn't begun to think, doesn't have to pay bills, hasn't been betrayed, hopefully; hasn't dealt with all the crises of life, hasn't had a parent die of cancer and hasn't dealt with having her breasts removed. The baby hasn't dealt with any the pain of life, all the tragedy of life, so that baby is hanging out and saying: "Wow." It is just because the baby doesn't know what is really going on here. Just wait till the baby grows up!

Pre-tragic and post-tragic Enlightenment & devotion

So here is the deep teaching in this: there is pre-tragic and there is post-tragic. There is pre-tragic devotion and there is post-tragic devotion, pre-tragic Enlightenment and post-tragic Enlightenment. You meet someone and you fall in love, you are 19 years old, and the first six months you are flying high and it's awesome. Going to the supermarket and making love is the same thing, just as long as we are together; it's awesome, and it's pre-tragic.

But what do you do when you are 35 and you have three lovers that left you, two that you betrayed, six people that died, and all of your complexity, you're not sure of anything, what do you do then? Either you live in the tragic or you go post-tragic. Post-tragic means that you step out of the tragedy into Hee Nay Nee, Here I Am. There is pre-tragic devotion and there is post-tragic devotion. I say to all of my students: "If you are pre-tragic, don't stand with me. I want to stand with people who are post-tragic, who have post-tragic devotion."

Surrendering to pain, embracing the moment

For after all the betrayal and the hurt and all the broken-heartedness, the pain has loved me open, I'm willing to show up and be here and now in the eternity of this moment, as my shem, as my name, in my unique story and my unique essence, and I'm going to stop trying to get there. To solve the tragedy, I'm going to be here and live it fully. Whatever the moment has to give, I will embrace it and bring it to God. I will bring it to God, the full tragedy of it, the full pain and the full heartbreak and the full betrayal. I'll go right into it, yearn into it, live and die into it, I'm going to surrender into it. And you can send me more pain, go on, I'm going to surrender to more pain, I'm going to be here, right now, I'm going to show up fully and bring it to God. Not the God you don't believe in, not the one who doesn't exist, not the God of the fundamentalist Church, but I'm going to bring it to the God who knows my name, the personal face of Essence that wrote the script of my story, together with me. No place to go, no place to hide, no place I'd rather be than right here, right now. Whatever the moment has to bring, I'm going to enter it wholly, no avoidance, not a void dance. This moment has a blessing for me, whatever it is, here I Am, fucking A, bring it on. *That's* Enlightenment.

The person sitting in perfect lotus position meditating on the bliss of eternity is just taking drugs, that's not Enlightenment. You meditate on the bliss of eternity in order to step into the present, with all of its change, with all of its evolutionary Becoming. I ground myself in Being in order to live in Becoming. How do I do it? I get to the top of the 100 foot flagpole and I keep climbing. Why? Just because. I'm making love, that's what I do, and you'll find unbelievable passion and unbelievable depth and unbelievable meaning.

And it's painful; if my position is a little uncomfortable, I feel into the pain. How many people have ever done yoga? What happens when you do yoga? How do you do asanas? When you do asanas, you stretch into the pain, just a little bit more, in Down-Facing Dog. You step into it, you don't step away from it, you just stretch more and it gets a little more elegant, a little more beautiful. The deep teaching of asana is 'right here, right now, Here I Am'. Whatever the position is, Here I Am - you step into it and it holds you. That's what asana means: whatever position I'm in, I'm held in that position. That's the yoga, wow.

Dyad exercise: running hands over face of person next to you

For the next seven minutes we'll do a meditation, in dyads, with partners, and I ask everybody to hold Silence of Presence, so as not to lose the flow of the dharma.

Close your eyes, and the first person is going to run their hands over the face of the second person, with the intention of giving them total pleasure and bliss, just because. After about three minutes we'll switch. So the purpose of this meditative practice is to know that in every moment, this is what's happening: in every moment, the Universe is running its hand over my face, intending to give me the pleasure of my own development and growth, just because. For every moment has its own growth, has its own evolution, which is its own pleasure.

So I'm going to make love just by running my hands over the other person's face. Why? Just because. And I'm going to know that this is the essence of reality. I'm showing up, I'm giving pleasure and receiving pleasure in the fullness of the moment, in every way it happens, just because. Hee Nay Nee, Here I Am, I'm going to keep climbing, not to get anywhere, but just because. Because that's what Buddhists do, because Buddhists are lovers, and that's what lovers do.

Keep the exercise going, and I'm going to chant into the exercise.

CHANT: [Marc chanting about devotional love in the moment, making it up as he goes]

Hee Nay Nee, Here I Am.
And I keep climbing every day in ecstatic devotion.
I love you now, I love you now, I'm making love in every moment to
the moment, which holds the healing of everything that's happening.
You can't be late, it's happening now, by the name of God.

And we rest into silence, the hands fall to the side, the eyes remain shut. Forgive any imperfections in this dharma talk and hold Silence of Presence. Drop into the hole and let it fill up with the utter ecstatic delight of your cells, your legs, your body, your hands, genitals, shoulders, face, and feel the Universe caressing you. That's what pleasure is, it is the divine caress. Feel the Universe caressing you in every moment, just because. And send blessing for all sentient beings, for the sake of the All.

The Third Awakening, to the Personal Face of God

Recapitulating the First Awakening, to a healthy ego

*I*n this series of sacred conversations on Enlightenment or awakening, we are talking specifically about five different forms of awakening. First we talked about awakening to your personal self, to ego. We always think of awakening as awakening beyond ego, but actually, the first awakening is from the pre-personal self into the egoic self. When I become an ego, in the most positive sense, I become a personality, I have an identity, and that identity is clear, I know who I am. I am responsible for my identity, I can love from the place of my identity, I can engage relationships. I don't give responsibility for my life to any larger framework, I take response-ability, I am able to respond, to engage. That is the beautiful awakening to the personal.

Recapitulating the Second Awakening, transcending the ego

Then we talked about transcending the ego, or trance-ending,

ending the trance of your limited self-identifying with your separate self, which is the Second Awakening. We talked about blowing your mind and actually realizing your true and deeper identity as part of the seamless coat of the Universe: I am not separate from, separation is an illusion in the mind of God, I am, ultimately, always part of a larger whole. The realization that I am not only a separate self, but that I am also part of a larger whole, which lives in me and flows through me and is awakened in me, that is the Second Awakening, the awakening to True Self, the true nature of my reality, and that changes everything. So you should already be awakened twice. ☺

Cash practices for the Third Awakening

Now I want to fill in some really important practices, which I call cash practices. There are credit-card practices and there are cash practices. When you pay with a credit card, it takes time for the whole thing to happen, there is a process. Cash is like an immediate buy; you are right there. So these are cash spiritual practices that plug you in your Second Awakening immediately, into your awareness of being part of a larger field that is holding you. These cash practices today will point us in the direction of the third Awakening.

Let's begin with maybe two minutes, three minutes of deep silence and from the silence we will move into chant, from the chant we move into dharma, and then we will have group sex. J (*Laughter*) Just checking if anybody was listening.

Ch: You have awakened them all, Marc.

M: You see that awakening is very direct and simple. So let's sit up straight, holy brothers, holy sisters. It's an awesome delight to be with you in this moment right here and right now. There is no place else I want to be in the entire world other than right here, right now in this moment. And that is part of awakening, to know that there is no place to go. You can't be late, it is happening now. You don't want to get over there, you want to be here, because here is where it is happening. We know in the deep teaching of the Eye of the Spirit, as revealed by all of the great traditions, that Enlightenment/awakening means to receive the healing in the moment, which is available in the moment, because every moment has its pain. We know that, don't we?

Life is gorgeous, life is fucking awesome and life is also painful. It is poignant and painful and broken, even as it is whole and perfect and radiant. The problem is, that we always want it to be the one or the other, when actually it is both at the very same moment. To be enlightened is to know that you laugh out of one side of your mouth and you cry out of the other. The laughter that is needed to heal the tears in any moment is in the moment itself, it is right here. The healing needed to heal the pain of the now is in the now, and the problem is that we are always trying to get out of the now, over there. If we would just drop in for a moment, into the infinite spaciousness and goodness and wisdom that are available through the deep consideration of the now. All the healing, the love, the power, the goodness and all the embrace, the drug of the hug uniquely prescribed for this moment, are actually in this moment. So it is.

So let's enter silence. I will ask everybody, holy brothers and sisters, to sit up straight. I know there is an old Venwoude custom of several thousand years to lie down in the most relaxed, sprawled-out position while you receive the dharma. (*Laughter*)

Ch: It is different today, Marc, they are all up straight. You are getting real influence here.

M: That is awesome, I knew there was a reason I was born. I will tell my therapist we have solved it.

So my spine is straight, it reaches towards the heaven and it reaches down to the ground of the Earth. My spine is what the Sufis call the pole, the axis mundi, the step, the rock that links Heaven and Earth, making love to the Earth and making love to the Heavens. As they say in Aramaic, the heavens and earth kiss through me.

My neck is back, my shoulders are dropped, my palms are open to receive. We move into silence and then we move into chant.

Follow your breath for three minutes. Other thoughts will arise, don't fight them, let them enter and leave, and drop back into deep Presence, into the Silence of Presence, the infinite stillness of the vast spaciousness that is present, awake, alive and aware in every moment. Three minutes.

Chanting: from 1st to 2nd to 3rd awakening

And we move from the silence into chant. Chant moves us from separate self into True Self, from the First Awakening to the Second Awakening, and then we are going to study the Third Awakening. And we will see that in its essence, the chant is about the Third Awakening.

So let's begin with chant as a way of awakening to our full presence as individuals, as personal selves, and then let the chant melt away the boundaries of the jagged separate self that thinks that it is only a part and not part of a larger whole. We will do a classical chant that we always do together, because together, we have invested it with so much Shakti, so much love, so much commitment. If I am off-tune, which I usually am, I rely on you to help me. We chant with our eyes shut because there are things we can see with our eyes open, and so much else we can only see with our eyes shut.

Chanting

The Awakening to the Beloved

*O*ur chanting brings us to the third Awakening, which is the awakening to the Beloved, the personal face of God, the Mother. You can awaken to the True Self in the Second Awakening, awakening to the reality that you are actually part of the seamless coat of the Universe, part of the great system, the great sunyata, what the Buddhists call 'the great Emptiness', which sounds a little empty, actually. In Japan, when you get married, there is a very strong tradition that you never ask your Buddhist teacher to marry you, because they are so boring; you ask the Shinto priest to marry you. They do their serious, spaciousness practice in Buddhism, but when they want to do a wedding, they ask the Shinto priest. That is like asking the Jew, you've got to know how to throw a party, you know what I mean? You've got to not just awaken to sunyata, to spaciousness, the deep Ground of Being that is beyond all concepts — which the Buddhists call No-Self, and is unbelievably important — but you have to awaken even more deeply to fall into the arms of the Beloved.

And when I talk to my Buddhist teacher friends, we have a kind of deep Dharma combat about the nature of reality, and what I am really saying to them is: "My dear friends, you've got to awaken into the arms of the Beloved. You've got to awaken into the ecstasy, the living Shakti that is in every particle of reality, that knows your name, that loves you, holds you, sparkles and dances in you, as you and through you, even as it hold, cradles and rocks you."

And this is the Third Awakening, the awakening to the knowing that every place you fall, you fall into the arms of the Beloved. That was the great teaching of Rumi and Hafiz and the great masters of Kabbalah, to awaken to the glimmering, erotic Intelligence that is in every particle of reality, that loves and caresses you and lightly dances her or his fingers across your chest and deeply wants your pleasure, knowing that your pleasure is your growth, your development, your emergence, your unfolding. It conspires to fuck you open to your own growth and to your own highest self in every moment of your life, which is arranged perfectly for the infinite pleasure of your growth, development, fulfillment and joy. Wow. That is worth knowing, that is worth awakening to.

The awakening to No-Self is not sufficient

Do you understand why the awakening to No-Self is not sufficient? This is one of the great tragedies that came with the export of Buddhist practice to the West. Buddhist practice brought many gifts, it is good practice and it is good to practice with a good Buddhist teacher. My friend Diane Hamilton is a wonderful Buddhist teacher, a good person to practice with, and JunPo is a fabulous, gorgeous Buddhist teacher and a great person to practice with. Junpo brings the gift of No-Self, and I bow before my dharma brother Junpo for that great gift.

The masters of the Kabbalah, the Chassida, bring the same gift: No-Self is true. Buddha brings the great, wonderful gift of awakening to your True Self, getting out of your personality, and when a Buddhist teacher brings new ways of doing this into the world, like Mondo Zen, wow, what a gift, what a pleasure, what an honor. So No-Self, or True Self, or Buddha Nature, is a critical piece of awakening.

We also need to realize that each awakening has its own teachers. Who are the teachers for the awakening to the fully competent, integrated ego or separate self? Psychologists. Most of modern psychology actually awakes you to a healthy, responsible self that can be functional, effective, ethical and alive in the world. That is beautiful. And good psychology will help you to integrate your shadow, the disowned parts of your separate self, helping you to wake up to your self-personalities that might be running your life unconsciously. So psychology is a great teacher, the great teacher of the first Awakening. And Buddhism and certain forms of mystical Kabbalah, of mystical Sufism, of Chassidism, are the great teachers of the awakening to True Self. That is awesome.

And now we are at level three, at the Third Awakening, awakening to the knowing that you are held in the arms of the Beloved.

It is awakening to your relationship with the absolute Godhead that knows your name, that loves you, that holds you. And in that relaxing into the infinite significance of your life, you matter to God. Remember, the God you do not believe in doesn't exist. I have said it every time we met: it is not the mystic God of the Church who tells you that only the Church can save you and that homosexuality is the great sin of abomination before God. Not that God, for the God you don't believe in, doesn't exist, but the God who is the awakened Shakti of all of reality, that holds you personally, that knows your name, that is not a dogma.

The level-line fallacy in Judaism/ Christianity versus Buddhism

Very often people will commit what I am going to call a level-line fallacy, where 'line' refers to lines of development, a particular approach or path, and 'level' refers to the different levels that exist within a line of development. For example, let's take music as a path. You have a novice like me, who can barely play the guitar, and then you have these awesome guitar players that you can sit and listen to in orgasmic ecstasy for hours. So we are both playing the guitar, but we are at different levels in that line of development. Meditation is a line, it is a path, with a beginning level and an advanced level. Awakening to the Beloved also is a path — you have a beginning level and you have a much more advanced level.

Now, in the late Sixties, there were tens of Jewish kids who lived on Long Island in New York, which is a very important place. And they all went East. One of them was Richard Alpert, who later changed his name to Ram Dass. Another was Jack Kornfield, he is part of the Spirit Path Center, with his teacher Joseph Goldstein and Sharon Salzberg. Yet another was Dennis Merzel and he later became Genpo Roshi, and Jeffrey Millet, who later became Surya Dass. You begin to get my point?

What happened is, these Jewish kids were going to synagogues in Long Island, most of them to conservative synagogues, which had lost their ability to communicate authentic experiences of spirit, doing big Bar Mitsvahs with a lot of bar and not that much Mitsvah, and these guys said: "Man, this is not cool." And then they went eastward and found these awesome Buddhist teachers like Papaji, and they said: "Wow, this Buddhist shit man; this is happening, this is gorgeous; fuck that Jewish thing, that is bullshit, man. This is the real stuff."

Now they were right and they were wrong. They were right in that they found a great teacher; that is awesome, deep bow. They were wrong in throwing out the Kabbalah, in throwing out the awakening to the Beloved that is the core of the Sufi path, the Jewish path. They compared Judaism at its lowest level with Buddhism at its highest level, and said: "Judaism sucks and Buddhism rocks." So that is a level-line fallacy, when you identify a particular line with its lowest expression and then compare it the highest expression of another line.

The same thing is true when we think about the Second and Third Awakening. I will call the Second Awakening the mystical, Buddhist Awakening, the awakening to True Self. We meet a bunch of great Buddhist teachers in the East and we say: "That is awesome, that is beautiful," and we are right. It is beautiful to blow your mind, through Kabbalistic or Buddhist meditation, and awaken to your True Nature, knowing that you are not just a part, but part of a whole. You are not a separate self but True Self, and the total number of True Selves is one. I am actually No-Self, I am beyond all concepts, all realms of being; the Thou lives in me, sunyata is awake in me, as me and through me. Oh my God, that is beautiful. But if I compare that to a primitive teaching, which says that God is Santa Claus in the sky who strikes you dead if you miss a word of prayer, and I say: "Oh, is that is the Third Awakening? That sucks, that is this Jewish-Christian bullshit, right, that is terrible; I am so glad I got out of that." Even really sophisticated Zen masters sometimes say that.

But that is silly, that is a level-line-fallacy. Then you miss the Third Awakening, the awakening to the reality of the Beloved who suffuses all of existence. Every particle of reality is awake Shakti that loves you. Love is not difficult to find, love is not hard to locate, love is impossible to avoid. You are showered with love, every part of you, by the Cosmos in every moment. The Universe is awake, the Universe feels, the Universe feels love, and that is not a dogma, that is a realization.

The personal God as a living experience

I met a man named John Welwood, a longtime Buddhist practitioner who wrote one of the most important books on psychology and spirituality in the last twenty years: 'Journey of the Heart, the

Path of Conscious Love'. John and I kind of liked each other and decided, in spite of crazy schedules, to try to meet every once in a while, just to talk to each other. John is a very strong Buddhist, probably one of the major Buddhist teachers in the Bay Area, and he said: "What is this thing about a personal God? What does that mean? I just don't get that, it seems so primitive." And of course, as we began to talk, we realized that the God that John is talking about, is the God you don't believe in.

I said: "John, when you are thinking about praying to the personal God, which is part of the practice of the Third Awakening, you think of prayer as a concept. Then your Buddhist self comes in and says: "Who can answer this prayer? The personal God is just a concept, it's a dogma," and you throw it out. But when you talk about awareness, John, you say: "That is not a concept, awareness is a living experience." And you are right, John, but only half right. Because the personal God is not a concept either; it is the living reality, just as awareness is. The personal God is the personal face of Awareness, of Essence, that holds you and knows your name."

Practice: Tracing Your Gifts Back to Source

Now I want to awaken with you to what it means to be held in the arms of the Beloved, and to feel that gifting that is happening in every moment. We are going to do a meditation on the Third Awakening, awakening to the reality revealed by what Rumi calls 'the Eye of the Heart': in every moment I am loved, in every moment I am held.

I am going to ask you to shut your eyes for this very simple reality consideration. First locate your center as an individual. And with your deep, loving, gentle permission, I ask you please to forgive me if my voice somehow does not work for you, if I have said anything wrong that is offensive to you. Please forgive me, don't let me get in the way! If my separate self-transmits to you an opening of love, receive it. If I am in the way, please press 'delete'.

Let's enter into Silence of Presence, because the silence itself opens up the field of meditative awareness of realization. So as soon as you have located yourself as an individual, turn to someone next to you and actually face them. Here are the words, they are always beneath the now; here is the practice, a new practice that we have never done before. I actually do this practice myself every day. I meditate, I pray, I pray more than I meditate, I chant, but this is the one practice that I do all the time, that I never miss, it is like my constant cash practice, totally cash. This is going to be the first time I do this meditation with a group. For me, it is the entry into realization.

After locating yourself in Silence of Presence, the first person is going to say: "I am really good at this, I am really good at that", for instance: "I am really good at teaching. I am really good at singing. I am really good at running the kitchen. I am really good at relationships. I am really good at writing in my journal. I am really good at calling my mother every week. I am really good at..." Whatever it is. Then the other person will say to them: "Wow," and then they ask the following question: "Why are you so good at that?" And the first person will say: "Well, I am good in relationships because I am really good at listening." Or: "I am really good at writing in my journal because my mind is organized." They will break down their gift into some other skill they have. Then the first person will say: "Wow, great. And why are you good at that?" And the first person will say: "Well, I am good at thinking in an organized way because I went to a school where I was taught organized thinking." And the first one will say: "Wow, and how did you get to that school?" "Well, my parents…" And so on. The idea is to trace any gift that you have back to its source.

It is actually a tantric practice with roots in Kabbalah that I have developed in the last five years. The point is, to realize that any gift that I have comes from Source. Any gift that I have is actually gifted to me in reality — everything that I think that I have earned, developed, worked hard at. Even the ability to work hard was a gift, including the values to know that I should work hard. If you trace it back to its source you will realize that all is grace, it is all a gift, everything has been given to me. And once you realize that everything has been giving to you, you realize that your entire existence is a gift.

And once you realize that your entire existence is a gift, you realize that you are being held and loved in every second, and you get humble, but also audacious, because you just realize: It is not just you, not just your small-self you, you realize that everything was gifted by God, by the Cosmos, and that you need to live your full self, because you did not do it yourself. All of reality gave you these gifts in order to live them. You experience yourself being fully held and you realize you can't be arrogant, you can't have a false ego when everything you have is a gift, and you are delighted to realize: "Wow, all of reality conspired to give me these gifts." And you feel completely held, wildly filled with gratitude, and then, of course, called to live your gift to the world with full audacity, with full courage, with full passion.

Modeling of practice 'Tracking back to Source' with Chahat

Okay, Chahat, you want to model this with me? Okay, so I'll start.

M: I am a really great teacher.

Ch: Wow.

M: Can you emphasize the 'wow' a little more dramatically? (Laughter) Okay, not bad, but try it like a swoon. We try it again, start again. I am a really great teacher.

Ch: Wow Marc, that's awesome. How come you're such a great teacher?

M: Well, there are lots of reasons, but one of them is that I have a photographic mind, I remember pretty much everything that I read or say. So because I remember everything, it is sort of easy for me to organize material in my mind into a kind of dharmic structure. And for whatever reason, I don't know why, I totally love people, I fall in love with people all the time. I love to talk to people, it gives me gifts and makes me happy more than anything in the world.

CH: Wow, that's awesome! Why do you love people so much?

M: Well, because I practiced, I have done this practice over the years, to develop loving, to really access the natural love in me. Now ask me: "Where did you get the energy to do that practice?" So you keep tracing it back to its source.

CH: Okay. Wow Marc, where did you get the energy to do that practice?

M: Well, I got the energy to do the practice because, when I was young, I prayed to God, I did this radical prayer that God would give me massive amounts of love.

Ch: Wow, awesome. And why do you think God gave you such an awesome amount of love?

M: (interrupting): No, ask me where I got the ability to do the prayer. You see, the practice is that every time I ascribe a talent to myself, you ask me: "Where did it come from? How did you get it?" Okay, there we go, let me recapitulate very fast: "Hey, Chahat, I am a really great teacher, I love people, I have this great organized mind."

Ch: Wow, and where did you get that great organized mind?

M: Well, I got it because I really studied for many years, you know, I remember in my youth I did eighteen hours a day of deep study, training my mind.

CH: Where did you get the energy to study so much from?

M: Well, I got the energy to study because I would actually pray to God to get the energy to study, and I also had really good genetics from my parents. And I really worked hard to get that energy to study.

CH: Wow, and where did you get all that energy from?

M: Where did I get the energy for praying in order to get that energy? You follow the practice? You want to stay really close, you want to keep asking me: "Where did you get the ability to pray?", until I realize that actually all of it comes from Source, I did not do anything. The energy to pray comes from Source, the prayer comes from Source, the genes come from source.

So every time I say: "I did something, I developed this talent, I developed this love," you trace it back to its source, saying: "Where is that from? And where is that from?" This time you do it. So tell me something you are really good at.

Ch: Okay. I am really good at making something out of nothing.

M: Wow, wow, that is awesome, Chahat, that is a huge talent. Wow, where did you get that, how do you do that?

Ch: Well, because there used to be so little that I could find anything to make something good out.

M: Right. And what is the talent?

Ch: The talent is, er, creativity.

M: So you are really creative, which allows you to make something out of nothing. So where is your creativity from? Where did it come from? From your childhood?

Ch: Well, it is because there is so much aliveness.

M: In you?

Ch: Yes, there is so much aliveness in me.

M: That is fantastic, wow. You do have this enormous aliveness, but where does that aliveness in you come from, Chahat?

Ch: I just got it! I just got it! (*Laughter*)

M: You see that, everybody? Actually it takes about ninety seconds to get there. Thank you again for bearing with me while we practiced, I have never done it out loud with anyone, I always do it with myself. So the practice is two questions. There is a 'what' question and a 'where' question. The 'what' question is what talents or gifts you have that allow you to be so good at something, and then you ask the 'where' question: Where does that come from? And then you do that three times, saying: "Chahat, give me another talent that you have."

Modeling of practice 'Tracking back to Source' with Pauline

Now I want to ask Pauline to come forward. Okay, so tell me something that you are unbelievably good at.

P: I am unbelievably good at... listening to people.

M: Wow, Pauline is unbelievably good at listening to people. And what is it that makes you so good at listening to people, Pauline?

P: I don't always really listen to the words, but more to the feelings, to what is radiating through the words, what is behind the words.

M: Wow, wow, I get that, that is a really big gift, that blows me away, wow, what a special person you must be, Pauline. (Laughter)

P: Meet me sometime!

M: So how do you know to listen between the words? Where did that come from? How do you do that?

P: Well, if people are talking, I just look at them, and what I see in their bodies and faces is mostly totally different from the words. It is easy. (Laughter)

M: So where does that come from, how do you know to do it? It's such a special skill, you know, such a special talent. Where does it come from?

P: Well, I think it started back home. My mother used to say: "No, I am not angry, I am just disappointed," and I thought: "Well, fuck you." It was so obvious!

M: Why is that the source of the skill of good listening? When I asked you about that, you thought about your mother. How are they connected?

P: I just knew I was right.

M: And how did that give you the skill of listening?

P: I just got it.

M: You just got it?

P: Yes, I just got it.

M: From where?

P: Well, from Source.

Does everyone see what happens? You got to develop the skill of doing this practice, the practice of 'Tracing it back to source'. So Pauline has an awesome presence, and she is an awesome listener, and she listens through the space between the words, which is based on the ability to really feel the presence of the other person. And then you ask them: "Where did that come from?" She said that it came from her home and her parents, but actually there are many people who had the same kind of home and they did not develop that skill, so at some point you just got it. You realize: "Wow, it's like that with everything: I just got it."

All your gifts have been gifted to you by Source

And because of that I can't say: "I am better than anyone else in the world." I can be really arrogant, but you have to be really humble at the same time, and really audacious, because you realize that the Universe gifted you specifically with this gift! And clearly you don't get a gift for nothing. Imagine that your beloved gives you a gift that you never wear. Your beloved gives you a beautiful new blouse, a beautiful new dress, and then you never wear it? That's terrible. You get this beautiful necklace from your beloved and you never wear it? Your beloved says: "Why? Don't you love me?"

So when you realize that all of your true gifts you received, you just got them, then you realize that the Universe, Source, the personal face of Source, gave you this set of gifts. And if you say: "Well, it is genetics," then look at genes, the most infinitely complex, living system which combines unique codes and every person in a particular way into a full living intelligence. For whenever you go back, you always get to Source. You get to Source and you realize: "Oh my God, my Beloved gave me an awesome gift." And so I am really humble, I am so thankful, I am so full of gratitude for this gift, and I don't get small, I get larger. When I wear the gift proudly I tell my beloved: "I love you so much for giving me this gift," and by doing what I am good at, I am living my gift.

Every single person has a unique working set of gifts. Normally, we ascribe them to ourselves: that is what I have, those are my gifts. But this practice of mysticism is to trace them back to Source, to awaken to the Beloved and realize that you have received these gifts. And if you really are alive, awake and aware, you're going to want to wear the necklace and wear the new shirt. Because if you don't, it's a total rejection of the Beloved, who is loving you in every second, who knows your name and seeks to pleasure you to your infinite growth. And so it is, Amen.

The Awakening to the Mother

*L**et's go* deeper into the Second Face of God and really try and understand and feel into the experience of Enlightenment in the second person. In particular, we're going to talk about the Mother. Not your mother; that's for the therapist, but about The Mother and what the relationship is between the two. I want to begin with that chant from a holy Chassidic master named Sinead O'Connor.

Let's find a meditative space, shut our eyes and let Sinead lead us into the Dharma of the Mother.

Sinead O'Connor sings 'This is to Mother You'

This is to mother you
To comfort you and get you through
Through when your nights are lonely
Through when your dreams are only blue
This is to mother you

This is to be with you
To hold you and to kiss you too
For when you need me I will do
What your own mother didn't do
Which is to mother you
All the pain that you have known
All the violence in your soul
All the 'wrong' things you have done
I will take from you when I am come
All mistakes made in distress
All your unhappiness
I will take away with my kiss, yes
I will give you tenderness
For child I am so glad I've found you
Although my arms have always been around you
Sweet bird although you did not see me
I saw you
And I'm here to mother you
To comfort you and get you through
Through when your nights are lonely
Through when your dreams are only blue
This is to mother you

The forgotten face of God: The Mother

The Dharma of the Mother, as we weave together an Integral World Spirituality, is utterly essential. Somehow, because of the evolution of consciousness, we know a little bit better than we did 200 years ago how to talk about God in the first person, the First

Face of God, the God who lives in me and flows in me as the Force, the Presence, the spaciousness, the bliss, the infinity. We're just learning, when we study together in person, to talk about feeling within ourselves the Third Face of God, the energy of evolution, the evolutionary impulse, and how to connect and align ourselves with that evolution. Which is one of the primary ways I move beyond ego: aligning myself with something larger, aligning myself with the evolutionary impulse, the evolutionary context. Each one of these is a deep Dharma, God in the first person and God in the third person, and they are essential within an Integral World Spirituality.

But what has been left out of our hearts, in virtually the entire Human Potential movement in the last 20, 30, 40, 50 years, is God in the second person, especially God as the Mother. The Mother who comforts me, whom I can trust, who knows that I'm good, who holds me no matter what. There are a lot of good reasons why the Mother God has been left out, and we'll talk about it in a way that allows us to reclaim the great teaching of The Mother. Because what would we be without the Mother?

I want to try to access with you today, in the deepest way we can, this Dharma of the Mother. When you hear Sinead sing her, you can actually feel her; in some deep way, you can actually feel her presence. So I want to feel her presence and then I want to update her, to evolve her, so we can engage her as the living presence that holds us in our lives. That's not mythic, not superstitious, not based on a deconstructed thing of the Church; it is based on a living experience of the Mother.

Exercise: distinguishing between real and ideal mother

I want to begin with a holy exercise, to clarify the difference between my mother and The Mother, because that's one of the first things that get in the way. So find a dyad partner, you get two minutes each. First describe in a few words your own mother, and bless her. Then call up the image of the ideal mother and describe her qualities. We all know the ideal mother, we can actually find her in ourselves, we know what she is like, we know how we want her to be. What are the qualities of the ideal Mother?

Various participants: Presence/Space/Humor

M: What are her most basic attributes, her core?

P: She is warm. She welcomes everything.

M: Right, there is a welcoming embrace. She offers safety, she holds me safely. There is tenderness, compassion, she is always available. As long I am willing talk to her, she wants to talk to me; she doesn't get upset if you don't call. We can find this dimension of the Mother in ourselves; it's not a dogma of the Church, because if you go inside, as we just did, you can find her, and the reason we can find her is because she is there. In some sense, as much as we may love our mothers, the complexity with our mother is that she often doesn't meet the image of the Mother that we're holding. So that deep image of the Mother that we're holding doesn't come from superstition, nor from a Church dogma; it comes from a deep, sacred intuition about the force of the Mother that holds us.

I want to read something from Ramakrishna now. Remember the rule: whenever I ask if you've read some great teacher, just lie.

Quote Ramakrishna

"The world has a beginning, and that beginning is the Mother of the world. Once you found the mother, you know yourself the child. Only when you know yourself the child, can you return to the Mother, not perishing, not dying, even though your body dies. Close your eyes, shut your doors. And yet you do not toil all of your life, you're held in the shining radiance, you return again to the light. This is called 'entering the eternal'. Nothing will harm your Self. This is called 'the Mother of the world,' the Dao, the Goddess, the inexpressible. Once you know the child, you return to keep the Mother."

Wow, that's Ramakrishna. He is not talking about a Church dogma, he is talking of the realization of chant, of meditation, which is the realization of the Mother. So first we heard Sinead, then we did an exercise distinguishing 'my mother' from 'The Mother', then we heard these words by Ramakrishna. Now, let's get the obstacles to the Mother out of the way, before we enter her even more deeply.

Obstacles to realizing the Mother at the levels of Spiral Dynamics

M: What are the obstacles to the Mother, why do we associate the Mother with an old Church doctrine? You tell me.

Ch: She has ideas about me.

M: Good. What are those ideas?

Ch: That I have to be in a specific way.

M: Okay, so mother wants things for me but seems not to know me well. Mother makes claims on me, and those claims seem to be in violation of who I am. Feel into this very deeply. The way mother appears to me, is based on my level of consciousness. How many of you know about the levels of consciousness according to Spiral Dynamics? Everyone? Good! Let's go through the Spiral together and let's see how the Mother appears at each level of the Spiral. I'm going to do it as a Voice Dialogue, I will ask to speak to the voice of the Mother at each level of the spiral. And for those who don't remember, I'll give you a summation before each level that we do.

The Mother at Beige

M: I'm going to start with beige. Beige is the instinctual level, the survival level. Everyone sit up and hold their center, find your place. Okay, I'd like permission to speak to the voice of Mother at the level of Beige, survival consciousness. Who am I speaking to?

All: The voice of the Mother.

M: So tell me, mother, what's your job?

P: To feed. To protect. To keep warm. To defend.

M: Okay, so at the instinctual level of beige, your job is to ensure the survival of your child.

The Mother at Purple

Now switch positions, we are going for the level of Purple. Purple is the level of magic, of blood connections between tribes. It's the level of being partially immersed in Mother Nature, just beginning to become human. It's the level of all the invisible lines that connect the river to the mountain, the Earth to the person. It's "Love the Earth, love the Sky". So I'd like to speak to the voice of the Mother at the level of magical, Purple consciousness. Who am I speaking to?

All: To the voice of the Mother.

M: So Mother, tell me, what is your job? What do you want from your child at this level of blood ties and magic connections?

P: They have to honor me in Nature. They need to be obedient, to bring offerings, they have to do rituals, sacrifice.

M: So at this level, the voice of the Mother says: "I want something from my child." And what happens if your child doesn't bring you the right offering?

P: They may be punished.

M: What if your child marries the wrong bloodline?

P: I will prevent it from happening at all costs.

M: Does everybody feel that the Mother feels different here? The Mother is on the one hand Mother Earth, nourishing and protecting, and on the other hand there are all these mysterious, invisible lines of connection and magical blood relations in these clans and tribes, which are all expressions of the Mother. And if you violate them, the Mother devours you. This is the Great Mother to whom you must bring ten thousand virgins to sacrifice. That's a big deal. If there are any virgins in the room, be careful with this Mother! What else?

P: It's really important that they understand me. There are a few people that really understand me and whom I can talk to.

M: And the rest of them?

P: They will listen to these people.

M: Right, so I need to be really understood and worshipped properly and most people don't really understand me. But those few people, the shamans, the priestesses and the priests, they really understand me, so I need people to listen to them, because they know how to approach me.

The Mother at Blue

Okay, let's shift in our chairs again. I'm going to skip Red for a second and to talk to the Mother at the level of Blue consciousness, which is the level of mythical membership. It is the Church, it's the Empire with its rules and regulations. You don't need to be part of the bloodline, but if you follow the rules, subscribe to the rules, then you can be become part of the Empire, or of the Church. It's all about rules, disciplines, rigorous practices, sets of laws. It has great beauty and is also very demanding. So I'd like to speak to the voice of the Mother at the level of mythical, Blue consciousness. Who am I speaking to?

All: To the Mother.

M: Tell me about yourself, Mother, what do you give and what do you want to receive?

P: I give a beautiful life after this one. If you give me obedience, I give you protection.

M: So there is an exchange. If my rules are obeyed, I give protection; if my rules are not obeyed, you get less protection. If the rules of the Mother Church aren't obeyed, I might go straight to hell. So that Mother is still a little frightening, but when you enter into her Church with all of its rules and you become part of it, there's also something comforting, isn't there? There is a sense of belonging, a sense of comfort; if I only can enter and be part of that. But if I don't believe or there is evidence that goes the other way, or there is something that stops me from entering, even though I desperately want to enter, I can't, and I feel the anger of the Mother. If I violate the rules, either the sexual rules or rules of faith, I feel that somehow she thinks I am unworthy; that's also the voice of the Mother. Does everyone begin to feel that the Mother isn't just a mother, that she is always seen and felt through a prism of consciousness? So the Mother is complex. We need to get to another Mother, we're not there yet.

The Mother at Orange

M: Let's shift positions. I'd like permission to speak to the Mother at the level of orange consciousness. Who am I speaking to?

All: To the voice of the Mother.

M: Now orange is the level of meritocracy, of capitalism, of industry and modern business. It's no longer based on the rules of the Church, it's based on marriage and hard work. The quality of all citizens of the world without any church, based on their own individual capacity to work and ensuring the rights of every person. At this point not actually every person, at this point at the level of orange it's still every man. But that's basically orange. So tell me, voice of the Mother, at the level of orange consciousness, what do you give, what do you expect, what do you return? Tell me about yourself.

P: - I want my children to have a proper education, so they can be successful in the world.

- I prepare their sandwiches, but only when they are going to school or to work.

- I expect them to be productive, I expect them to have wealth.

- I want them to be autonomous and independent.

M: And what do I give them if they do all these things?

P: I praise them.

M: Wow, I'm the proud mother: "My child, look! He went to Oxford, that's fantastic." So I praise them if they are successful. And if they disappoint me, what do I do? The Mother of Blue would be angry, but what does the Mother at Orange do? If you do well, she supports you; at her best, she loves you unconditionally, but there is this deep sense that if you don't do well, if you're not productive, she is not going to punish you formally, she is not going to send you to hell, but what will she do?

P: She makes you feel very bad about yourself.

M: Right, you let your mother down, you disappointed her. You get emotional blackmail if you don't give her what she needs to be proud of you. "Why am I living in Venwoude, when I could have been a lawyer in Amsterdam, and my mother would have been so much happier." So the mother gives me love and support, but if I don't give her that motherly pride, there is something that she takes away. She makes me feel like a failure.

The Mother at Green

Green consciousness is about doing your own thing, whatever your future is. We are multicultural, Flower Power. As long as you're happy, it's good with me. If you're good with Venwoude, go to Venwoude if that is your path, it's totally fine. If you want to study with some freak Rabbi, whatever, your problem, but I understand. If that makes you feel good, that's good, that makes me feel good, too, so it's all good. Help the homeless, I'm so proud of you because when you were seven, you gave your piece of bread to that homeless person. That's the mother at the level of Green.

Let's go to the level of Green, let's shift positions. Who am I speaking to?

All: To the voice of the Mother.

M: So tell me, what does she give and what does she want?

P: She wants you to call her all the time.

M: Right. Have you all heard of the Oedipus complex? There is a Jewish story about Mrs Goldstein, a Jewish mother in Long Island, New York, very liberal, very progressive, very lovely, good person, very Green consciousness. She goes to see the psychiatrist, who has been seeing her son for some time, and the psychiatrist says: "Mrs Goldstein, I think your son has an Oedipus complex." And Mrs Goldstein says: "Oedipus, schmoedipus, as long as he loves his mother."

At the level of Green consciousness, what is the Mother's interest? Love me and show me. At the level of Purple she wants blood sacrifice, at the level of Orange she wants success, at the level of Green she wants love, just consistent love. And what does she give? She gives friendship, freedom and a kind of love. She says: "Choose your way and I'll be happy if you're happy." That's beautiful, that's very different from the level of Purple that says: "If you violate the bloodline, I'm going to fucking kill you!"

The Mother at second-tier consciousness

Now let's go all the way, let's go down to what we call the second tier of consciousness, which contains yellow, turquoise, whatever. Second-tier consciousness transcends and includes all of the first-tier levels, so all the important dimensions of all the previous levels are here. I'd like to speak to the voice of the Mother at the second tier of consciousness. Shift in your seats. Who am I speaking to?

All: To the voice of the Mother.

M: Give me an image of the Mother, who is she?

P: She sees me for who I am.

M: Good. She sees me, I'm recognized by the mother. She loves me, and it's a different love. On the one hand she wants me to succeed, she makes demands on me, but on the other there is a sense that she is always holding me, no matter what. In her essence she has this deep demanding and this deep holding at the same time. So she wants me to rise, and when I'm going on, she is embracing me. But I know that wherever I fall, I fall into her arms. She sometimes wants me to offer sacrifice, she sometimes wants my ethical obedience, she wants my productivity, and yet she holds me, because she sees me, because she knows me. I'm not afraid to be at my greatest before the Mother and I'm not afraid to be at my most vulnerable before the Mother. She will receive my confession of greatness just like she'll receive my confession of vulnerability. This Mother cares about my personal needs; there is no request that is too small to bring before the Mother. Even when I am a full adult, the Mother cares about every detail of my life, including my body. The Mother affirms the dignity of my personal needs. She sees me in my greatness at the very same moment that see sees me in my vulnerability. Wow!

Hold that energy, let's hold Silence of Presence, and let's hear Sinead again, but this time as a deeper meditation on the Mother of second-tier consciousness.

The Mother image as the personal face of Essence

In teachings on Enlightenment, we're usually told to get beyond the personal, to access the vast, impersonal space, the unqualified consciousness, the open space in Presence. Yet after looking at the Mother at all first-tier levels of consciousness, we got to second tier: the realization of the Personal Face of the Cosmos, the Personal Face of Essence. The Mother who holds me and knows my name was distorted and lost; we wrongly identified the Mother with the way she appeared through the distorting prism of the lower, first-tier levels of consciousness.

When I actually engage in the evolution of my consciousness and the evolution of the consciousness of the Cosmos, I once again realize the personal lighting of the Cosmos, the personal face of the Mother that holds me and knows my name and cares about every detail of my individual needs. Not to affirm my narcissism, not the Mother as the Law of Attraction that gives me a shining red car, but as the Mother who truly knows me, recognizes me, knows what my deepest needs are. She stands for those needs, and she passionately, radiantly, wildly, ecstatically, insanely desires my good. And my dearest, most holy and beautiful brothers and sisters, to live in the Universe without knowing that the Universe desires your good, without knowing that the Universe desires your highest prosperity, without the realization of the Great Mother, is to live in radical pain, but what's worse, it's to live in ignorance.

Let's do some practices now. So shut your eyes and I will guide you through a three-step meditation

Guided meditation: The Mother's yearning for you

First step: Imagine someone that you love dearly, that you feel very protective towards, that you like to take care of, that you like to hold. Feel your love for that person arise, and feel the tenderness in your heart, the compassion that you feel for that person. Even though you know something of their weakness, you're able to see through that weakness and see their beauty and goodness. Even though you know something of their brokenness, you're able to see through the cracks of the brokenness and see their essence, which is so wildly beautiful. Feel in first person your actual love for that person rising and emerging and playing and expanding and deepening. Just feel the full tenderness of your heart, what you would do to take care of that person, what you would do to protect them, what you would give up for them. Feel the energy of the Mother in you, which radically loves and feels total, open, tender-heart love for that person. Then hold this feeling and place it gently in the back of your heart and let it sit there.

Second step: And now in this moment, feel the beautiful, gorgeous rising of sexual desire for someone you love sexually, someone you desire to be with. Your body yearns for them, you feel the thriving, the openness, you move towards them. Let the sexual energy and desire and passion and yearning rise in your body, and bring yourself to a moment where it rises stronger and stronger, until you're literally in that moment before fulfillment, where everything you want is going to explode. But you're not quite there, you can't quite get there, and you feel the full yearning for contact. You cannot quite make contact, but the full, passionate, alive, pulsating, yearning of total openness, desiring entering, penetration, contact, lives in you. And hold that and place it in the back of your heart.

Third step: And then feel rising in you the ability to totally, completely, absolutely merge those two together. Merge them together completely and absolutely in a beautiful, wonderful way. Let the love and the sexual desire merge as one, as your care and your tenderness cross into one inside of you. And then take all of that desire and yearning and love, and feel that that is the experience of the Mother yearning for you, wanting to know your name, holding you, caring about you, lusting for you, particularly you, wanting to merge with you, to be penetrated by you and to enter you in this very moment.

Let's come back together and just feel how radical that is. Some of us were able to touch it, some of us weren't, but that's totally fine. Just feel how radical that experience is. That is the experience of the great saints and mystics. That is the inner Enlightenment experience, born of the deepest meditation, the greatest realization of the most solid and spectacular of minds and hearts that ever were. What would it mean to walk around the world holding that realization? It would change your entire life. Nothing will be ever the same. So even in the fullness of what you can't hold, you can hold in this moment a glimmer of it. You now know that it's there, you know what it is. You now know what Rumi knew; all of Rumi is about this, the entire thing from beginning to end, this is the entire story. And the reason you like to read a Rumi poem, even though you're not quite sure why, is because it reminds you of this, it reminds you of this knowing.

Poem Hafiz: There Is a Beautiful Creature Living in a Hole

How does Hafiz say it? Talking about the Divine he writes:

There is a Beautiful Creature
Living in a hole you have dug.

So at night
I set fruit and grains
And little pots of wine and milk
Besides your soft earthen mounds,

And I often sing.
But still, my dear,
You do not come out.

I have fallen in love with Someone
Who hides inside you.

We should talk about this problem

Otherwise,
I will never leave you alone.

This is the Divine voice: "I have fallen in love with Someone who hides inside you. We should talk about this problem, otherwise I will never leave you alone." That's the Mother. Can you see why sitting in Zen meditation is such a beautiful thing to do, and you should totally do it, AND you need all three Faces of God? Without the Mother, oh my God, it's kind of cold out there. But you don't want the Mother as a crush, you don't want the Mother at the level of Blue, or Purple; you want the Mother at the highest level of realization.

Dyad practice: Confessing your greatness

We'll do a second exercise, so find a dyad partner. Here we go. To whom in the world would you tell that you're awesome? To whom would you tell how incredibly, wildly great you are, and who would be utterly delighted to hear it and let you go on about it for two hours? The Mother. The Mother, in mystical understanding, is the Mother and the Lover at the same time.

So in this practice, your job is to confess, it's a confession before the Mother, instead of confessing your sins, like Mother Church wanted you to. You actually have to do a much harder confession here, which is to confess your greatness. Confessing your greatness is actually much harder than confessing your sin. Because as you confess your sin, you're off the hook. If I am a rotten worm, who cares? But if I am awesome, beautiful, stupendous and gorgeous... Oh my God.

The person who is listening is the priest of the priests, the Divine Mother. And the Divine Mother who is listening holds you, holds your confession. If you get stuck, the priest, the Divine Mother asks: "Is there more?" And you respond. Then when you're finished, the Mother says: "I see you in your greatness and I love you," and embraces the confessor. Now feel into this, this is a very advanced practice. You're speaking your greatness, you're speaking not from the level of ego, but from the level of Unique Self, from the nature of the Divine that lives in you, as you and through you.

What was your experience of being received by the Mother and what was your experience of being the Mother receiving?

P: Receiving was beautiful.

M: Receiving is easier, sometimes. To be received is a big deal, so let yourself be totally received by the Mother and to confess your absolute greatness. Because the only thing in the world that actually obligates me is my greatness. That's what caught me: to actually confess my greatness. In the old Church, they would confess sins every day, but in Integral World Spirituality, we are engaged in the evolution of confession and we actually begin the practice, from the level of Unique Self, of confessing our greatness.

Turning back to the Mother

Exercise: writing a letter to your mother

*L**et's hold* Silence of Presence, we are in meditation, and write a short letter to your mother, thanking her for the ways she did mother you and forgive her for the ways that she didn't.

Remember, as long as you're separate self, you're a skin-encapsulated ego, and your entire world is about that: your separate self and then the nuclear family, the small family that lives around you. And everything that happens in that family system is so enormously huge: "Wow, oh my God, what did she do to me? What did I do to her? How did it all happen?"

But when you move from separate self to True Self and you realize that you are part of the Ground of Being, you realize that after all your thoughts and all your emotions are gone, you are still there. You realize that you are the Divine Heart of Being itself, which lives and beats and breathes in you. You realize that all of reality lives in you, and you live in all of reality as a felt, first-person, glimmering experience of ecstasy, and you feel that love pouring through you.

Amen: sucking at the breast of the nursing mother

Amen, hallelujah, praise, amen! The word 'amen' in English, or the three-letter Hebrew root 'amn', means 'the breast of the nursing mother'; it means both 'total trust' and 'doing practice'. It's beautiful. Why? Because you practice to access the trust that you are held and sucking at the breast of the nursing mother, right? Here is what master Isaac the Blind says, in the 13th century. He writes: "We know Source not by knowing, but by sucking." Wow, that is so gorgeous.

The Mother as the goddess Kali who rips you open

Have you ever heard of my friend Kali? Kali is this wild Hindu goddess who appears in these wild pictures; she's got snakes and dragons and she is killing people left and right. She's doing her shit, man, she's scary, okay? Kali is ripping you open! But here is the deal: you *trust* her to rip you open, you see that? You trust the Mother, because we need to be ripped open sometimes. But most people we can't trust to rip us open, because they have got so many ulterior motives, they've got so much else going on, they've got so many agendas they're running. So when they give us a critique, we're like: "Yeah, okay," and we know the agendas that they're running, and the smarter we are, the more we block them out.

But when I'm nursing at her breast, the Mother says: "Man, you've got to transform. Man, you've got to step up. And man, I'm going to rip your heart out and eat it if you don't! And I'm going to give it back to you and kiss you." That's Kali, that's the wild, Divine Mother. And we trust her with radical trust, because she's the Mother, she loves me and she's not like the father. The father says: "If you don't do it, I'm going to punish you." The mother says: "If you don't do it, you're going to break my heart. And if you break my heart, you're going to get destroyed by my broken heart, so I'm going to ask you not to break my heart."

And so you step up for the Mother, because you want to heal her heart, because her heart's in you. You see that? The Mother holds you. To walk through life not held by the Mother, by the Mother who knows your name personally, is insane; it's utterly, wildly insane. For what's the definition, holy brothers and sisters, of insanity? Not to know the nature of reality.

A mother's love allows her child room to choose

And what does a mother do? A mother loves so much that she steps back to allow her child room to choose, even if the child chooses against the mother. Do you get that? That's called the mystery of withdrawal of the Mother, in mysticism, in Sufism, in Kabbalah, meaning that the Mother loves so much, that she steps back and allows room for choice, even when that choice seems to be against the Mother, and the Mother waits for the child to consciously align with the Mother. That's like "Oh my God!"

Do you know what it means to be a mother? I'm watching Marianna now raise Zion for the last two years; she's with him 24 hours a day. And Marianna, my son's mother, is a wildly ambitious person; she's wildly talented and ambitious. Before she was 37, she wrote seven or eight books; two years ago she won the national, number-one book award in America for spirituality books. And then she had Zion. It's like: "Oops, oh yeah, I have a book that came out last year; I guess I should post it some place, maybe. Oh, there's Zion." She's madly in love with Zion and she knows that Zion is going to leave her. And to be an awesome mother, she has to love him in a way in which he can leave her, and hope that he's going to come back. Wow!

Oh, the Mother is madly in love with us, madly, wildly in love with us. And how do I know that? I know it. I know it as a sure realization of the enlightened Second Person, absolutely true. Don't trust me, Rumi knew it, Hafiz knew it, Ibn Arabi knew it. What does it mean to go through life and not know Mother? Mother, Mother, like wow! Her love is wow! The Mother loves me, and I love the Mother and I serve her with absolute devotion, even as she releases me into my freedom and waits for me to return. Wow!

Talking to the Mother through prayer

I want to go on one more step with you, okay? Because I just want to really feel this with you. This is so deep, it's like the deepest of the deep. So, let me ask you a question: How do you talk to the Mother? How do you talk to God in the first person? Someone here said: "Meditation." So, the train to God in the first person is meditation, is that fair? You can also do some dervish whirling, kind of feel it going through you. Or you could do a little spinning at a Jerry XX?? concert, but basically you're trying to access this thing going through you in the first person.

What's the God train to the Mother? Prayer, right? But when we hear prayer, we hear fundamentalist church. You got that? "The Lord Jesus will save me and the Lord God will punish those gay people and the Lord God will punish those people who are not in the Mother Church of Christ, serving and receiving absolution in this Church, and if you send me a check, I can serve the Lord a little bit better." Like yo! That's a bit of a problem.

And 70% of the world today lives in a fundamentalist church that says: "We're in and you are out." So 70% of the world lives in a fundamentalist church, which is ethnocentric, meaning: "God is my God, and my God kind of hates you, because you do not recognize him." We got that? That's because we don't just have perceptions, we're *interpreting our perceptions.*

But when we serve Allah, whether it's the Father face or the Mother face of God, it's always the Mother, because the Father and the Mother aren't separate. They are part of the same deep ??, and the yearning we have for Mother is the Mother speaking to us. You hear that? A fish doesn't say: "I'd love to be on dry land," for fish is in water. When you yearn for something, it means you're connected to it. Did you get what I mean by that?

Our yearning to come home is real

When you have an unquenchable longing... How many people feel: "I'm totally at home, my life is perfect just as it is; I'm not yearning for anything"? No one. It means that every single person is yearning, every single person has an unquenchable longing for some other place. Do you get that? Is that wild? But why? Because we are not yet home, because we're yearning to be home. That's not a mistake, but we go to a psychologist to get that out of us: "Let me get some equilibrium here, let me get some homeostasis." And you do therapy your whole life to get rid of that inchoate yearning, when that yearning is the Mother whispering in your ear, saying: "Come home." Wow!

Of course, there are also pathological forms of yearning that you should work with in structural therapy, and if you go to the central process that Mauk has developed, which comes after the process that Marijke does, you get this awesome tour on how you can use all these structural therapies. They are awesome, for sure. But the core yearning that lives in me is the Mother whispering in my ear, saying: "Come, I know your name. Come home, I can hear you, I can hear you."

Group practice: asking the Mother out loud for everything you want

We're simply going to stand together and everyone is going to be invited, without anyone else listening, to just speak out loud to the

Mother. Speak to the Mother directly; not about her, not around her. It's like: "Wow, the same way I hear my neighbor talking, the Mother hears me." If you like a poem by Rumi, that's what the whole thing is about: the Divine Mother. Now, the Divine Mother isn't owned by a religion and the Divine Mother also lives inside of me. The Divine Mother is not outside of me *and* she is beyond me, both at the same time. Can you hear that? The Divine Mother lives in me as me; I am the Divine Mother.

You're able to turn to the Divine Mother in devotion. You turn, my holy friends, and you kneel. You take all the books you've written, you take all of your intellectual skill, you take all the wisdom that you have and you kneel like a baby before the Divine Mother and say: "Hold me, hold me." And who doesn't have a yearning to be held? That's the yearning for the Divine Mother, and no single human being will ever fill that yearning themselves.

Do you look to a human being, one human, to be the whole Divine Mother? The relationship will shatter. The human being can incarnate the Divine Mother and can hold you as the Divine Mother, but each human being has to be herself/himself participating in the Divine Mother.

So, in Silence of Presence, we're going to stand and spread out through the room, staying inside of the inside: "My arms have always been around you." Let us shut our eyes and let us pray, not in a fundamentalist-church way, but in a Venwoude, evolutionary world-spirituality way. If you want to know what God is: God is the infinity of intimacy. We know the little intimacy that we have between us, and the infinity of intimacy, that's the Mother. And the Mother hears us at this moment.

We ask for everything, because the personal matters, not at the level of the separate self, of the grasping ego, but of the unique expression of life that is 'God having a Marc experience', 'God having a Mauk experience'. You matter, you're special, not at the level of ego, but at the level of an infinite, unique expression of the Love-Intelligence and Love-Beauty that never was, is or will be again. To deny your specialness and to say that your needs don't matter, is to deny the Mother. To get lost in your wounds is to not be held by the Mother, but to deny the dignity of your need and the utter, infinite, wild, ecstatic importance of your story. Wow! The Mother is here, I can feel her in the room. She is every place always, but she's revealed herself just now, she's happy with us for a moment.

So on three, as the chime goes, I'm going to invite everyone to pray fully out loud and ask for anything and everything, and everyone is listening and no one is listening. So pray to everyone, don't pray quietly to yourself. We will use the tradition of the great study halls, we pray out loud and we hurl our prayers, shout our prayers, or at least speak our prayers out loud until the room becomes the song of prayer. One, two, it's a huge opportunity. The intelligent Universe hears us. One, two, three.

Try and just open your hands, in the gesture of prayer, just open your hands, and open your heart, and let yourself fall in love with the Mother, because she is madly in love with you.

Dyad practice: asking the Mother for everything you want

This practice is very simple. We go into dyads, one person holding the place of the Divine Mother and the second person holding the place of the prayer, and then we are going to switch. So find a partner, and the partner is going to stand as the high priestess in the temple, the Mother, and you're looking at the Mother incarnate in this person, and you're going to ask for everything that you want.

It's really easy to get naked taking your clothes off, but I want to invite you to get naked with your clothes on. So the person who is going to be with the Divine Mother, don't be like: "Oh, he can see my cock and my cunt, that's totally fine, but I'm not going to share with you what I *really* want." That's not okay - just get naked and really ask for everything and know that the Divine Mother is holding you. And as the Divine Mother, you're not listening passively. You're the Divine Mother, you're the high priest and high priestess, receiving. You're the Mother that Sinead was singing about.

The person with the shorter hair goes first, and if you stop for a second, the Divine Mother just says to you: "Is there more? Is there more?" And when you finish, the Divine Mother embraces you, and then you switch, with the person who was the Divine Mother becoming the child turning to the Mother asking her for everything. Then when you're done, the Divine Mother embraces you.

And we're doing this not only for those of us here; we're doing this to invite the Mother back in. We've exiled her and she weeps and cries and she awaits, as Ramakrishna said, for us to open up the door of the temple of our heart to her again, so we can feel her love and she can feel us loving her.

I'm going to tell you a wild secret. Much more than man is in search of God, much more than woman is in search of God, God or the Mother is in search of us. She yearns for us as desperately as we yearn for her. She is Krishna dancing with the milk maidens, she is Shekinah, Kali, she's the aboriginal Grandmother. She's your own mother in all her brokenness trying to be a mother, and she is in the Earth and in the Sky, she's everywhere.

So really get vulnerable and really ask for everything. The great thing about the Mother is that after you break down before her, you just feel relieved and you just begin to smile and you love the Earth.

The Fourth Awakening, to Unique Self

Unique Self as the second-person perspective

*T*he *essence* of the Unique-Self teaching is the second-person perspective. If in our True Self we are all impersonally a part of the One, and there is no room for a second person. The second person implies a distinction within the One. Second breaks the monism of the One and is utterly personal, which is precisely the teaching of Unique Self. If all is One, then there is nothing personal and no relationship. And while relationship does not require separate selves, it does require Unique Selves.

When you move to the second-person perspective, you realize that the inner fabric of all of reality is love, and that there is ultimately no distinction between impersonal and personal love. Both participate in the same essential energy. The love that animates the evolutionary impulse is not merely personal, in the sense of separate self or personality, but it is not in any sense merely impersonal either. It is rather the inner essence of All-That-Is, which expresses itself both as the vast impersonal cosmic love which suffuses and sustains All-That-Is, and as the radically personal love in which Spirit holds every being, as well as the personal love which exists between all beings who have realized their true nature. For in your true nature you are not separate from the true nature of All-That-Is. Your true nature and the true nature of All-That-is is love, which expresses itself as the drive to ever higher and more sustained unions.

Overcoming obstacles to Unique Self

Group exploration of obstacles to Unique Self

We are going to enter into Silence of Presence and sit for a minute or two in deep silence, and when you come out of the silence, you answer the following question: "What obstacle stands in the way of the full realization of my awake, alive, ecstatic Unique Self?" The person with the shorter hair goes first and we speak for about two minutes. If the person stops talking, the other person asks: "Is there more?" Okay, take it away.

So, what obstacle stands in the way of the full realization of my awake, alive, ecstatic Unique Self?

E: For me it was anxiety, as if I'm afraid that when I live that fully, I will lose my grounding, that I am not taking everyone with me, that I will leave our community space. That is a big one.

M: So, if I would step into my full Unique Self, then I will lift off and wind up alone? Make sure I get it right, so correct me.

E: Yes, then I am sort of by myself.

M: Right, by myself. So if I would really be the fullness of myself, you would somehow not be able to be with me, I would somehow wind up in my Uniqueness all alone. Something like that?

E: Yes, but when I am in my uniqueness, I am not alone.

M: So there is a little contradiction, between this feeling of anxiety of "I will be left alone", but when I think about it, I realize that when I am in my Uniqueness, I am most together. That's a pretty good realization. Anything else?

E: Well, I also discovered that when I am too busy, when I'm not relaxed, I drift off in emotions and stuff.

M: Let's go careful, perfect. So, the goal is to be in my Unique Self. If your Unique Self is connected to being busy...

E: No, it is connected to focus.

M: It is connected to focus, that's another good realization. I'm afraid of being busy, but actually my Unique Self has nothing to do with business, it has to do with focus. You've done pretty good. You see that relaxation that has come into you? Deep bow, thank you.

So the question is: what is the obstacle that stands in the way of your realization of your Unique Self?

D: I have the idea that I cannot live all the time ecstatically, awake and all that stuff, because I have to work efficiently for a better environment and it cannot be together at the same time.

M: So if I would be in my Unique Self, I would have to be kind of ecstatic all the time, and then I wouldn't get anything done, right? I wouldn't actually be effective in doing the good things that I need to do in the world. Can you recognize that this is a story?

D: Yes.

M: Yes, and as soon as you say it out loud, you realize: "Wow, I am a wise woman, I know that I don't need to be ecstatic all the time, and actually my Unique Self IS involved in healing the environment. My Unique Self has ecstasy and it has efficiency; it has effectiveness and rapture, and I can actually move between all of them." Let's just watch this together, just you and me, no one is listening. What happens is that you tell yourself a story, like we all do, and we get caught up in that story, which says that if I really let myself be my Unique Self, I have to constantly be in ecstasy and I couldn't do things in the world. But that is just a story. Deep bow, thank you.

So, what obstacle is in the way of realizing my Unique Self?

M2: What is in the way is, it is too vulnerable. I'm afraid that people will misuse it, will misuse me.

M: Let's feel into that one. That one is more about sorrow, right? In other words, if I would be in my Unique Self, in my authenticity, that's way too vulnerable, and people will misunderstand it, will misuse it, or will misuse me. Wow, that almost convinced me, brother. So let's go into it together. Part of my Unique Self is to know when and where to share my vulnerability, right? That's part of it. You see, we each have a vision of Unique Self. Her vision was: it's always ecstatic. So we all create a vision of Unique Self that we know we can't meet, right? And your vision is that being your Unique Self is always being vulnerable, exposed. Isn't that wonderful to see? That's what I mean by a story. Because actually I know you, you are a very discerning, wise man, and you already know that part of your Unique Self is to know how to move between your different parts and how to play them effectively. So it is great to notice that you actually tell yourself a story, a story that you know isn't true.

M2: (*laughs*) But I still believe it, so...

M: Then let's stay with it. Do you really believe it? In what book is it written that to be your Unique Self, you have to show your vulnerability all the time? I wrote a book on Unique Self, let's see if it is written there, hold on... No, I don't see it. So if you would go into this a second and a third time, the guru in you, your own guru, the guru that lives in you, would give you good instructions. Check in with him and ask him what he thinks about that belief. He is very wise, I trust him, totally trust him. Gafni I don't know, but this guru inside you is awesome. So part of your Unique Self, part of my Unique Self, is to know when to share my vulnerability and when to hold it privately. Does that make sense?

M2: That makes total sense.

M: Awesome. Deep bow to the God in the center of the circle. Thank you, brother.

Okay, there must be someone with a persuasive story that we can really believe. What is the obstacle to live and realize the fullness of your Unique Self?

T: It's about losing control.

M: About losing control. Yeah, you're right, you are lost, forget it. No Unique Self for you, everybody else was wrong, and you are actually right. I think you are probably lost. It is kind of a shame, but it happens. I guess everyone else in the room will realize their Unique Self, but not you. *(Laughter)* Hey, we two are trying to have a quiet conversation, so we appreciate it if you guys be a little quiet, seriously. I apologize, so let us try it again, okay? So the fear is losing control.

T: Yes, living my Unique Self is beyond my control.

M: It is out of control. Let's stay together, let's slow down and relax, and let's try and keep this conversation between us, okay? Do you mind if I ask you a personal question?

T: Go ahead.

M: Are you a virgin?

T: No.

M: Okay, I'm just checking. So in sexuality, do you lose control?

T: Yes.

M: Okay, but you still do it anyways?

T: Yes.

M: Okay, I'm just checking. So the problem seems to be not about losing control, because there ARE places where you like to lose control. So what if all of life was one great, erotic fuck?

T: *(Laughs)* Interesting!

M: Nice, right? And let us go a little further. I don't want to get personal here, but just a couple of things, okay? So in sex you have to know when to lose control, right? For example, there is this very big thing in society today, they actually have new medicines for it, and it is called 'premature ejaculation'.

That's when someone loses control too early, right? So that's something a person wants to work on, because you can give more pleasure to God, to reality, to yourself, to your partner when actually you have enough control to stand the game long enough, to lose control at the right time. That's kind of nice, isn't it? But just stay with this, it's a big deal. So what we are seeing here, of course, is a story. Of course you lose control sometimes, and losing control can be great. And being your Unique Self is knowing how to retain control for long enough to lose control at the right time. Awesome. Now when I speak from reality, in the name of reality, we need you to lose control at specific times, when you are just kind of full out in your full, radical, alive Unique Self. And other times we need your Unique Self to actually hold appropriate control, in ways that allow you to function in great, effective Unique-Self ways. You see, it really is just like sexing.

T: So the idea that Unique Self means not having control is too rough, too simple?

M: Right. It is more nuanced. The story that if I am in my Unique Self, I am out of control, is just a story of the ego. That's kind of a relief. To live in your Unique Self is to make love, and in making love you need to know exactly when to hold control and when to lose control. A great lover knows the precise balance between the two, okay? Awesome. Deep bow, brother.

Now, I am sure, I hope there is at least one person who has a good reason for not being able to live their full Unique Self, in which case that will be fine. So tell me, what's in the way? I mean, there must be some real obstacle that's in the way; please share that with me.

E: I'm blessed with a fantastic mind, which keeps thinking and thinking all the time and comes up with a thousand 'no's'. And it is always telling me: "Just stay modest. You will make a fool of yourself, you will make them look like a fool, you will be ashamed of yourself afterwards. You will look arrogant, and you probably will have it all wrong."

M: Right, you have a great mind! And your mind is working all the time, all the time. This is really important, this is great. Your mind is working all the time and it keeps saying 'no' in a thousand different ways. Wow. We were able to help T in the end, but I think you are hopeless.

E: I knew it.

M: Yeah, it happens. Nothing to be done. But let's try anyway, since we are here. I'll tell you something wild, and you tell me what you think of it, oaky? In order to realize your Unique Self, you have to first get a glimpse of what we call your True Self. And I want to ask everyone to really be present, for everyone in the room is really the High Priest; let's really hold the space together, my friends. Let me just share a little Dharma with you for a second, all right?

Ego says NO, Unique Self says YES

So Level 1 is your separate self, or your ego self, your personality, and your personality always says 'NO'. No, no, no, no, no, no. And your ego self is smart, it's clever, correct, perceptive, but it is always saying NO, and all of its perception and cleverness is used by it to say NO. Then at some point, through practice, through your chanting, your meditation or your deep thinking, you realize: "Oh my God, I'm not separate, I would give my life to save a school bus of children." I am lonely, which means I must be connected to a larger whole. As I chant, as I practice regularly, I fall into this realization that I am part of the great system of the Cosmos and all of its depth.

In other words, you have moments that you realize that you are not a separate self, you are actually part of this larger context, and that's a glimpse of True Self. And one of the places where you get this, my friend, is in silence, deep silence. When you go into deep silence, your mind is still racing, right? But at some point it settles down and it stops saying no, or yes. It just says: "Here I am." A thought comes up, whether it is a yes or a no: "Oh, there is a thought. I am not my thought, I am in silence, it's just a thought," and you let the thought go. You realize: I am not my thoughts, I am not my emotions, and I am not my body, I am!

So when the NO comes up, you recognize it, you say: "Hi, have a nice day," and it just kind of floats on through. You are not identified with the NO, it is not you talking, it is the ego. And the ego is fine, we need your ego, without your ego you will get into a lot of trouble. But you move from Level 1, personality, ego self, separate self, to Level 2, True Self. And you and I are part of the same True Self, part of the same Silence, part of the same One. And from that place what emerges is a YES. The YES never emerges from the ego, the ego always says NO, but the Unique Self always says YES. And that's how you know the difference. And then you have to begin to trust your YES.

E: Yes.

M: Yes, you can feel it, I can feel you feeling it. Awesome, deep bow to YES. Thank you.

Spirituality got a bad name for ignoring/denying Unique Self

There is always a story, and the story tells us: "This is what would happen if I lived my Unique Self," and it's always just a story. Because to live your Unique Self is not to be foolish, it's not to be vulnerable in a place where it's dangerous, it's not to be ecstatic when I need to be very clear and focused; that's not what Unique Self is.

What's happened is that is spirituality has got a bad name. Spirituality has come to mean: leaving all of the sensible, wise strategies, discernment and wisdom in engaging with the world, in order to find some ecstatic, altruistic state, which we call 'spirit'. When am I spiritual? When I'm on XTC, when I do a psychedelic trip, when I'm so lost in chant that I don't really remember who I am. That's what we call spiritual, that's how we define the word 'spiritual'. But spiritual means to be fully awake, to be fully wise, to be fully discerning. Spiritual means to protest in front of Parliament against actions that hurt human beings and the environment. Spiritual means to use computers, to create great texts, to share a teaching. Spiritual means to pay my bills on time, with integrity. Spiritual means every single engagement in every single part of life, for it's all spiritual.

But we've exiled the spiritual to a particular set of mind-body states, which is why mainstream people say: "I don't want to do the spiritual thing, I need to engage with the world." People are actually afraid of being spiritual, because the fear is that I'm going to lose myself when I get spiritual. Now, I do lose myself, when I'm really engaged in spirit; I lose myself and find my True Self at a deeper level.

Personal practice: Telling yourself your own excuse story

Now let's do some personal practices. The first, which is a great and awesome practice, is to tell yourself your story and then realize that it's just a story. Now watch this carefully with me: usually you don't express your story, for your story actually lives in you and is unconscious, but it stops you from being who you are, it stops you from finding your Unique Self. So you have to tell your story out loud; it's a great daily practice.

So you ask yourself the question: What is in the way of being my Unique Self? What is the real obstacle, what is stopping you? And you say: "Oh, this is what is stopping me, the idea of being vulnerable all the time, or out of control." You come up with all these smart reasons, and then you realize: "Oh my God, it's just a story." I'm not going to leave people behind if I'm living from my Unique Self, actually, that's the place where I'm going to find people to be with. When I'm in my Unique Self, I can sit in any cafe in Tel Aviv and hang out with anyone, and they're going to love being with me. The reason that I don't sit in a cafe is that I'm afraid they're not going to love me because I'm just not wild enough, I'm not interesting enough, I'm not unique enough, I'm not special. But when I'm in my specialness, when I'm in my uniqueness, I create a complete, radical connection with everyone, because everyone is attracted to that and wants to connect.

Being your own guru

So that's the first practice, to speak your story, bring your story from the unconscious to the conscious, and then realize that it's just a story. Because you yourself know that it's not true, you don't need me to tell you, because my voice lives in you, which is your voice. You are your own guru, your own teacher, you are the authority over yourself and no one else. No one else in the entire world can have authority over you, other than the author of your story. The word author and authority come from the same verb. You are the author of your own story, you are the authority, and you know that it's a story.

It sounds really simple, but it's a big deal. It's what always happens. When I'm angry at someone, I know just that I'm angry and I think I know why. Then I stop and write it down: "This is why I'm angry." You actually write down the story, then you look at it and you realize: "Oh my God, it's just a story!" You can only be enlightened if you're willing to leave the story behind. You cannot leave behind your Unique Self, for that's who you are, but your story is the story you tell yourself that allows you to keep yourself small.

A lack of energy to connect to Unique Self

And there's a second thing that stands in the way of Unique Self, and that is a lack of energy, the sense that I don't have enough energy for it. Does everyone get what I mean? "It's too much energy, it's too hard, it takes too much from me, please let me live smaller." But Unique Self actually doesn't take energy. I'm really going to go deep with you now. You guys ready to go deep for ten minutes?

On the one hand, Unique Self takes an enormous amount of energy, that's absolutely true. I mean, when I'm finished teaching, I'm exhausted, always. So where do you get the energy from? I'll tell you guys a secret, it's between us, okay? Don't tell anyone, but tell everyone. I'll tell you exactly where I get energy from, and thank God, it's a complete blessing from God, I have a lot of energy. You can get it from the same place. There's a place you can get energy from, and it's always available, it's always there.

Now, before we talk about what it is, remember that your story takes energy away. Your story is exhausting, it's tiring to remind yourself in a thousand different ways about your fear of losing control if you are in your authenticity, the fear of people misusing you if you are actually vulnerable in the right way. That's exhausting.

But your Unique Self is your truth. Anything less than your Unique Self is a lie, and there's nothing more exhausting than keeping up a lie. You get that? Everybody knows that. It's like telling some people that I'm going to support them, that I'll work with them and help them with their teaching, but really I'm just lying, I don't really care about them. Each time I see them I smile and confirm my commitment, but I'm just lying.

That's exhausting, it's so tiring. I'm pretending to love them, but really, I think they're just a pain in the ass. And I had to tell it to someone, because not admitting it to anybody is even more exhausting, but please don't tell anyone else. Oh my God, now I worry that you guys might tell them; please forget what I said. That is so tiring, when you're living a lie. But actually, if I love these people with all of my Unique Self, I want to give them every gift I can give to them, so that I'm living my truth. And my truth, which is my uniqueness, gives me energy. Uniqueness is the source of energy.

Plugging in to Universe through your own socket

We've talked about Unique Self being a puzzle piece, a puzzle piece to let you fit into the Cosmos. I'll give you another image: imagine your Unique Self as an electrical cord that allows you to plug into the current of cosmic energy, to plug into the wall of the Universe. But every plug is different, so if Chahat tries to use Ted's electrical cord, she gets electrocuted, BLAAAAH. You get that? This is a big deal, this is what I call 'cash dharma'. It's a simple image and if you get this image, it changes your life. Try plugging in, into the socket of the Universe, with anything but your unique puzzle piece: BLAAAAH. The only thing that allows you to get alive is your unique plug, that gives you your unique connection to the unique frequency of your Unique Self, and that's what gives you energy. So it's a great and wild joke of the Universe, that's why the Buddha was smiling. The joke is that I think I'm not going to have enough energy to live this Unique Self thing, but actually, the true source of my energy IS my living my Unique Self - that's where the energy comes from.

Ch: Then everything falls into place.

M: Right, everything falls into place, the energy organizes itself, and I actually have energy. When I'm finished teaching, I'm exhausted and I'm filled with energy at the same time, because I get energy from doing what I do, from living my unique story. And if I try to not live my unique story, I get exhausted. The two most exhausting years in my life were the two years when I didn't teach. I was tired all the time. I had a great job and I was working in big companies, it was all good, but I was exhausted. And the only time I got energy was when I was giving a big presentation for some business, and I found a way to talk not about the business but about a some deep spiritual idea. I skived with the business and walked out with filled of energy. That's a wild realization.

So living my Unique Self is what gives me the energy to be alive, to exercise my control when I need it, and to let go of it when I need to let go. And that energy, that wisdom, that discernment, all come from Unique Self. When I enter my Unique Self, it's like putting on my Iron Man suit and then I have huge energy, huge resources. Because my uniqueness connects me to the Cosmos, as a puzzle piece or as an electrical cord.

Stepping into a life that fits you

Let's go one step deeper. Just feel this, okay? As long as you're not in your Unique Self, you're in your separate self. So then, where do you get your energy from? You get energy from your own body, from your personality, from the particular people you meet, but you get energy from a very small circle, because you're disconnected from the core source of reality. You're disconnected from the larger game, from the evolutionary context in which you live, from your wider, deeper participation in all of reality. So all you have is your own strength and wisdom, because you're just a separate self, alienated, disconnected from the whole.

And then you step into your clothes that fit. How many people here have bought great clothes that fit them perfectly? Does everybody know what I'm talking about? My partner likes Armani shirts, so every two or three weeks I come home and there's a new black Armani shirt in my closet. I don't know why I need another black Armani shirt, that's another problem, we're not going to talk about it now and we're definitely never going to send her this video, okay? It's actually a beautiful gift, and when I put on my black Armani shirt, it always fits perfectly and I have this surge of energy running through me because it fits so perfectly.

Now imagine the feeling, okay? This is both for the men and the women. Imagine the feeling, guys, when your pants are too tight and too short. You feel funny, and you get that surge of energy? I don't think so. You kind of feel weird, your energy gets low and you want to hide in a closet or at least take the pants off. Just feel that, okay? And women, you're wearing a blouse or shirt that just doesn't fit right, it just fits weirdly, you just feel funny. But if you're wearing something that just fits you perfectly, that's exactly right for your shape, you feel great, you feel energy, right? Everyone knows what I'm talking about, right? And that's just about your shirts and pants, that's nothing. Can you imagine you're wearing the wrong life? Wearing somebody else's story?

Your Unique Self is called, by the great mystics of the Kabbalah, your malbush, your clothing. And when it fits right, oh my God, you feel awesome, beyond awesome. When it fits wrong, you feel funny and weird and small and contracted. So your Unique Self is the source of your energy, it's your clothes that fit right, it's the puzzle piece, the end of the electrical cord that plugs in uniquely to the wall of the Cosmos, and no one can use anybody else's cord.

Ch: I used to say it's like I'm 20 kilo's overweight, it's like plowing through sand or having constraints on my legs and arms, when I'm not connected.

M: Right, and now, when you get up to organize the festival and teach about Unique Self, what do you feel?

Ch: I feel like a fountain.

M: Right, and the words are coming from you, all these wise things are just spilling out of you, because your Unique Self is in place and is filled with energy.

Ch: Or when our cook is in the kitchen and she is all into it and she's just a radiant being of love.

M: Right, she just stepped in, it doesn't matter what you do when you're in your Unique Self. Anyone ever heard about a sapphire stone? Language often reveals the inner nature of reality, and the Hebrew word for story, as in 'your story', your Unique Self, is 'sipur', from the same root as 'sapphire', the radiant, blue stone of life, the blue diamond. According to Swami Muktananda, the teacher of my spiritual friend Sally Kempton, when you're meditating and you step into your Higher Self or Unique Self, you can see an image of yourself bathed in blue, sapphire light. Wow. So the words 'sapphire' and 'sipur', story, are the same word, and your radiance comes from the unique frequency of your life, which is your unique story, the source of your energy.

Your Unique Self is the source of your energy and joy

And one of the main reasons why we don't live our Unique Self is that we feel we don't have enough energy, but actually, Unique Self is the source of our energy! So the reason I don't have enough energy is that I don't live in my Unique Self. Isn't that great?

Now, what do you do to achieve orbit, to lift off? When a rocket ship wants to achieve orbit, to get out of the atmosphere and achieve a stable orbit, it needs an extra push. The atmosphere is like the ego, the atmosphere is all the stories we tell ourselves that keep us on the ground, but in a bad way. It keeps us from flying in the way we need to fly, so we need energy, we need power to achieve orbit. Now, that power comes from your Unique Self, but the problem is how to get there. You can't get to your Unique Self because you don't have enough power or energy to achieve orbit, right? Okay, let's go very deep now, friends. What we were doing before was just superficial, now we're going to go deep.

The source of energy is joy; joy is a form of energy. In Kabbalah, joy is called chiyut, like the Eastern word for energy, 'chi'. So joy is energy. Now, you get joy from where? One place you get joy from is living your Unique Self; we've just talked about that. So where else can you get joy from that can give you enough energy to get to your Unique Self? What I'm going to tell you sounds so simple, and it's not simple at all, my friends. It's going to sound so obvious, and it is obvious, but not simple. It's the essence of wisdom, and it's the most important simple practice that you can do. And the practice is, very simply, appreciation.

Appreciation takes you to joy

The source of joy is to appreciate what you have. Lack of joy is to appreciate what you do not have. Let's say you have a beloved. Three days go by and you text each other four times and Skype a couple of times and you say: "Wow, that's awesome." Or you say: "Oh my God, we didn't get to talk on the phone." You get that? It's deep. Appreciation means that you appreciate a hundred things in a day, a hundred blessings a day. If you can't get to hundred, try ten, and it will work pretty well.

This is the practice of gratitude, to develop an attitude of gratitude. When I have joy, it gives me energy, which takes me to my Unique Self, which gives me even more energy, which is the energy of the living Cosmos, alive and awake through me, which gives me even more energy, which takes me into a radical, powerful, alive, awake Eros of joy. You will get there, but the cycle starts with appreciation. Now most people don't get started, they don't do appreciation ten times a day, because we all suffer from the Missing Tile Syndrome. The whole room is covered with tiles and there's one missing, and where does my eye go? To the missing tile, every time. And all the other 999 tiles, you think I appreciate them? No way, they're just there, and my attention goes to the one tile. You get how that works? That's powerful.

So let me ask a question. How many of you have one kidney that's working? Everybody? Now notice how you react, you're laughing, right? Have you ever been to a hospital where people's kidneys are not working? A kidney is a big deal. If it's not working, or only working a little bit, you go to the hospital and take tests and take drugs and needles and try an operation and then another operation and get hooked up to this dialysis machine. Your whole life becomes nuts and painful and insane and crazy, and then you wake up one morning and the doctors say they have a cure and your kidney starts working again. Are you in joy? You're ecstatic, you're beyond joy, you're dancing in the streets, and are you asking what the meaning of existence is? I don't think so. You are just enjoying the hell out of your one kidney.

How many women in this room have skin?

Ch: We all have skin. Some have too much.

M: Stay with this, okay? The Missing Tile Syndrome here is that I have too much. Just for a second, I want to ask the men in the room to touch the skin of the forehead of the woman next to them, and just appreciate the skin. Do it really quietly, just try to feel it, don't verbalize it. Skin is awesome. Ask any one of the millions and millions of people in the world that have bad skins how awesome it is to have skin.

The personal practice of radical appreciation

So the third practice of today is the practice of radical appreciation. I appreciate my skin. I appreciate my heart. I appreciate my cock which gets hard even if it doesn't take backrub, I appreciate my wetness. I appreciate my shoulder. I appreciate that my mind is able to think. I appreciate the fact that I'm able to feel. I appreciate the fact that I live in a house. I appreciate that I have enough money to get through the month. I appreciate two friends that I'm close to. I appreciate the richness and depth and beauty of the world that surrounds me and loves me open every day. We can call it appreciation, or wonder, or radical amazement. This is a practice of radical amazement.

The first practice is to let go of your story, in a very particular way. The second practice is plugging into the wall through your Unique Self socket and getting your energy. The third practice is getting energy and aliveness through the practice of radical amazement, radical appreciation, radical gratitude. Every time that you're amazed, every time you're in wonder, every time you're deeply grateful, you get a hit of energy. That's the secret. Appreciation creates energy, gratitude creates energy, it gives you joy, and joy gives you energy. Without joy, you get depressed, listless, empty, tired, just waiting for the moment that the ice cream comes, for life sucks just now. But actually, the ice cream comes for you to lick every second. Radical amazement brings you radical joy, which brings you radical energy, which is the way I achieve orbit to find my Unique Self. Then I can pull the whole Cosmos into me, from which I give my unique gift, for the Cosmos desperately needs to give.

Go into Silence of Presence, and then make a list of 30 things or people that you appreciate, that you got radical, wild, ecstatic appreciation for. And if you don't have an orgasm when you get to 30, you're faking it.

The Fifth Awakening, awakening to Evolutionary Intimacy

Dharma is alive, and Dharma matters

*T*oday, we are going to do a session on the Fifth Awakening, the awakening to your Evolutionary Unique Self, or to Evolutionary Intimacy.

We enter the Dharma and the Dharma is alive, it's not a dogma, it's a living thing. Dnyaneshwari, the great teacher from the Bhagavad Gita whom JunPo and I both love, who created the second turning of the wheel called Mahayana, talks about non-conceptional knowing, knowing something directly in your first person. That's what Dharma is. Dharma is not intellectual, although it also has a mind component, but your mind and your heart and your body merge into one as you hear Dharma. And the hearing of Dharma is a practice in itself, the listening to Dharma, the reading of Dharma is a practice, for then we embody it in a new way.

I really want to share this with you with such sweetness and such love: what I'm trying to do, together with you in our Mystery

School and our whole gorgeous, sacred, shared community space at Venwoude, is that in some sense, I want to completely love you open and also fuck you open with this idea: *Dharma matters!*

Dharma matters. Dharma is not a University lecture, Dharma is not a mind trip, it's not a masculine, intellectual journey. Dharma is the living contact with the voice of Spirit whispering in our ear visions of meaning and patterns that connect. Dharma is the user's guide to being alive, Dharma is 'how do I actualize?' Dharma is connecting the dots. All awakenings that are part of our Dharma, are about connecting the dots, and we now step into the Fifth Awakening.

I invite you to just step into the Dharma and into any resistance, because when you're about to step into the Dharma, you will feel resistance. "No, don't penetrate me, I don't like Jews!" Let the Dharma penetrate you, the Dharma is beautiful, and it loves you, it loves me, it wants to hold us. The Dharma is a living, awake organism. So here is the Dharma.

Living a small life, yearning for more

We live in an evolutionary context, and knowing that we live in an evolutionary context and aligning with it, is the truth that changes everything. Because what do we usually do? Usually we live in a very, very narrow relationship to life. We are trying to live our life and find a little happiness, find a little joy and a little satisfaction, we work out our financial issues and maybe have some direct contact with Spirit once in a while, and that's our life. It is a small life, and it's good; we can act in integrity and we can be good to each other, but it is still a small life.

And if I ask you, my dear friends, to go inside, you know that you are not satisfied with the small life. You know that there is something deep inside you, deep inside me, deep inside the nature of human essence, and that is that we want to play a larger game, we want to awaken to a larger relationship to life, to a deeper intimacy with All-That-Is. So the Fifth Awakening is the awakening to your Evolutionary Unique Self, which really is to awaken to a sacred, evolutionary, mystical relationship to life. We need to be evolutionary mystics, we need to actually realize that we live in a larger evolutionary context.

Trainings on Venwoude

In the old world, it was enough to work on my own issues. When Venwoude started, we did Emotional Bodywork, we did this training and that training, working out our early issues, doing trauma work, and those are all important things, so it is important that they keep going on.

After we did all that work, we realize: it is not enough. And then Marijke's Fundament training is utterly critical, as is Mauk's Centaur training; these things are all critical.

And we awaken to this even larger context when there is a new spiritual impulse arising, in which I realize that it is not sufficient to only engage in my own work. My own private world isn't enough, even when I try and improve myself and do my work on my shadow and my embodiment. In the old world, I went for my own Enlightenment, but what we understand now is that we need to awaken in a much deeper way, we need to actually awaken to living in an evolutionary context.

Awakening to the evolutionary context

What does that mean, to awaken to an evolutionary context and to shift my basic orientation? The way my teacher said this was: "I shift from looking at the world through my perspective, to God's perspective." It's moving from our side to God's side, shift perspectives, begin to play a larger game, and we align with God's eyes. We become evolutionary lovers, we see through God's eyes, and we begin to align with the core evolutionary impulse, what Aurobindo calls 'the evolutionary imperative', the evolutionary impulse that moves through all of reality. What does that mean? Let's go into it in a really deep way, to really understand what this is about.

Intro for guided meditation into the Four Big Bangs

I want to do a meditation with you, I want to ask you to shut your eyes and take you into this Evolutionary Interior, the Evolutionary Interior of the whole Cosmos. Allow yourself for a moment to imagine what it would look like if you stepped into this. You may be relating to life from only your narrow perspective of your egoic, separate self, trying to take care of your issues in the best way you can, to be spiritual in the best way you can. But imagine if you actually shifted perspectives and awakened to the Enlightenment of the Evolutionary Impulse, and you begin to relate to life, to engage with life from the perspective of God, who expresses Him/Herself as the Evolutionary Impulse.

What am I talking about here? What does it mean? Let's go inside and begin to *feel* this, begin to feel what this actually feels like. So I want to invite you to join me in this meditation. Let's review, let's enter into the history of reality, of everything, from the point of view of the living, divine, personal Evolutionary Impulse that unfolds everything. And this is really part of you, this lives inside you. The Evolutionary Imperative lives in you and is awake and alive in you if you open up to it in meditation. I'm not going to tell you about it, I'm not going to talk about it in the third person, I'll do that afterwards; now I'm going to take you into it in the first person.

The First Big Bang: the evolution of the physical Universe

Sit up, let your shoulders drop, and go back with me to the beginning of manifest time, 13,7 billion years ago, when all of reality was what's called a singularity, condensed in one point. All of the energy and matter, all of reality was condensed into what the mystics call 'one point', smaller than the eye of a needle, it seems like nothing at all. But in reality it is not nothing, it is 'no thing'. Science tells us that all of reality, all of future potentiality is condensed in one point, before the Big Bang.

Begin to feel that, because you were there! You were there, because where else could you have been? When you strip away your personality, your public accomplishment, your changing emotions, your ego and your body, YOU are still there. Isn't that wild?! Take everything away that you identify as you, as your small, separate self, and you're still there, because you are Being, you are inseparable from all Being. As Being is about to explode, before the Big Bang, and all of Being lives in that singularity, in that single point, then where are you? You were there, because where else could you have been? And there is this sense of infinite possibility, the possibility of all possibility.

And in one moment you scream out and you say: Yes. YES, YES! And the world explodes in a Divine Orgasm, screaming YES, YES, YES… The great adventure of reality begins to unfold with a great, holy YES. Nothing, No-Thing becomes Something, and the unmanifest, your original face before your mother and father were born, becomes manifest. In one split, infinitesimal second, manifest reality, what Dnyaneshwari calls *form*, is born out of the Emptiness.

Remember, remember back, because you were there, and if you can't quite remember, imagine, because your imagination IS the memory. Remember what it was like as this explosion of chaotic wildness begins to burn for a billion years. The galaxies, burning balls of hydrogen gas, are burning and exploding with great intensity, and become filled with primordial stars, and ultimately the stars go supernova. They explode themselves in intense heat and give birth to higher elements, carbon and oxygen, and the supernovas are scattering those elements throughout the galaxies. Wow. And this goes on. This burning fireball of reality, described with such elegance and gorgeousness by Thomas Berry, Brian Swimme and other evolutionary cosmologists, takes up all of reality.

And at some point, in this field of self-organizing, creative intelligence, all of these higher elements coalesce, come together, integrate. They are allured to each other, there is this Cosmic allurement, they are attracted to each other and mix in these huge galaxies of stars, burning balls, supernovas, breaking apart and then attracted to each other over and over again, and at some point Planet Earth is born. Wow. That is the first Big Bang, the Big Bang that gives birth to manifest reality, and that stardust lives in all of us. In 1964, new telescopes began to discover the radiation, the memory of that original explosion, the light of the Big Bang. For the first time in history we were recovering the actual, felt, visible, detectable, sensory memory of that big Cosmic Fuck, the Big Bang that birthed reality.

The Second Big Bang: biological evolution

Open your heart. And then, after billions of years, a second Big Bang took place, in which, at some particular moment, all of the quarks organized into atoms, and atoms organized into molecules, and molecules organized into complex molecules. Why is that? Why were they drawn together? Why were they attracted to each other? What was the allurement? It didn't need to be that way, there was no reason for it to be that way. But there is this Cosmic Erotic Attraction, in which quarks become atoms and a single boundary forms around them, and they create a higher level of complexity and consciousness. And atoms come together and form molecules, because they are allured, attracted. And molecules form complex molecules, and at some point, the second Big Bang occurs. People think there was one Big Bang, but there are four Big Bangs, and the Second Big Bang was when one of these strings of complex molecules awakened and exploded into Life, and the first cell was born.

Now my good friends, we didn't know this 200 years ago, we didn't know this a 100 years ago. This is the new great Universal story, this is the Genesis story which the great mystics talked about a thousand years ago, but they talked about it only in allusions, in hints. And now science and mysticism are meeting, and science is beginning to describe the exterior, the outside of the Big Bang, and mysticism describes the inside. The Second Big Bang is the beginning, not of Cosmological evolution, but of biological evolution; the biosphere begins to evolve.

Darwin, who came along some 150 years ago, mid-19th century, begins to realize deeply that all of the biosphere is evolving. But then 50, 60, 70 years after Darwin, in the 1930's, we begin to realize that not only the biosphere is evolving, but the whole Cosmos is evolving. Evolution is not taking place within the Universe, but the Universe itself is evolving! So cosmological evolution is the first Big Bang, followed by the biological evolution. We go from bacteria to early plants and later plants, to early animals and later animals, and there is this explosion of gentle, unique precision and love, and some 60 million different species arise on the Planet. Oh my God, 60 million different species on the Planet.

The Third Big Bang: the evolution of human culture

And then the Third Big Bang takes place. Feel this inside of you, feel how the Third Big Bang is about to take place and remember it, you can remember it. Go back and imagine the memory, for the imagination *is* the memory. The Third Big Bang takes place maybe 40,000 years ago, not much more than that, which is the explosion of human creativity, of the human mind. The human culture that we know now is born, and we begin to see art work on cave walls, we begin to realize that we need to bury our dead, and musical instruments are found in burial grounds. There is this huge explosion of a new, unbelievable creativity.

And then this human culture begins to unfold, beginning with this Third Big Bang, and first we are hunter-gatherers, cavemen; we gather our food and we hunt. Our vision of time is maybe a day, or half a day, an hour, and we live in very small units of three, four, five people, and our major drive in the world is survival. And then we get deeper, and we begin for the first time to form clans and tribes, and we begin to create loyalty within the clans.

We begin to make and use primitive farming instruments, we begin to save some food. Our sense of time expands, we begin to make contact with Spirit in a deeper way and great shamans begin to take us into the interior face of reality. We begin to create laws that govern us in a deeper way, in a way that we are good to each other, and a sense of Truth, of a higher level, starts to be born. We begin to deepen our understanding of reality, and we awaken and begin to think about who we are and what our purpose is in the world, what the meaning is of our lives.

And on each level of consciousness, the human being as a society, as a collective, as a We-space, gets deeper and deeper. We move from horticultural instruments to more sophisticated farming instruments. From tribes we move to form the greater societies with laws that govern us beyond the tribe, beyond being a blood relative, beyond living in a certain place. We begin to talk about higher principles of order, of justice, of love, of shared understanding and meaning and vision, and as long as someone buys into these higher principles, they get to join. We create these larger memberships of societies, of the Church and the Empire, and goodness and truth and beauty go up one level and get deeper.

And then, another 1500 years later, the Industrial Revolution begins. We move away from being the mythic members of our societies and through revolution we move into this new world, which is not about being part of a Church but about being oneself, with infinite rights and infinite dignity. Every human being can achieve something, every human being is creative, all people are created equal and we create this new world.

Then we get even deeper, we explode again, and we begin to realize that, actually, men and women ARE deeply equal. We begin to create gender equality, we begin to allow for different forms of sexuality, we begin to realize that everyone has a right to have their story told and lived and heard, that no one people is better than any other people, and that everyone has a unique and beautiful and holy story. All of this emerges, and this explosion is not an explosion of cosmological evolution, nor of a biological one; this is the Third Big Bang of human cultural evolution.

The speeding up of evolution and interconnectivity

The First Big Bang, of cosmological evolution, which is the beginning of the physical world, takes up billions and billions of years. The Second Big Bang is biological evolution, the beginning of life, and things begin to move faster, for it takes only millions of years. Then we get human cultural evolution, the Third Big Bang, which takes place in tens of thousands of years. You see what is happening? Things are speeding up, and as human cultural evolution starts going faster and faster, things begin changing faster and faster.

I want you to really get this, it is so wild and so deep. 3000 years ago, 1000 years ago, nothing much changed. 25 years ago no one had heard of the Internet, seven years ago there was no such thing as Facebook, it didn't exist. The entire world is changing completely; the world that your great-grandparents and your great-great-grandparents knew, doesn't exist anymore. There is no such thing as being local any more, there is no more local world, all of local is gone. The world is becoming a global village, everyone is connected, 500 million people are on Facebook. Everyone gets more and more connected, until in another 10, 15, 20 years, every single person on the planet will be connected on the Internet. That's unbelievable, that's beyond imagination.

Everything we do affects everything else. The environment of the entire planet: either we destroy it, or we will heal it. Everyone is connected to everyone else, no one is separate. You go home to your computer, you go to Google Earth and you can find any point on the planet. The entire planet is one. The mystics of 1000 years ago talked about the world being one and all being connected, and they could only find that in their mystical consciousness, but now mystical consciousness is becoming reality. The interior, inner face of the Cosmos, our inner heart and soul where we know we are all one, is now manifesting and becoming true in the exterior world. We have complete outer connection. We can all love each other and we can all kill each other.

Waking up to our role as evolutionary agencies

Every year or two, the world is changing with new technologies, new stem plants, new genetic mutation experiments, the entire human genome project, new ways of healing. New potential for insight and artificial intelligence are waking up. We are coming to the time, very soon, called the singularity, which can happen in 10/20/30/40 years, in which for the first time, machine intelligence will awaken to actual consciousness.

And we live our little lives, just thinking: "Oh my God, I'm trying to make sure that I have a little more love, feeling a little better, make a lot more money. My stomach is a little fat, maybe I should work out, and I haven't enough orgasms, what am I going to do? And that's all great, that's beautiful, let's hold it, but oh my God, good morning Vietnam, wake up! Wake up! We are living in an evolutionary context and for the first time we have to begin to act as an evolutionary agency.

The Eternal Now holds the past and the future

The evolution, the emergence of intelligence, of love and beauty that defines the future of tomorrow, has to awaken in us. And with all due respect for my friend Eckhart Tolle — who says it all happens in the Now; we sit down and do Satsang and it is all in the Eternal Now —the future is also happening, and we need to awaken and create the future. We need to learn from the past and realize that the Now has the future in it. It is not just about the Eternal Now; that is only valuable when I realize that it is from the Eternal Now that we begin to create the future, from the realization that I'm one with everything and everything is one with me. I can feel it inside, all Being is in me and I'm Source and Source is me. From that place I awaken as an evolutionary Unique Self and I realize that I have a unique gift to give to the entire evolving Cosmos, which is evolving rapidly, fast, changing all the time, in a way that it never did before.

Recapitulating the Three Big Bangs

But actually, I began the process as the Big Bang, I was at the start, exploding, screaming out YES, YES, YES, YES! The Big Bang emerged and the cosmological evolution began, for billions of years. And at some point I awoke into life, the first cell was born, and then another, and it started to move fast, in periods of millions of years. We went all the way through animals, to mammals, to later mammals, to the first human being, and then we have an explosion in the early human beings, just 35,000 years ago. And then things took thousands of years to change, until oh my God, we went all the way from hunter-gatherers to early agriculture to labor farming to the first large empires, bound by laws, and membership societies, bound by rules. Then we get to the Industrial Revolution and the Western form of Enlightenment, which explodes into the information world, the information technology.

And each of these is a different level of technical, structural consciousness and a different level of interior consciousness. And as we exploded into new levels of structural, technological competence, new levels of interior consciousness exploded at the same time. Fifty years after the Industrial Revolution, democracy and feminism explode in the world, because they are connected to each other. And now we are in the information world, and informational highways are moving faster and faster. In our own lives everything is changing. There was no Facebook six, seven years ago. The entire nature of communication is changing, and what can happen now, is one of two things.

The Fourth Big Bang: aligning with the Evolutionary Impulse

We can take this world of information and technology and ultimate wired connectivity, and make it into a reality that is flatland, that is just surface, superficial, where real friendship doesn't exist anymore, where you have only Facebook friends. We can create the greatest explosion of child pornography that ever existed, we can have 17 million sex slaves in the world, because corrupt governments profit from human trafficking and sex slaves. We can have a world in which there is no shared meaning and no shared vision. Or we can actually deepen into this connectivity as awakened, evolutionary lovers and realize that we can give our unique gift for the awakening of all of reality, aligning our individual lives with the evolutionary imperative that lives within us.

We can actually explode into what is the fourth Big Bang. The first Big Bang is cosmological evolution, the second Big Bang is biological evolution, the third Big Bang is cultural evolution, but now the fourth Big Bang is where every human being awakens as an evolutionary agent and says: "I'm going to align my life, my arms, my belly, my cunt and my cock, I'm going to align my eyes, my legs with the Evolutionary Impulse. I'm going to actually participate and make love to the world in giving my unique gift, in giving the unique, evolutionary kiss that I have to give."

When we say that we want to emerge in the basic principles of Integral World Spirituality, we mean that we want to have a shared vision of meaning. We want to have a shared vision of what it means to be evolutionary lovers. We want a community model, a new vision of what love means, a new vision of what it means to live together, a new vision of what it means to co-create an evolutionary We-space.

We are actually going to create a great website, so we can share that vision with the world. We want to create a world in which people come from all over Europe to experience what it is like to love each other open, through our Venwoude trainings and through our Mystery School. We want a model for the world as an evolutionary community, to know what evolutionary intimacy feels like.

What does it feel like when we come together not just as individual egos? When we evolve beyond our exclusive identification with ego, awaken to the Fourth Big Bang, recognize ourselves as people who have evolutionary gifts to give to the world, then we can create an evolutionary We-space and say YES, YES to our lives and to the Fourth Big Bang: "I want to live a larger game, I want to play in a larger field." Wow.

Being evolutionary mystics, in public and in private

That's the Fifth Awakening. The Fourth Awakening is to awaken as Unique Self, the Fifth to awaken as an Evolutionary Unique Self with a unique gift to give, which is the very engine of evolution. The erotic impulse of evolution, throbbing, pulsating and pounding in me, is awakened through the unique Eros of my Unique Self, which is my evolutionary creativity, and my evolutionary creativity makes a mystic of me.

Let's be evolutionary mystics, which doesn't always mean that I have to be doing it out loud; it's not necessarily about creating some new public, although it can be. We are creating an Integral World Spirituality based on Integral principles, and we created a Mystery School where people can come and experience an awakened, enlightened way of loving each other, that lasts for weeks afterwards. And if I let that gift of awakened love begin to transform my life, if I become an awakened evolutionary lover and I begin to act in the world, that is awesome.

But at the same time, being an evolutionary lover is also completely private. It could be that in my family, there were three generations of men who failed to create intimacy, so there's a brokenness, a trauma in the masculine line of my family. But when I awaken to my power and I say I'm going to be intimate, to give love, then when I feel lazy and I don't feel like making love with my partner, I actually wake myself up. And instead of making love for six minutes, I make love to her for an hour and a half, slowing kissing her body, kissing his body. I don't bother if my partner is a man or a woman, I kiss his or her body for an hour and a half, with the intention of an evolutionary lover who offers his love up for the sake of All-That-Is, offering up this love for the healing of all the broken hearts and broken bodies and broken vessels of the light.

I happen to have the intention of an Evolutionary Lover and I don't get lazy, I don't say I'm tired, I actually wake up and say: "I'm going to fuck you open for the sake of all of reality. First I'm going to be holding your fragility, holding your brokenness, kissing you open, but not just because it's about you, but because you are All and All is you. And I offer it as a gift to all of reality, to all of the cosmological evolution that started with the inanimate world of rocks and stones, awakening as life to biological evolution, and to all of biological evolution, plants and mammals, until it becomes a human being.

And then in the Third Big Bang, human culture evolves, until in the Fourth Big Bang I become an awakened human being, fucking you open in the Big Bang that is happening in you, in the holy YES that is happening in you. I fuck you open, not to separate self, but to this greater evolutionary intimacy, and there are two holy YES's, two personal faces of Essence coming together here, Shiva and Shakti, the upper waters and the lower waters, the lion and the snake, the masculine and the feminine. The Big Bang re-happens as we make love, the Big Bang re-happens as we walk on the Path and stop and take the time to go beyond our narrow, egocentric self and do something for someone else, reaching beyond ourselves.

What happens in the Fourth Big Bang? The Fourth Big Bang is that evolution awakens and becomes conscious of itself in you, and you begin to act for the sake of the All. You begin to act as the evolutionary impulse, an awakened Big Bang, fucking the world open, fucking the moment open, gently, beautifully, sparklingly. That's the Fourth Big Bang.

Sentence Completion practice: "As the Evolutionary Impulse, I…"

We're going to do a very beautiful developmental exercise, a Sentence Completion practice. Let's form groups of three. I will begin a sentence, and then everyone in the circle is going to complete the sentence, talking as the Evolutionary Impulse itself, living in first person. What we are about to do is a very basic shift, and this shift, according to Kabbalah, is to move from our small-self perspective to God's perspective. Abraham Cook, my lineage master, said that all of the world is evolving and we have to align ourselves with the evolutionary imperative, the evolutionary impulse that lives with us.

You don't have to have this big life experience, of lions and tigers and bears, nor do you have to have the big meditative experience. You actually just shift, you change your own basic alignment from your own small self to the larger evolutionary Self, and then you begin to talk from that place for about a minute. So everyone in the circle speaks in the first person from the evolutionary impulse. Go inside yourself and find that deepest inside place where you are the evolutionary impulse, aligned to the fourth Big Bang, the evolutionary impulse that realizes: "I'm bounded by limitation and I want to bring into the world higher and higher levels of the good, the true and the beautiful."

So I give you three sentences and each person finishes the sentence.

Here is the first sentence: "As the evolutionary impulse, what I'm most passionate about is …"
The second sentence is: "As the evolutionary impulse, what gets me most excited in my life is …"
And the third sentence is: "As the evolutionary impulse, my relationship to my personal problems is …"

Identifying with the Evolutionary Impulse shifts your relationship to personal problems

Just feel into that for a second. As the evolutionary impulse, my relationship to my own personal stuff completely shifts. It's really true that my mother didn't let me keep the light on in my room at night, and that was really traumatic for me because I really was afraid of the dark. It's even true that when I was 21, maybe somebody raped me, it was horrible, *and* I'm playing a fucking larger game. I'm a unique evolutionary being, 13,7 billion years of evolution live in me, the stardust, the first cells, every level of evolution lives in me, the DNA of particular animals, particular properties of the fish, dimensions of different levels of genealogy — they all live in me, it's all in me, and I am the future. It's not only that I want to awaken to the Eternal Now, which is a great, but I realize that the future is in the Now, the future is in *me*, as an evolutionary mystic.

And it's not that I'm not engaged to the personal. I want to get this really clear. I have a couple of friends who teach evolutionary spirituality and I like them very much, they are dear, beautiful people. But the way they teach evolutionary spirituality, is that they say that the personal doesn't matter, because you live in an evolutionary context. That's not what I'm saying, that's not my teaching. The personal totally matters, a 1000 billion per cent, but it matters within a larger context.

Working on your issues for the sake of the whole

To be able to work in the world as an evolutionary lover, we have to work out all of our issues in our life. Just like Ted had to work out his stuff in the world, challenging his father, a big industrialist in Holland, going to Osho; and he had to do all his shadow work and false-self work. But you do it in order to heal the whole story, you do it for the sake of the 'tikkun', the fixing, the evolving. That's what the word means in the original, Aramaic Hebrew: for the sake of the evolving reality.

If you work on your relationship, you work on it for the sake of all of reality, for all of reality needs that to work. And if my friend Ken Wilber works out his issues, he does it for the sake of reality. And if Marc Gafni tries to work out his complexity stuff with his father, he works it out for the sake of the all. Because by clarifying my own internal reality, something shifts in the entire world. Physicists call that the 'butterfly effect': when a butterfly flaps its wings in Tokyo, something changes in Venwoude. So can you imagine, if you flap the wings of your interior consciousness, if you are able to heal a broken part of yourself, what you are able to heal in our collective consciousness?

When you are awakening, you begin to do your internal work with your wounds, but not for the sake of your own masturbation. Now listen, masturbation is a good thing, it's sex with someone you love and good cuddling afterwards. You really want to make love with yourself, and when you make love, you're doing it for the sake of a larger reality. I do it because I know I'm not separate from anyone else.

There's this old story of mysticism of a boat with 20 people in it, and one woman starts drilling a hole in the boat. The others want to kill her, but she says: "What do you mean? It's my part of the boat, what's the problem?" And that's really what it means. When you awaken to evolutionary consciousness, to evolutionary intimacy, you realize that we really are in the same fucking boat. And now for the first time in reality, I know that's true environmentally, in terms of the arms race, the ozone layer, the oceans, the interest rates and mortgages and international money flows, in terms of the ecology, the information flow, the Internet, Facebook. It's all connected, we are all face to face, my friends; it's one book. Oh my God, that is a new reality of consciousness.

An evolutionary spirituality that denies the dignity of the individual becomes Communism

So when a couple of my friends teach about evolutionary spirituality, they say: "It's not about the personal, it's about moving beyond ego." No, no. It's about realizing that the personal and the Process are one. Do you get that? Now, I want to tell you a really deep, crazy secret, but keep this between us, okay? Evolutionary spirituality has been really deeply rooted in the Kabbalah for the last 2000 years, but when evolutionary spirituality kind of hit the world, it went from Kabbalah and the Renaissance to Germany, to Fichte and Schelling and Hegel, and when they awakened to evolutionary spirituality, that gave birth to Marxism and Communism. But they awakened to evolutionary spirituality without a realization of the infinite dignity of every single human story.

I want you to hear this so deeply. It's a really hard thing to say and it breaks my heart to say it, but actually, evolutionary spirituality in wrong forms, in bad versions, has killed more people than all the religions together. Communism was a bad form of evolutionary spirituality, just as the Crusades were a bad form of Christianity. So when I hear some of my friends, who are evolutionary spirituality teachers, say that religion has killed so many people — guys, get serious, get real. But it's not about Christianity, it's not about evolutionary spirituality, it's about the highest version of each one.

Claiming the dignity of your personal story without drowning in your wounds

So evolutionary spirituality has to claim the infinite dignity of everybody's story, and at the same time, not drown in your own wounds. Get hold of the evolutionary context, put your wounds in perspective, live in a larger story. Can you understand in your body, feel in your body that they are both true? On the one hand, you matter eternally, you have infinite dignity, infinite value, and on the other, in this larger context, playing a larger game, it doesn't matter so much that you get a little hurt.

Let me tell you a little secret; don't tell anyone. I had a really bad childhood, it didn't work well. I have great parents, they were holocaust survivors, they were good at a lot of things, but parenting wasn't one of them. So I went to a therapist to tell him the story, but I did that only once. You have to do that once, that is enough. Erica Jung says once is not enough, and still once is enough, maybe twice. Because when you keep retelling the same story without being willing to move forward and live in a larger evolutionary context, it means you are using your wounds as your identity. And your wounds are not your identity; your identity is that you're a child of God, that you are a unique expression of the evolutionary impulse, with unique gifts to give.

My big problem with all the Twelve Steps programs, Alcoholics Anonymous, Over-Eaters Anonymous, Rabbi's Anonymous, is this. When you come to an AA meeting, the first thing you say is: "I'm an addict." True, but partially so. You might be an addict, but you are also a beautiful, gorgeous Unique Self, with unique gifts and unique beauty and unique evolutionary love-intelligence and love-beauty moving through you. And that is not an intellectual idea. You are aligned with the love-intelligence that is uniquely you. So that gives your problems, your personal wounds, some perspective, it gives them some air to breathe. And at the very same time, you really hold the infinite dignity of every person, and in realizing that every story matters, you begin to heal the entire story.

This Dharma is life-changing. If you can align with the evolutionary impulse as an infinitely personal Unique Self, then you can create not just intimacy but evolutionary intimacy, evolutionary relationship. This summer, at the Mystery School, we are going to talk about moving beyond Venus and Mars and create evolutionary relationship.

A glass of water for a thirsty old man

Let me end with a story, which may be my most favorite story. It's so wildly true, it's just so wild. Levi Isaac of Berdichev, a great non-dual master, was leading the prayer services on Yom Kippur, the holiest day of the Jewish calendar. On this day, the person who leads the chanting goes into the very source code of the Cosmos in order to evolve everything, to change everything, to bring history to its ultimate perfection. The high priest who leads the prayer services with his or her chanting becomes a great evolutionary agent, entering the source code of reality to change it all, to fix it all, to transform it all. It's a 24-hour fast and everyone enters into 24 hours of ecstatic chanting.

So he was doing this for 24 hours, he was at the inside of the inside, he was changing everything, he had become evolution itself. He was awakened as the living Evolutionary Process, he was awakening to the Fourth Big Bang, when you realize that you are evolution awakening to itself, evolving and changing the future, and it was all happening. The fast was about to end after 24 hours, and he just needed another 15 minutes to change all of history. So he goes on and keeps going for 10 minutes, he just needs five more minutes, and then he sees out of the corner of his eye an old man of about 77 in the congregation, and this old man is thirsty and picks up a glass of water, but it's empty. The rabbi needs just five more minutes of evolutionary activism to change all of history, but he says: "No, NO!" and he stops and climbs down from all the highest heavens, leaving evolution to fend for itself. He ends the fast, he pours a glass of water and brings it to the old man. Wow. When I first heard that story, I burst out crying. See, that is what it means to hold the evolutionary context in all of its power, and at the very same time hold the infinite, gorgeous dignity of every individual who needs a glass of water.

Every one of us knows somebody that we can bring a glass of water to, and when we find that person and bring him a glass of water, that's really the change, that shifts everything, that's the Evolutionary Impulse.

Deep bow to the God in the center of the room, Amen.

Introduction to the Six Christmas Meditations

*I*n *this series* of meditations from Christmas to New Year, we are going to collect ourselves, to bring ourselves in full presence. Our goal of the first couple of days of meditation is to lift the veil, to let go of and deconstruct the dragon and to feel the natural essence of our True Nature. To deconstruct everything that stands between us and our True Nature, to reveal the ever-always-already present True Self, True Essence, True Nature that we are in our luminous, blinding, dazzling, gorgeous Essence.

So, welcome, a kiss into your heart, total love. And in these daily, one-hour sessions we are going to radically love each other. I want to invite you in these hours to seduce each other, to fall in love with each other, in the highest, most beautiful, holy sense of the word. I get to love you, to feel your presence in the room, with your subtle and unique energy patterns, your sacred community in which everyone who is there, needs to be there. This community was actually formed billions of years ago, at the Big Bang, when things began to move to allow this particular, unique, gorgeous, holy community to come into being, in the week between Christmas and New Year at Venwoude, at the end of 2011 and entering 2012. It's perfect, the perfect people are here, and everyone you need, everything you need for your full liberation is here this week.

I'm doing no teaching. What we will be doing in these sessions* is simple, meditative sharing and meditation instruction. I will be asking you to listen with your eyes closed, because some things you can see with your eyes open and other things you can only see with your eyes closed. I am talking with my eyes closed as well, so we can meet each other in inner space. Wow, thank you, I love to meet in inner space, when the third eye opens, what Rumi and Ibn Arabi call 'the eye of the heart.'

*The Six Christmas Meditations were held in the form of
six Skype sessions, with Marc talking from behind his laptop
in the US, and Chahat and her Circle students listening
in front of a laptop in a room at Venwoude, Holland.

First Christmas Meditation: The Path is the Goal

The Path is the Goal

*P**lease* shut your eyes and let me start by a simple pointing-out instruction. Just answer the question, we'll do a show of hands even though no one is looking. How many people in the room have had sex? Okay, good. Now the second question. How many people in this room have had at least once in their life what we call 'great sex'? Okay. So everyone's had one experience of that thing that we call great sex, and I know it's a little elusive, it's harder to find than we think. We all think there is some man who lives with some woman in New Jersey and they are the only people in the world having great sex, but everyone has that experience someplace and, hopefully, at least once.

So let me ask you a question and you answer in your heart. When you were having great sex, was that the path or was that the destination? Everyone gets this, right? That's called a pointing-out instruction in Buddhism, pointing out an enlightened knowing that you already have in your consciousness, so you realize that your own first-person experience is the teacher, your own inner self is the teacher. When you actually access the experience of great sex, you know that the path, the sexing, is the goal. You are not sexing in order to get somewhere; you are sexing in order to be sexing. Which is why there are people in the world who've had sex not just once, but twice. "Twice? But why? You already did it once, why would you do that again?"

In the same way, meditation, or the experience of enlightened consciousness, is not merely a method, it's not merely a practice in order to get somewhere; it is the destination itself. Imagine that you're having a conversation with someone and you are not trying to manipulate them, you are not trying to get them somewhere; the conversation itself is the goal, which is the full joy and depth of that communication by itself.

In original Hebrew mysticism, the word for Messiah — the symbol of the end of days, Nirvana, complete liberation and perfection — comes from 'moshiach', which means 'conversation'. And that means that when a conversation is the goal, and not just the path to get to the goal, the world changes. Imagine talking to someone who just wants to be there with you, whatever the communication is, in deep presence, with open heart, listening and wanting to understand exactly what you said, totally focused, curious about who you are, ready to receive you and to commit to your growth and your liberation; now *that's* conversation.

So our meditation is also not the path, it is the goal.

Now I am going to welcome you with a very simple chant and then we'll begin the meditation of today, which is a Pranayama or Shema meditation. Tomorrow, we will chant together, but today just listen and receive the chant. You don't need a voice in order to chant. I don't have good voice — my family would sing songs around the table on Hanukkah and ask me to sing quietly, to not ruin the melody; I have been in therapy ever since. So just kind of hear the quiet in your heart, meditation and chant come from the heart, they are the instruments. I am going to chant to create our place to welcome you into my heart and I invite you to welcome me into your heart, and if there is anything this week that I say that annoys you, please just forgive me.

If I make you a little uncomfortable, good — sometimes that's my job: to comfort the afflicted and afflict the comfortable. But if anything about my voice or my being somehow gets in the way, just forgive me, we're all on the Path. Ramana Maharshi was also a pretty annoying guy to spend an afternoon with, so let's just forgive each other between Christmas and New Year. If I'm in any way in your way, I ask you to just let it go, to forgive me in advance. I will do anything I can, with everything I have, to be radically committed to serving you, to your liberation, ecstasy, freedom, and that's what this is really about. It's about your freedom, your full freedom to live and enjoy in goodness and depth and integrity.

Chant

The secret is always in the aftertaste, so rest in the Silence of Presence and let it wash you with warm, hot, beautiful water, let it wash your stomach, face, chest, upper back, lower back, between your thighs, legs, knees, ankles, the soles of your feet.

Picking up the pieces

We will do a Neshama-Nishima or pranayama meditation. Neshama means 'soul' in the original Hebrew and Nishima means 'breath'. The great Hindu practice of pranayama is meant to collect your energy, your prana, which fragmented during the whole year. Because in the hard moments of the year, you left a piece of yourself behind. How many people can feel that? Just feel in your heart and answer the question in your heart. When something happened, when you lost someone, when you had a conflict, when something exploded or broke open in your heart, you left a piece of your energy behind, you ripped out a page from your Book of Life, you lost something elemental and essential in your breath, in your vital life energy.

So this is the intention and I am inviting you to let it in, from deep within Hebrew mysticism: I want to collect the pieces of my life that I have left behind this past year. Okay, good.

Now you expand the intention to: I want to collect any piece of my life that I have left behind in the last five years, the pages that I have edited out or that have been ripped out of my Book of Life - a relationship that went bad, a job I was fired from, a city that I left, a part of myself that I had to hide because I felt it wasn't safe, so I let it go into exile.

And I expand again, holy brothers and sisters, I expand to ten years and identify: Is there anything in my life in the last ten years, a relationship, a job, a place, a part of myself that I sent into exile, because it felt not safe, too dangerous for the survival of my small-self ego? And set the intention that in this practice, you will recollect, reintegrate, remember and gather up that part of yourself that you left behind.

And now expand the circle again to your entire life, back until you were 18, and gather in any part of your life that you left behind all the way back until 18 years old. It might be a gift that you have, or a song that you sing, or a relationship that went bad or a living context that exploded, or a place, and commit with your intention in this moment to gather it up. Because anything you leave hidden in the back seat, controls the car. You want to stop driving by looking in the back mirror. Bring everything into the driver's seat and integrate it into your life: all the un-owned pieces, all the pieces of your story that you've edited out, undermining the power of your sacred autobiography, so let's add the chapters back in.

And finally expand for the fifth time beyond the year, beyond five years, beyond ten years, beyond even until you were 18, and expand all the way back to your earliest moment on this planet, when you were born, when you were one, or, like my son Zion, 16 months old, two years, three, four, seven, 10-12-14-16 and 17 years old, and gather up any part of your vitality that you left behind.

Recollect you dreams, remember what you were dreaming about when you were 18, gather it up and reclaim that dream. It might be fulfilled in a different way than you ever imagined, but the dream must be reclaimed. Gather up any part of yourself that you left behind, because it was too fragile, broken, vulnerable, or too large, grand, beautiful and luminous, and it would have gotten you into trouble, or so you thought, so you dulled your radiance, you dulled the luminosity, you darkened it, you covered it up so that it shouldn't threaten your surroundings, it shouldn't threaten the people around you and the people around shouldn't threaten you.

Introduction to Breathing Meditation

So this practice of Neshama-Nishima, soul breath, pranayama, will move not only the energy in your body in this moment, but all the energy in your heart, mind and spirit, from any point in your life. Because we enter into the timeless time and the placeless place, and every home you've ever lived in, every bed you've ever slept in, every emotion you've ever felt, all energy that ever moved through your body is now in you and with you and available to you.

We will breathe into your body from all of these places, and finally, in setting your intention, know that you are making love; you are not masturbating. Blessings to masturbation; as Woody Allen said, it is sex with someone you love and good cuddling afterwards, but meditation is about making love! You do it not only for you own sake, but for the sake of the All. You realize that your body-heart-mind-spirit is the body of Christ, the body of the Cosmos, the body of Buddha and the body of Moses. It's the heart of Christ, of Adam, of the Cosmos. It's the mind of God, of the

Earth, of the Cosmos. Your spirit is the spirit of Earth, of your individual Essence, of the Cosmos, of God — and remember: the God you don't believe in doesn't exist. So when I say God, I mean Essence with a personal face.

Now I am going to ask everyone to sit up. If anyone is lying down — total blessing and love to lying down, but here you actually want to sit up. You don't need a fancy position, you don't need to be in Lotus position or even half Lotus, but you need to be sitting up with your spine as comfortable and as straight as it can be, reaching up towards the heavens and down to the ground of the Earth — as they say in Aramaic, the heavens and earth kiss through me.

Your shoulders back, let them drop down, your head erect, your neck back, your hands either facing up or facing down on your knees or at your side. The key is to be at the most natural, comfortable, relaxed position; not in order to fall asleep, but in order to wake up, to let go and let God in. This is a practice that locates you in a deeper reality — "through my body I vision God."

We'll breathe separately into each section of the body, inhaling, and then I will say 'release', exhaling, which means to release the contraction, to release the tightness, to untie the knot, to release the contraction of ego — the ego of the body, the heart, the mind and the spirit. As you release, you do it for the sake of the all, at all four levels that live as Essence, as all of reality, because when you enter into the interior castle of your own body-heart-mind-spirit, you are on the inside face of all reality, all of Essence, of God.

And then after we've done that body-part release, either once or twice, I will name the same body part and I will say 'radiance'. And radiance means to let the natural radiance, luminosity, love, aliveness of that part of the body-heart-mind-spirit come alive. In this way, you release and radiate not only the body now, but you release and radiate anything that was ever broken or misused or not appreciated or not enlightened in the body. Just follow your own breathing pace.

We go through the physical body in this way because in every great mystical tradition and particularly in Kabbalah, every physical part of the body is part of the body of God. The microcosm of the human body is the doorway into the macrocosm of Spirit or Essence, the reality of God.

Guided Breathing Meditation – Release & Radiance

Crown of the head – release. *Aaaagh - actually I should hear you on the out breath.*
Crown of the head – release
Cheeks, face – release
Forehead – release
Top of the head – radiance. *Let the natural radiance of that part of the body come online.*
Forehead – radiance
Shoulders – release. *Aaaagh. Shoulders drop down.*
Back of the neck – release
Shoulders drop again
Shoulders – radiance

Back of the neck – radiance
Upper chest, breast – release
Upper chest, breast – radiance
Stomach, tummy – release
Stomach tummy – radiance
Upper back – release
Upper back – radiance
Lower back – release
Lower back – radiance
Yoni, phallus – release
Yoni, phallus – radiance
Full face - release
Full face - radiance
Anus – release
Anus - radiance
Left leg, thigh to knee – release; shoulders, drop
Right leg, thigh to knee - release
Both legs, thigh to knee – radiance
Right leg, knee to ankle – release
Left leg, knee to ankle - release
Both left and right ankle - radiance
Soles of the feet – release
Soles of the feet – radiance
Full body - release
Full body - radiance

And now rest into the silence. Follow your breath for three minutes. Other thoughts will arise, don't fight them, let them enter and leave, and drop back into deep Presence, into the Silence of

Presence, the infinite stillness of the vast spaciousness that is present, awake, alive and aware in every moment. Three minutes.

Now feel into the inner space of your heart, enter the inner space of your heart. Open your heart with your intention, feel the inner space of the heart, and feel the inner space of your heart connect to the inner space of the heart of every person in your surroundings, in your world. Because in the inner space of the heart, we are the same, we are True Self, part of the Great Heart, in endless, boundless compassion. Not idiot compassion, but the compassion of the wise, full body, reclaiming every part of our life that we edited out, forgiving, releasing, setting new intention. We call it metanoia, turning, and the turning itself is the path, and the path, the destination.

So allow me as a teacher, as a simple friend, to bless you, and you bless me and you bless each other and you bless your teachers with the full greatness that you already are, the full greatness of the Universe that lives and pulses in this moment, that enlivens every cell, that makes every blade of grass sing, that makes the hills alive, that moves through every complex molecule, every chemical equation, every elegant, mathematical dance. The power of All is now unified within you and as you, is now alive and elegant and awake and moving through you and saying: "Yes, this is right, yes, you were right."

This time together is to sing a holy YES to life: yes, yes, yes. May this week be a week of your radical, audacious and alive holy yes, filled with big heart and gentle, audacious, wild, ecstatic love. That is already true and the word is good, all obstacles are removed, everything that stands in the way melts in the sun of Light and Compassion and so it is. Amen.

Second Christmas Meditation: 'Here I Am'

A language meditation

Relax, sit up straight, find your location, and most importantly:

open your heart and shut your eyes. Slowly, gently, shut your eyes, knowing that some things you can see with your eyes open and other things you only see with your eyes closed. There is no rush, no place to get, no place to go. It's all right here. We're all students and teachers, masters and disciples on the Path.

We will be doing what in Kabbalah is called a language meditation, a pointing-out instruction in Buddhism, or an analytic meditation in Tibetan Buddhism. It means diving into the moment, and the Hebrew word for the moment is 'rega', whereas 'ragua', the exact same Hebrew word, means deep tranquility, deep peace and deep healing. The reason that it is the same word, is that the deep tranquility, bliss and healing that your Self requires right here, right now, is available in only one place — in THIS moment, right here, right now. It's not over there, there is no place to go, you can't be late.

I invite you, I demand with holy audacity, I beg you, kneeling in front of you as your servant, for the sake of your own liberation, imagine these two experiences and you will have the key to both Nirvana, liberation and Samsara, slavery.

The experience of Samsara is the experience of being late: "I'm late, it has started already. So much depends on my being on time, but I am late and I am rushing and I am in traffic, the meeting has already started and I've got to get there, I can't control the traffic, the meeting has started without me, I worked for four years to create this meeting, but here I am, stuck in traffic, because I stayed up too late and got up too late and I did not plan. I may blow the whole meeting 'cause my cell phone is not working, so I can't even call to say that I'm late, late, late." That's the experience of Samsara, of slavery, of ego grasping, of being closed off, of being locked in, trapped, out of control.

And then there is Mukti-Ananda, the ecstasy of liberation, the knowing that I am in the exact right place at the exact right time, and that all of history, my personal, family, lineage history, all of the history of this planet and of the Cosmos, all those 13,7 billion years, are leading up to this very moment. And the inner face of the Cosmos, which is aligned with love and perfection, being Sat-Chit-Ananda, or Truth-Consciousness-Bliss/Love, this loving Cosmos gives me in every moment the healing and transformation necessary for that moment, right here, right now. The original Hebrew word for this is 'Hee Nay Nee', meaning 'Here I am'. It's happening now, you can't be late, there is no place to go, it's the opposite feeling of being late. You are perfectly on time because the time is NOW.

In original Hebrew, the word for 'time' is 'zman', and its second meaning is 'invitation'. They are the same word, because time is an invitation, it's an invitation to say the holy Yes to the holy Now, to cry out the holy Yes to the holy Now ecstatically.

What does a person say at the moment of maximum erotic, sexual expression? People say the name of other: "'Oh Jack, oh Thomas, oh Jasmin", and people say: "Oh God, oh God," and the third thing in every language that people say is: "Yes, yes, yes!" Because it's the response of the full showing up, the full presence, the holy Yes to the holy Now, which is Je-Ho-Vah. 'Je' means the Divine point, Ho-Vah, which moves in the present, containing the past and the future, which is not over there, but right here – Hee Nay Nee, Here I Am, showing up right now.

And the inner essence of the Universe, whose inner lining is love, makes available to me, as a divine gift of reality in this moment, all the healing that could ever be necessary in this moment. And the only possible way not to be healed and held in this moment, is to NOT be in the moment, to be over there, not here. In the infinity of the present, in the eternity of the moment, is the presence, is the invitation to the full bliss, power and Yes to the radical, holy success of your life.

This is the teaching of the great mystical traditions, and it is from that place that we realize that there is no distinction between the path and the goal, between the taste of the bark of the tree and the taste of the tree, between the way and the destination, between means and ends, between getting there and being there. Because 'there' is here, right now, in the very step you are taking in this very moment. All of the love, power, glory, goodness, sweetness, bliss, perception, insight, ecstasy, depth, knowing and wisdom is here, right now.

Being Here Now, following the breath

'Be Here Now' - that is the invitation, the practice and the enactment of meditation. Let's rest for a few minutes in the silence of the Now, and you will feel your mind wandering away from the Now. And the practice of meditation, the essential practice of the meditator, is not to rest in the bliss. That's a mistake. The practice of meditation is, when your mind wanders away from the fullness of the presence in the present moment, that you non-judgmentally bring your mind back to center, back to presence, back to the fullness of Eros that lives in the infinity of this moment, in the eternity of invitation inherent in this moment in time. The act of non-judgmentally pulling your attention and energy back into the Eternal Now is the act of meditation.

Entering into the practice of meditation is not to enter into the bliss or the spaciousness; that's a by-product of meditation, a possible, natural result of meditation. But meditation itself is non-judgmentally bringing back your love, your attention, your energy to the Now, and all you're doing to do that is following your breath.

You feel the inhale; you feel the exhale. You place your attention energy on your breath, and you follow your breath. You don't think about time, you don't care, because you are ecstatically on the inside of the inside, in the deepest of the deep, the Holy of

Holies, the eternal NOW, that Presence in the present, the Divine point in the present; in the ragua, deep tranquility, in the rega, in the moment, which says: "Here I am, as a holy Yes to the holy Now, following my soul, the shama, and my soul essence, my shima, my breath."

Just stay with the breath and every time your mind wanders, 30 times every second, or every two minutes, you non-judgmentally bring your mind back to center, again and again and again, watching your breath inhale and exhale. Feel the part of you that wants it to be over there, that wants to get there, and then drop deeper into HERE, into Hee Nay Nee, "Here I Am".

On the inhale you expand your stomach; on the exhale you contract it and you rest. Hold your posture, you should be sitting up straight, shoulders back and relaxed, hands gently relaxed, palms up or palms down. The spine is lifting you up by the crown of your head, and locating you down at the earth as you follow your breath. Your stomach expands on the inhale and contracts on the exhale as you release any tension in your body. When a thought comes into your mind, you let it pass through your mind non-judgmentally and pull your attention back to center, following the breath a thousand times, time and time again, in the ceaseless wonder of meditation.

A meditation of self-inquiry

We will now enter into the meditation of self-inquiry, of Fichte and Schelling, of the holy Ramana Maharshi, of the holy Baal Shem Tov.

Collect your energy around your posture, feel your back straightening, your head and neck lifting back until it's completely perpendicular with your spinal cord, not hunched forward or bent over. Your shoulders drop down, your hands open, you are in Lotus or in half Lotus position, or you're sitting with your knees up or down, it doesn't matter as long as the energy can move up and down the spine, so long as the prana, the chi, can move through your body.

Just feel the air against your face, as you breathe in and breathe out, breathing in oxygen and breathing out carbon dioxide, as the plants breathe in carbon dioxide and breathe out oxygen. Feel yourself breathing in, breathing out. Feel the entire world of trees and plants and grass, feel the air around your face, listen to any sound around you — the low hum of the computer, perhaps a bird outside, a beat, a sound in your nose, the sound of the person breathing next to you, a vague rustling movement in the trees.

Feel the sensation of your breath as it comes in and out of the body, the sensation in your nostrils of the breath going in your nose, going into your upper chest, your stomach rising and falling. Notice any energy sensation, a feeling of restlessness, of sleepiness. You are aware of your body, aware of your posture, aware of the air against your face, aware of the sound of coughing around you, the subtle hums, the subtle sounds. You're aware of the sensation of your breath coming in and out of your body, you're aware of the air going into your nostrils and into your upper chest, you're aware of the rising and falling, you're aware of energy sensations.

And now become aware of any emotion you might feel, an emotion as energy-in-motion. Find any emotion that you had in the past days. It may be sadness, confusion, joy, degradation, anger, bliss, anxiety. Become aware of the emotion, of the energy-in-motion, become aware of the calm inside you right now, become aware of the impatient voice inside you now.

Become aware of your hope and expectations. Feel the hope and expectations move in you as your shoulders drop, and become aware of the hope and the expectations moving in you. Become aware of your thoughts, any thought moving through your mind in the last hour, any thought that is arising in your mind's consciousness. Become aware of your thoughts. "Is Marc Jewish? Yes. Am I an anti-Semite? Yes. Do I owe money? Yes. Do I need to repay it? Yes." Become aware of your thoughts, and know that you are not your thoughts, 'neti neti', not this and not that. Here in the Now, in the present, Here I Am.

You are not your thoughts; become aware of your thoughts. You are not your emotions; feel your emotions rising and falling in the matrix of consciousness of awareness, and let your awareness hold your breathing, hold your anger and hold your love, because you are not your breath, you are not your anger, you are not your depression, not even your joy.

Hear the sound and become aware of the sound, because you are not the sound — you are the awareness of the sound. Just like you are not you emotions, you are the awareness of emotion. You are not your thoughts, and any distraction — for life is always distracting — moves through your consciousness like a cloud through the sky and falls away as your realize once again that you're not your thoughts, you are aware of your thoughts. You are not your emotions, you are aware of your emotions; you are not your body, as wonderful as your body may be.

The gorgeousness, the delight that is your body, the manifest, living, visible sign and inward invisible essence that is your body - you're not your body. You are not your breasts; if one is removed, you are still a woman and you are still Essence. You are not your stomach, you are not your cock; even if it's cut off, you are still a man and still Essence. You are not your legs, you are not your head. You are aware of your breasts, you are aware of your arms and back and ankles, you are aware of your cock and you're aware of your face.

Your body is held in your awareness, and you are conscious of your awareness, you are aware, awake and alive to the fact that you are 'awaring'. I am aware that I am aware of teaching right now, I am aware that I am friends with you right now. I am aware that I am loving you radically into bursting open right now, I am aware that I am aware with you in meditation. You are the awareness of the awareness, the knowing of the knowing, the consciousness of the consciousness.

You are not your body, you are aware of it, you are conscious of your body. You are not your thinking mind, you are aware of your thinking mind. As you say in your mind: "Two plus two equals four," you are aware of your thinking mind, but you are not your thinking mind. You are not anger; call off your anger, call off your suicide and realize that you are not your anger, that is not you. You are aware of your anger as your shoulder drop, your spine is erect, and you are aware of your awareness.

We are lifting the veil, we are deconstructing the illusion of the separate self and we realize that who we are is HERE, right now. And what is here, right now, is consciousness arising in every moment. I am the name, which is essence, the awareness of the awareness, the awareness of my name, of your name, and no other identity is ever true. Who am I? I AM.

And the knowing that lives in me, is the knowing that lives in you, that lives in all of us. The awareness of body that lives in me is the awareness of body that lives in you, that lives in all of us. We make love in the One —the knower in me makes love to the knower in you, and it is not a Oneness in which we are lost, but a Oneness in which we are found. Meditation only comes alive when we realize this Oneness right here, right now, saying a holy Yes to the holy Now.

Third Christmas Meditation: God's Yearning for You

Footprints in the Sand

*One night I dreamed I was walking
along the beach with the Lord.
Many scenes from my life
flashed across the sky.
In each scene I noticed footprints in the sand.
Sometimes there were two sets of footprints,
Other times there was one set of footprints.*

*This bothered me, because I noticed
That during the low periods of my life,
When I was suffering from
anguish, sorrow or defeat,
I could see only one set of footprints.*

*So I said to the Lord,
"You promised me, Lord, that if I followed you,
you would walk with me always.*

But I have noticed that during the
most trying periods of my life
there has only been one set of
footprints in the sand.
Why, when I needed you most, have
you not been there for me?"

The Lord replied, "My child, the
times when you have seen
only one set of footprints, is
when I carried you."

his text, written in 1936 by a girl named Mary Stevenson and quoted zillions of times, is not a story or Dharma of some old, ethnocentric church or synagogue or mosque. This is the realization that I'm always held in the arms of the Beloved, or in Rumi's words, that "every place I fall, I fall in the hands of God."

To feel that experience, to know and to be able to access in your own experience what it might mean to be held in the arms of the Divine, is the intention of this next set of meditations. So dear, sweetest, holy lovers and friends and teachers and students, dear holy community, on this third day we begin to become a new, sacred community, a new sangha, which is interconnected and interwoven and inter-textured in a way that never existed before. In this precise community of people, no one is extra, everyone is needed to weave the fabric of this holy sangha.

Meditation: Accessing God in the third person

This is a guided meditation, so follow with me step by step. And those of you who have done this with me, find the ego that says: "Oh, I have done this already," and ask yourself: have you ever had sex twice? Meditation is making love, it is not information; even the Dharma talk in the meditation is not teaching. We make love with each other as we meet in deep truth. As we meet in the deep knowing, we meet in the love.

With your eyes shut, imagine for a moment the room that you are in, and let the room expand; feel the larger presence not only of the room, but of all of Venwoude, feeling all of the parameters of this beautiful property.

Thank you, Ted*, for your holy initiation, for your holy work, for making this a reality. And you know Ted, sometimes we forget you, we forget the energy that you suffused and gave your life to, to create this holy context. So we bow to you at the beginning of this meditation, we thank you, holy friend, holy teacher, holy delightful one. Know that on the next stage of your journey, you still have influence and we are loving and holding you and praying for you and say: "Thank you, deep bow."

We dedicate this meditation to everyone who has gone to the next stage of the journey, who passed to the next place. May the merit of your ascending lift your soul beyond any obstacles, beyond any impediment. You will be fully held, forgiven and loved, as your soul and essence deepens in the next stage of your journey, and we hold you in love. Thank you.

And imagine beyond Venwoude and expand to all of Holland - it's not that deep, but *all* of Holland, vast in its smallness, huge in all of its beauty and its rivers and its people and its buildings and its nature, its atmosphere, the whole of the Netherlands, all of it, everything contained therein it. Then expand to all of Europe, every country in Europe, all of it, everything contained in it. Then expand again, to all of Europe and Asia, teeming with billions of people in India and China, and then include Africa and Australia and New Zealand and the Americas and Antarctica, and all of the oceans, all of the teeming communities of life beneath the ocean and in the atmosphere, the entire Gaia, all of Planet Earth.

And feel into God in the third person, because this is God's manifestation and expression, emerging for 13,7 billion years, constructing and deconstructing, creating and destroying stars and supernovas, out of which emerge the elementary particles, the first subatomic structures, atoms, molecules, molecular structures, molecular structures coming alive into the first cellular structures, all of it. The vast Planet Earth with all its complexity in shimmering, incandescent beauty, is part of the third face of God.

And I can imagine beyond this, I imagine all of the planets and all of the stars, hundreds of millions of stars and more in this Galaxy, the vastness of the Galaxy. And imagine matter and energy, space and time; matter and energy are one continuum, $E = mc^2$, and space and time are also one continuum. And we begin to travel, millions and then billions of light years at 186,000 miles per second, across the vast, extended Galaxy, and then the next galaxy and the next galaxy, and a thousand galaxies, ten thousand galaxies, a hundred thousand galaxies, a million galaxies, ten million galaxies, 50 million galaxies, billions and billions and trillions of light years and hundred million galaxies, beyond where any human being can even grasp to grasp in order to grasp, beyond what you can even vaguely imagine or know in words in any language, which can't even approach the awesome, unfathomable, insanely, wildly, ecstatically, infinitely, beautifully complex, gorgeous, perfect expanse of this God in the third person, manifesting in these billions and billions and billions of light years.

And then hold that vastness and go inside and feel not only in outer space but in inner space, as you go into every organ in your body, and begin to realize that in your body alone, at this very moment in time, there are 50 trillion cells, each one unique, each one cellularly arched and designed, perfectly functioning in precise relationship with the 50 trillion other cells, aliving and awaring in your body at this very moment, and feel again into the third face of the Divine, the third face of God, and feel the energy-Eros, the evolutioning Eros that moves and drives and animates and suffuses and unfolds and evolves all of these realities, steadily over billions and billions of years.

Through your imagining you are touching vaguely, shimmeringly, glimpsingly, the God in the third person, and then in this moment, in this very moment, take all that shimmering, hundreds-of-billions-of-light-years of expanse, and put it in a chair sitting next to you. All of it, all of God in the third person, put it in a chair sitting next to you in this moment, looking at you and knowing your name and caring for you, and you have God in the second person. Oh, my God.

From God in third person to God in second person

That is God in the second person, sitting in a chair next to you, in this very moment, knowing you, loving you, caring for you, holding you, receiving you, in the same way that you are hearing me, through the quality of intelligence that lives in you, that expressed itself on the physical level in the structure of the ear and eye, as well as at the level of consciousness, the same intelligence that is receiving this message.

And you, as gorgeous, holy and intelligent as you are, you are not more intelligent than the Cosmos itself, you are not more intelligent than Source, which is the source of your intelligence. Just as you hear me, the living Cosmos hears you; because the living Cosmos, in all of its vast, beautiful, shimmering complexity, which produces the depth of Dante and Shakespeare, the infinity of the laws of physics, mathematical constructions, the most advanced calculus, the incandescent beauty of Nature and all of its detail and gorgeous expression — all of this happens not by chance, no chance!

It's the evolutionary guidance, unfolded through the animating Shakti of the self-organizing Universe, what some physicists began to call the fifth force of the Universe, the Eros, and what other physicists call the unseen hand which pulls all, self-organization through self-transcendence. And all of that sits in a chair next to you, knowing your name, caring about you. All of the Divinity, all of infinite reality, in love, contracts itself into a point to know you.

In Christianity that's called the mystery of Incarnation, when God becomes man and lives in Jesus, and in Judaism it's the God that dwells between the two fucking Cherubs at the top of the Ark in the Holy of Holies in the Temple of Jerusalem. In Hinduism, in Islam, in the prostrations of Buddhism, in the Aboriginal teaching, in the teachings of the Sufis through Rumi, in the teaching of the evolutionary, Integral consciousness of world spirituality that talks of the three faces of God, we realize in our very being that that infinite Face of the Divine holds us, knows us, makes contact, cares about us and knows our name.

We have just felt that imagination is reality, for God may be a figment of your imagination, my friends, but your imagination is a figment of God. God is in your imagination and your imagination is a Face of God. Adam in Hebrew means 'the imagining one'. We are not merely Homo Sapiens, we're Homo Imaginis. You can only imagine what exists.

God in the second person is the yearning to make contact

So we felt into the infinite God of the Universe in third person, who sits in the chair next to me as God in second person and knows my name, and I feel that every place I fall, I fall into God's hands. God in the second person is the impulse to make contact, when I feel the yearning to make contact, not in a primitive or mythical way, but as the consciousness that is living in me and in you, which is revealing to you, IN the yearning, that contact is true and real, and that you're being held. When you turn to the Cosmos, to the personal face of Essence, and you say: "Help me," that's not primitive, that is the second face of the Divine.

We need to free the second face of the Divine from the hands of a clutching, ethnocentric, gay-bashing Church. We need to liberate the second face of God and let ourselves be seduced by the Divine, let God love us open, fuck us open, even as we fuck God open and make love to the Divine. That is prayer. Prayer is the erotic merging with the Divine, in which we put before God our request. But to all of that we return tomorrow.

What does it feel like for God to love you? And because the Divine is both beyond you and within you, we are going to go inside on an inner journey, to feel into the interior face of the Cosmos and touch the experience of God, holding and loving you. When you touch this experience, you will blow open in shock, awe and ecstasy.

Guided meditation: God's yearning for you, merging tenderness with lust

With eyes closed and our hearts open, I ask you first of all to forgive me for any way that I might be in the way — press delete, forgive me, forgive me any limitation, any imperfection.

Now imagine someone that you love tenderly. It might be your mother, or if you have been in intensive therapy over a mother for the last 30 years, pick someone else, or maybe in your intensive therapy you love her tenderly at the same time, right? Just pick someone you love dearly. If you have no human being like that, maybe you have a cat. I hope you have a human being, the gift of a human being, someone you care about and you love tenderly. Feel into that love in your heart, access that love and feel it. Feel that love rising in your breast, rising in your body, feel how much you care about them and how delighted you are to do something good for them, how much you want to hold them, how much you want to be good for them, and I'm not talking about a sexual love, but about a tender, gentle, caring, holding and protecting love.

You want to know every detail in that person's life. Feel that love and let that love expand and deepen, and let it deepen in you again and again, deeper and deeper and deeper. Feel it, know it, be it, touch it and then let it increase in you beyond the level that you ever experienced. Let it get bigger and wider and deeper and more full and more rich and more textured, and then let it deepen again and again and again. Now let it double as it rises in your body and your heart, and your hands open to help and hold that and let it double again.

Now you are exploding with tenderness, you ARE the infinite, fragile tenderness of the Cosmos, holding that person in radical, purified, clarified love, and as it explodes, it doubles again. Tenderness beyond imagination, you are an infinite essence of God holding, melting, loving, sweating, licking in every moment, touching, non-sexual but gentle, gorgeous, agape, a Yes to the end. And it doubles again, it explodes again in the ecstasy of infinite tenderness, as you give everything and anything, just to hold that person for a moment.

Then it doubles again and again and again till it explodes, and then take all of that and put it into and feel into the interior heart of God, and know that is how God feels about you in this very moment, holding and loving you infinitely, with the infinite tenderness and care beyond any and all grasp in imagination. That is God's interior, essence feeling of you, for you personally, knowing your name at this very moment right here and now.

Oh holy Mother of God, love you, love you, thank you, thank you, thank you for being here. And you can't hold it, so you want to giggle or laugh, but that's just the body's voice whispering in your ear, caressing you in this moment, and it's too much to hold, how can this possible be?! Love you, love you, that is Rumi's teaching!

And I invite you to go the next and last step of this mediation with me, with us together in this holy, sacred sangha community, holding each other, eyes shut, inner eye open, heart wide open, held in the second face of the Divine.

Now this time, we'll access a different kind of love in you, we access an erotic, sexual love that you once may have had for a particular person or that you have now. Feel into that beautiful, holy desire, that gorgeous lust, that stunningly beautiful, physically intense, sharp and sometimes painful, insisting, demanding urge; the urge to merge, to touch, to make contact, to open, to see, to penetrate, to thrust, to take, to hold.

Feel that rising in your body, feel it rising in your phallus and rising your yoni, feel it rising in your breasts and your nipples and your eyes and your cheeks and your back and your legs and your butt, between your thighs and in your toes and your ankles. Feel the sexual desire, the radical lust of Eros rising in your body. And you feel its gorgeousness, you feel its goodness, the utter, radical goodness of the urge to merge, to make contact, to touch or make love, to fuck, to be one. And you feel it rise in you and you give it space and do whatever you want to do in your mind to make it alive. When you do the mediation, take the place that works for you and make it alive with your body, until you feel nipples excited, yoni wet, cock erect, your body shivering, tingling, holy, holy, the Holy of Holies, so gorgeous; and feel its aliveness and let it increase.

Let it increase, the yearning, the desire, not the small desire that Buddha said to let go, but the great desire, which is God, Him or Her. It's self-desire rising in you, and let it increase, deepen, widen, arise, let it be you-enriched, let its texture be rich, open, yearning, seducing and let it double inside of you until it begins to course madly, maddeningly, insanely, yearningly, lustfully, thrusting, receiving open and throbbing, wet alive, right through your body, and it doubles again and now you are exploding with desire and with yearning and with raw sexual need and it explodes again and again until your body is aflame, you couldn't let anyone touch you or you'd explode in a 17-hour orgasm.

And then it doubles again and again, until you become yearning itself, you are at the edge of fulfillment, you are the very vibrating of the Cosmos, you are the Shakti vibrating in its inner essence, vibrating and pulsing like in the wetness and erectness of all of you, in the aliveness of all of you. And then double it again and again, until that explosion explodes to a supernova of shivering Shakti and energy, and then turn it all and feel it all into God, feeling to the interior face of God, and know that this is the Divine, feeling, yearning and lusting for you in this very moment, wanting to receive you and make love to you, to fuck you open, to love you open and to give you infinite pleasure, infinite lust of the Divine for your pleasure, for your fulfillment. This IS the reality on the inside of the Divine at this moment, God is lusting to make love to you.

And then take all of the infinite tenderness and all of the infinite desire and merge them into one in a seamless whole in which God is One and love is One. God is One and that is the feeling of God, loving you tenderly, infinitely lusting, fucking, making love, sharing, caring, caressing you in this very moment. That is God in the second person, this realization that lives and is true, here and right now, in every second — that IS Enlightenment.

This is Enlightenment, and it's not a dogma, it's a realization. It's the teaching of the Zohar, the teaching of Rumi and Shams, the teaching of all the great Kabbalah teachers, of all the great mystical Christian teachers, of the Aboriginals, of Kashmir Shaivism, the deep teaching of Vajrayana, the teaching of Isaiah the Prophet and of Jesus the Christ.

Not Jesus the Christ of the fundamentalist Church, but the Christ consciousness that holds you, the second face God, the Beloved, drunk in the taverns, pouring his ecstasy into you in every moment.

*'Ted' refers to Ted Wilson, founder of
Venwoude, who passed away in 2007.

Fourth Christmas Meditation:
Stages of Evolution

We *are going* to do a Dharma meditation today with several parts to it, and it will be a natural continuation of what we did yesterday, when we talked about the radical experience, the radical feeling, of the second person of God, the personal face of the Cosmos. In the great, impersonal Cosmic process of creation and distortion, we find the face of the personal.

You are the center of all evolution

I want to ask you to lovingly shut your eyes and find a gentle place on the inside. Sit up straight, good posture, spine is straight up, lift the neck to the crown of the head into the heavens and reaching down into the Earth — 'you are the place where heaven and earth kiss'.

Now experience yourself for a moment as the very center of the Cosmos and imagine the following truth, in the infinite, magnificent, frightening, awe-inspiring, wildly ecstatic, fearful, impersonal processes of the Cosmos: *you are the center of it all,* even as it's completely beyond you, this process of unfolding, through billions of years of stars exploding and then creating again, supernova after supernova.

Because at the very same time, you, you particularly, are the very center of the entire process, and you have the ability to let the process awaken in you. You as a human being are placed where Heaven and Earth kiss, you are the Axis Mundi, you are the pole of existence. All of evolution moves from unconscious to conscious as evolution awakens to itself, in you, and this evolution has gone through three stages.

Involution and the first stage of evolution: physical evolution

We imagine the first stage of evolution as physical evolution, from inanimate, non-living matter to life. But if you look at it again, how can you say that it's non-living? See the immense process of creativity and force as the physical world explodes from the Big Bang. The teachings of the great traditions, revealed by the Eye of the Spirit, all tell us that before the Big Bang, there is something called involution: when I truly love someone, I make myself just the right size for them to hold. I hold back my power, I don't overwhelm them, I allow them to emerge independently. The parent who truly loves the child steps back, withdraws, creates the space for the independent emergence of the child all the way, all the while knowing that the child is an expression of the parents, and desperately yearning, hoping and waiting for the day on which the child returns to the parent with free love and embrace.

And so the Eye of the Spirit reveals to us, through deep and profound meditation, that this is the story of Cosmic creation: first involution, then evolution. The infinite Divine, the force beyond the 100 billion galaxies, the Emptiness and no-thing-ness beyond anything, which is the Source of all things, contracted into itself, into a point, which is involution. And from that point it exploded into evolution, into this particular, revealed existence, the world of this Galaxy, and then physical evolution began to unfold, powered by the evolutionary Eros of creation and destruction.

The second stage: biological evolution

And at some point, this physical evolution awakened to life, when the inanimate world, the non-living world revealed its living essence as complex molecular structures awakened into cells, into life itself.

Now we move from physical evolution to biological evolution, to the evolution of life. Life evolved through cells to complex cells, to more complex organisms, to early plants, to later plants, to oceans teeming with life forms, to all the animals, to the early and later mammals, to more advanced mammals, to early human beings, to human beings with a triune brain, the neo-cortex, and then, culture emerged.

The third stage: cultural evolution

Culture began to emerge with the animistic totems of hunter-gatherer clans, with their very short time spans, trying to live through the next fifteen minutes, based on survival instincts, sex and food, surviving for the day, fighting off the enemy who was the primal threat. Then more sophisticated clans were created as a sense of the magical interweaving of the world arose, and the first tribes began to emerge with their rituals and more advanced structures of power. We moved from hunter-gatherer to farming communities, and farming communities gave birth to still more advanced forms of culture as the mythic membership societies evolved, with guiding rules and principles that were beyond the blood relations of the clans and tribes.

Empires and churches with both their laws and their revelations began to emerge, and then culture took another momentous leap forward when we moved beyond the mythic membership societies into the secular, Western Enlightenment. We began to talk about the Renaissance, about the universal rights of all men and all women, regardless of their membership of a particular mythical structure. Rationalism and science and democracy and universal human rights began to emerge, and then again culture evolves into multicultural, pluralistic, gender-empowered societies, and all the way, human consciousness gives birth to new and ever higher forms of expression.

The fourth stage: the Great Awakening of conscious evolution

So we have physical evolution, biological evolution and cultural revolution, and this begins to place into context this whole movement of the three great wheels of evolution: for billions of years it was the evolution of the physical planet, for millions of years it was biological evolution, and then, in the much shorter time of 30,000 years, we have cultural evolution. And now we're coming to the fourth phase, the fourth great turning of the wheel: the Great Awakening.

The Great Awakening is the awakening from unconscious evolution into conscious evolution. For the first time in the history of existence, evolution is awakening to itself, evolution is waking up through the human being — *you* are for the first time becoming aware of evolution. We realize that what I've just spoken about in the last 20 minutes, could not have been spoken about 300 years ago anywhere on the planet. We were unaware of this great, universal story of moving from physical evolution to biological evolution to cultural evolution. And today, as evolution awakens to itself, we begin to realize that we live in an evolutionary context.

And if we fully awaken to our full consciousness, we begin to sense into the inner face of evolution, the inner face of the evolutionary process, which is ultimately not impersonal, but infinitely, cosmically intimate and personal. The inside of the evolutionary process is nothing other than love, and love is the movement towards higher and higher levels of recognition, mutuality, union and embrace. Love is the overall meta-trajectory, the overall meta-direction towards higher and higher care, wider and wider circles of caring and concerning, as the human being moves from egocentric to ethnocentric to world-centric to kosmocentric. In egocentric, I care only about myself and the few people I need for survival; in ethnocentric, my care and concern relate to my entire community and people; in world-centric, my care and concern relate to the entire world, and in kosmocentric I am awakening and becoming aware and responsible and loving to the entire process of evolution as it emerges and takes its next step for me.

You are the Axis Mundi of conscious evolution

And so, as you sit straight and erect, with your spine lifting up to the sky and reaching down into the earth, you realize that you, particularly you, are the Axis Mundi, you're the central pillar, you are in that great movie of 10 years ago, 'The Truman Show'. An entire world is watching your life, and not only the entire world, but the entire history of the world, and not only the entire history of the world but the entire history of the Cosmos, of 13,7 billion years of evolution unfolding, creatively powered by the evolutionary Eros of Love, giving birth to uniquely you. No one like you has ever been given birth to, no one like you will ever be given birth to, and you possess unique consciousness, a unique perspective, unique gifts, which can affect the entire destiny of All-That-Is.

Remember the butterfly in physics: as a butterfly flaps its wings in Tokyo, a storm is caused in New Orleans, in the great sea of cause and effect, the interdependent arising of All-That-Is. As evolution becomes conscious of itself and awakens to itself, we realize the full interconnectivity of the All with the All. As revealed in the great experiments of quantum physics by John Stewart Bell and others, we begin to awaken to a sense of evolutionary responsibility and evolutionary power.

So we move to conscious evolution, evolution awakening for me, knowing that my unique gift, my unique joy, my unique inside, my unique way of being and becoming, can set up a ripple effect of goodness, creativity and love that affects the very course of the Cosmos. And to awaken into evolutionary responsibility, is to know that the entire world is in a scale with the good and the not-good, weighing this moment as precisely even, and your next action tips the balance, your very next action determines the entire trajectory unfolding. That is your true nature. If we realize the truth of quantum physics, of the butterfly effect living through you, then that is the nature of your power. Wow.

Meditation into the interior face of the Cosmos

In today's Dharma meditation, I'm going to take you to the inside, to the interior face of the Cosmos, in three steps. The first step is just going to feel the connection, which I'll try to unfold and share with you. This is not a Dharma talk, this is a meditation when you hear it with your heart open and eyes closed, so try and feel into the inner essence of the nature of the Cosmos. And then in the second part of our meditation, we'll begin to have a personal conversation, each of us, with the Cosmos.

Sink deeply, use your mind as a chisel on a diamond to cut through the illusion, and realize the true nature of reality that you live in. In the old religion, there was only the person, it was all about the person. For many years, the new Cosmology was taught to be only impersonal, the impersonal process of evolutionary unfolding. In the awakening to conscious evolution and the new world spirituality based on Integral principles — the next evolutionary leap of love and consciousness — we realize that the impersonal and the personal are one.

Your body is air, fire, water and ground. As air, fire, water and ground, you're part of the impersonal unfolding and emerging and arising, part of the creation and destruction, part of the grand narrative of emergent and emerging life, indivisible from that physical part of reality which is your body, which is driven by blind, impersonal forces seeking sexing, food, safety, survival.

But there is a unique expression of All-That-Is that is awake, conscious and alive in you. You see the world from a particular angle with a particular insight that no one else has, which is your unique perspective, your unique prism of insight, which creates your Unique Self, which has unique gifts of consciousness, love, caring and concern, and you greatly desire to give it, more than anything else.

Until you feel needed uniquely by the Cosmos, until you realize that you have a unique gift to give that no one else that ever was or will be, can or will give, until you realize that that gift is desperately needed by the impersonal, Cosmic process of All-That-Is and can only be given by you, until you live that full realization of awakened Enlightenment, of awakened Unique Self, your life will remain desperate. And no amount of food or fucking, no amount of lovely community, will replace the nagging sense of un-We, of disease, of anxiety, of wondering 'why am I here?' And then I will be gone, it will be like I wasn't here, the worst nightmare of a human being.

Wake up and face it directly in this moment. The worst nightmare in a human being, the most grotesque possibility confronting a human being, is the possibility that I am irrelevant, that I am an extra on the set, that I am un-needed, that I get my comforts to calm myself from the nightmare, but that ultimately, the nightmare was the truth: that the world would be just the same without me. That is the greatest human nightmare. That's why, when two persons are together for many years, one of them dies and the remaining partner can't find a genuine need to address, this partner statistically almost always dies several months later.

The only response to the great and vast nightmare of creation and destruction is to awaken from the nightmare, to des-illusion and to realize that you are the butterfly, by flapping your wings in your unique way of Being and Becoming, by singing your unique song, by giving your unique gift, by writing your unique poem, by being the way of laughing, living, loving, awake, aware and alive that is you and you alone.

You're not a narcissist, you're a God. A narcissist contracts you're your separate self and says: "Let me collect more and more comfort for survival." The Unique Self expands into love and says: "Oh my God, what can I give, what can I love, what's the Unique Love gift, the gift of inside and essence that's mine to give?" And it awakens to the full, radical, ecstatic joy and aliveness in that giving, and in that giving it receives in return the fullness of the erotic ecstasy of being alive.

And that's what was missing from the movie 'Home' that we saw yesterday. Yes, the impersonal as It; yes, the impersonal unfolding of All-That-Is; but at the very heart of the impersonal is love, is the mutual attraction of elements to each other, is the evolutionary Eros that connects everything everywhere.

I ask you with love to feel into this, again not as a Dharma teaching, but as a Dharma meditation. The Universe webbed for a billion years of work to create you, and it did it only because there's a particular, unique function that you and only you can fulfill. Know that your creative power, the unique creative power residing in you, will be evoked and invited to play for the unique, specific work mission that it has been created for.

And where did your unique creative power come from? What's its source? Its source, my friends, is the same place that everything comes from, the same place out of which the fireball comes: the realm of Source, of Emptiness, of No-thing-ness. The mysterious order of reality of No-thing-ness is simultaneously the ultimate Source of all Things. How strange this is, but we've recently encountered this not only through the Eye of the Spirit of the great traditions, but also empirically in physics, where we call it quantum fluctuation, where elementary particles fluctuate, moving in and out of existence. What a strange realization. You think physicists have an easier time with it than you?

Elementary particles, the very particles that emerged in the first seconds of the Big Bang, leap into existence and then disappear. Wow. Where did they come from? How did they sneak into reality all of a sudden? They simply leapt out of no-thing-ness, and what we call today 'quantum fluctuation', the ancient traditions called 'creatio ex nihilo', something that emerges from no-thing-ness, something that emerges from ultimate reality, from Source: there was no particle and then there was.

I'm not talking here about the manner in which mass and energy can be transformed into another. We're speaking of something much more basic, much more mysterious. Particles boil into existence out of sheer no-thing-ness, emptiness. No longer is this the teaching of the great traditions that revealed it by the Eye of the Spirit; it's now the simple reality of physics. Spirit now reveals itself in part from the quantum. It's the way the Universe works. We didn't construct it, we find ourselves here. Elementary particles come leaping out of mysterious realms, that's simply the way it is. I'm calling it now No-thing-ness or Emptiness, but that's only the limits of language.

Here we approach, through physics, ultimate mysteries, something that defeats our attempts to probe and investigate. There was no fireball, then the fireball erupted, the Universe erupted and all that has existence emerges, bursts out, erupts out of no-thing. All of being erupts into shining existence. Coincidence? Chance? Not a chance! There is no chance that we move from dirt to Shakespeare by chance. There is nothing in science that suggests it. The chances of that happening are billions and billions of billions to one, meaning no chance.

Does that mean that we go back to the old vision of an ethnocentric God that stands outside of the Universe and creates the Universe? No. We now realize that the force which is outside, is also inside, and that the Universe itself is a rising creator — that the Divine force of Eros, of living, alive Eros, is here and now, at the very sub-cellular level, at the very subatomic level. It is the unseen, evolutionary Eros, the Love-Intelligence guiding the process, and that Love-Intelligence lives in you, that Love-Beauty lives in you and becomes awake and alive, conscious and aware, through you.

Feel into it as it's happing in this moment. I want you to understand, holy brothers and sisters, that this essential nothingness, this ultimate mystery, lives in you. You are that mystery and that very emptiness is in you.

Take a single atom, for example one of the atoms living in you, and make it as large as a football stadium. We consist almost entirely of empty space, for the center of the atom, its nucleus, would be smaller than a baseball sitting out in center field. The outer parts of the atom are the tiny bugs buzzing at an altitude higher than any baseball has ever been, and between it all there is nothingness, no things, empty. You are more emptiness than anything else! Indeed, if all space were taken out of you, you would be a million times smaller than the smallest grain of sand. Let's say it again: if all emptiness were taken out of you, you would be a million times smaller than the smallest grain of sand, according to physics.

But it's good to know that we are this emptiness, because this emptiness is no-thing; it's the source of all being. And this has been revealed not only through Spirit, but for the first time also through science. The way particles spontaneously leap into existence is a radical discovery of our own lifetime. And this was and is the teaching of the great traditions, which intuitively understood the Emptiness, No-thing-ness, the ultimate, mysterious order that is the Source of everything.

Wow, we need to move beyond the division between science and religion, which has created so much suffering, so much pain, so much meaninglessness and so much hurt. It was important to establish scientific activity, but now we need to let science and Spirit re-collide and reintegrate as a new, grounded story of the Universe, one that emerges and explodes beyond any previous telling of reality. This great new story of existence is at the center of a world spirituality based on Integral principles. And within the context of this new story, we can continue our journey to our fullest destiny.

What is our fullest destiny? Our fullest destiny, and I say this based on science and Spirit together, is to become love in human form.

"Love in human form, what are you talking about, Gafni? I thought we were talking about science, religion and emptiness?"

Yes, that's true, but the journey out of Emptiness is the creation of love.

"But that's very confusing. What are you talking about?"

Well, what do we mean by love? In order to understand love, we have to begin with our common context, which is the emerging Universe in which we find ourselves. This realm of existence is our own — all beings, including humans, have this in common. If you want to learn anything, we've got to start with the Cosmos, the Earth and Life.

Love in its essence is allurement, because allurement is the force of attraction. A woman who is alluring, is attractive. A man can be alluring, a painting can be alluring. Allurement is the essential force of attraction of Eros, that attracts you to that person or thing. Let me use the word allurement for attraction.

So think of the entire Cosmos, all 100 billion galaxies rushing through space at this cosmic scale. The basic force of the Universe, the basic dynamic of the Universe, is the attraction, the allurement that each galaxy has for everything. Nothing in all of science could be more clearly established and studied, with greater attention to detail, than the primary attraction of each part of the Universe for every other part, which is what holds it all together. We don't even think about it, do we? On the Cosmic scale, the core-essence stuff of the Cosmos is an attraction.

Now gravity is not the attraction. Gravity is the word used by scientists to point to the primary attraction. Both Newton's and Einstein's theory, aside from their mathematical differences, are essentially theories of gravity. Both are attempts to say something intelligent about why rocks fall to the Earth. And why is there attraction? Before and after any theory, there's the ultimate mystery of the falling rock and the revolving Earth, which is the attraction that orders the Universe in an intelligent way. No matter how intelligently we try to theorize, the mystery of the core attraction remains.

Do you see what I mean? Okay, let's go a little further.

If a rock is dropped, why does it move towards the Earth?

"Well, because of gravity."

And what is gravity?

"Well, it's the basic force that pulls things."

What is doing the pulling?

"Well, there is just this pulling, that's all, it's just there."

That's right, it's just there. It's an attracting, alluring activity. The fundamental mystery of the heart of the Cosmos is this allurement of everything to each other, this attracting activity. We understand details concerning the consequences of this attraction, but what remains a mystery is the attracting activity, the allurement itself! Years after Newton wrote out the equations and the universal laws of gravitation, he was still wavering out loud, and I quote him: "Whence is it that the sun and planets gravitate towards one another?"

The Universe might have been different, the Universe might have included no attracting activity, in which case it would be a completely different reality, if at all. The fact is that our Galaxy is attracted by every other galaxy in the Universe and our Galaxy attracts every other galaxy. The attracting activity is the stupendous, mysterious fact of existence, and it is no less than love. That's what love is. Love is expressed attraction, allurement between things. In discovering the very basic level of elementary physics, we awaken to the fact that the alluring, attracting activity is THE basic reality of the macro-Cosmos of the Universe. Amen.

"One second, Gafni, are you saying that this attraction is love?" Well, as the cosmologists point out, like Brian Swimme, the problem with the word 'love' is it has been ruined, because we have made the word love into something that's only human. But love is actually way beyond the human world. Love is the essential nature of reality, love is what drives subatomic particles to become atoms, it's what drives atoms to link together. When subatomic particles linked together are attracted to each other and they become an atom, that's attraction. When atoms are attracted to each other and become a molecule, that's attraction. When molecules are attracted to each other and become that more complex molecule, that's attraction. The first power that moves the whole story is an essential gravity of love. And human love is but a human expression of that essential allurement at the very dynamic base of the Cosmos.

If you begin to think about love and its Cosmic dimension, you've got to start thinking of the Universe as a whole. You have to think about the attraction, the allurement, the same allurement that attracts you to a man or a woman, or a man to a man, or a woman to a woman, or to a gorgeous painting or a sunset. That same attraction permeates the entire macrostructure of all reality. It is the basic binding energy, found everywhere in all that is. It's the primary allurement that all galaxies experience from other galaxies.

So for example, what do you enjoy doing? Say that you enjoy listening to music. Okay, good, now watch. You can't get any explanation for liking music, you simply enjoy music of certain sorts. The attraction is primal. You will weigh into the existence of the attraction to discover the attraction. Explain your attraction to music? You can't, it's an ultimate mystery. It's the ultimate, complete and total mystery. Are you beginning to see? There are so many cells in the world and yet a very particular sort of cells interests you most deeply. Why can this be? Why not any of the other infinite number of cells, and why music? Why does the Sun attract the Earth?

The web of your allurements is your Unique Self. You are a unique set of allurements that attract you to your unique expression of love intelligence and love beauty that yearns to live and love in you and as you. Allurement is the language of love. You were born to allure reality to its next stage of evolution.

Fifth Christmas Meditation: A conversation with God

Breathing Meditation: release & radiance

W e will *start* with our breathing meditation, so sit up straight and feel your spine elongate, reaching out to the crown of your head, to the heavens, and reaching down to your buttocks, to the earth, your shoulders dropping down, relaxing the jaw of your mouth, relaxing its tight grip, your hands open.

I'll open the space with a very short chant and then we'll go into Pranayama, Neshama-Nishima, the soul breath. Then we'll enter the Divine, we open up to the Divine through the body and receive what we referred to earlier on, as the Second Face of God, the personal face of Essence, the quality of the Cosmos that hears me in the same way that you are hearing me now, or that I hear you, the quality of living intelligence. We'll access that quality and then our meditation will be an actual conversation with that quality, a conversation with the Infinite, with the personal face of the Infinite, not with the God that you don't believe in and therefore doesn't exist, but simply a conversation with God.

And in the interstices, which is a fancy English word for 'the spaces in between', we'll sit in the silence and watch our breath rise and fall with no place to go, nothing over there, it's all right here, Hee Nay Nee, Here I Am, in the infinity of the Eternal Now. Let's just drop into the silence and from there will come the chant.

CHANT

Instructions Breathing Meditation: release & radiance
(See Second Christmas Meditation)

Contacting the personal face of Infinity

Follow gently the instruction. This is a daily, simple instruction that I've done with you once in these last five days, but I do it a second time, because this is a particular practice that I want you to take with you.

Imagine the third face of God, and remember that your faculty of imagination IS God. God is an aspect, a figment of your imagination, that is true. But your imagination is also an aspect, a figment of God. Imagination is the sacred tool — you only imagine that which already is.

Imagine, conjure up, the third face of God, the face of infinite complexity, of mathematical equations beyond mathematical equations, infinite expanses of space and time in one curvature of continuum, hundreds of billions of years of space-time continuum, of complexity, shimmering, incandescent Light, the deepest beauty and goodness that you can imagine, of strength, of heroism, of grandeur.

Any association to the word 'strength' becomes nothing in relation to the third face of God. Any association with the word 'infinite complexity' becomes nothing in association with the infinite complexity of the Godhead. Any association with the word 'power', a thermonuclear explosion, becomes nothing in relation to the infinite insanity of hundreds of billions of years of mixing metaphors of power.

I will do the meditation briefly now, just so you see how to do it. You do it yourself starting with something relatively small, such as your room. Expand from your room to your house, from your house to your city, your city to your country, your country to the world, the world to the Galaxy, the Galaxy to ten galaxies, to a million galaxies, to ten billion galaxies, to 100 billion galaxies. This is infinity, the infinite power and gorgeousness of the third face of God.

And take all of that and seat it in a chair next to you, looking at you, adoringly, lovingly knowing your body, knowing your heart, knowing you intimately, caring about you desperately, and you have the second face of God, the personal face of Essence that knows your name, the God about whom the great poet Rumi wrote, desperately seeking to fall into the arms of the Beloved. Right at this moment, right now sitting in the chair next to you, looking at you, seeing you in your naked beauty and vulnerability, holding you in his arms, is the Lover-God who loves you, the Mother-God who holds you, the Father-God who guides you — all different faces of the personal face of Essence that knows your name.

Not the God of the old Church, not the Cosmic vending-machine, not Santa Claus in the sky, but the personal face of Essence who knows your name, who desperately loves you, who contracted His/Her/Its Essence to allow you space in the world, in order that you choose your highest essence. And in choosing your highest essence, the greatest glory, the greatest goodness, the greatest pleasure, the greatest delight should live in you.

Because it is the personal face of Essence, of the Divine, who more than anything, as an expression of love, loves and desires to give. Because the core expression and essence of love is to give, in the same way that I love Pauline and I want to give her everything, I want to give her everything in the world. If Pauline loves you, she wants to give you everything. If I love Chahat, I want to give her everything. If Chahat loves you, she wants to give you everything, she wants to give me everything. If you love each other, you want to give each other everything. When you truly love someone, you want to give them gifts.

So the source of all love, the infinite Love power that powers a 100 billion galaxies, desires to give to you personally, cares about you personally, designs and tailors your life perfectly in order for you to be able to earn the ultimate gift, because there is no free lunch that you can really enjoy. If it's free you don't really enjoy it; you enjoy it only when you feel like you've earned it. It's the Universe that's constructed for you to earn your Enlightenment, to earn your bliss, to earn your pleasure, to earn your joy, and so the second face of God that knows your name sits in the chair right next to you in this moment, seeing you and knowing your name.

Now we go to the third, new and essential part of the meditation today. Just follow me gently, brothers and sisters, and forgive me if anything I say is in the way, just press delete on it. If you don't like the sound of my voice, pretend it's different. If you don't like Jews in general, don't worry about it, certainly don't admit it. Just sit gently in your place, relax, spine erect. I'm going to give you instructions for a conversation with God, and this is a cash meditation, or cash Dharma. 'Cash' as opposed to credit cards - there is credit-card Dharma which you practice for a long time and eventually it pays off, whereas cash Dharma works immediately. So this is a cash meditation.

Introduction to the Meditation for
a Conversation with God

When I was a child, like many children who grow up in a place of Spirit, I found talking to God very normal and natural. Often a child will talk to God till ages six, seven, eight or nine, and then in your teens or twenties, you experience a great distance. Many people grew up in a place that was completely flatland, secular, lacking the ability to access the interior face of the Cosmos, the personal face of Essence. And your image of God might have been an old Santa Claus in the sky, and when you were six, you realized that Santa Claus didn't exist - it was really your mother and father who brought you presents.

But the practice of talking to God is actually a simple practice. It's a particular form or frame. One form or frame is to ask for your personal needs, as we did last year in our tele-course 'The Three

Faces of Love', where we focused on evolutionary prayer. Now I want to focus with you on a different kind of praying to God, which is a conversation with God, a simple conversation where you talk to the personal face of Essence in precisely the same way you talk and converse with a close, intimate friend, with whom you share your deepest secrets. Your close, intimate friend can hear you, because your intimate friend loves you and is intelligent. But your intimate friend who hears you is not the source of all intimate Love-Intelligence — the source of all intimate Love-Intelligence is the personal face of Essence. If your intimate friend hears you, how much more will the great Love-Intelligence of the Universe hear you! Open your heart, hear this pointing-out instruction, for it will change your life: The quality of the personal IS the infinite quality of Divinity.

For too long, meditation and satsang teachers — and I love them dearly — have been saying that the quality of the Divine is impersonal. This is not true. Only one face of the Divine is impersonal, and that's the face of the Divine that's beyond your small ego, your small personality. But beyond the impersonal God, the impersonal process of the Cosmos, the impersonal Essence, the energy of Divinity, is the internal, personal face of God. And the quality of the personal lives in Chahat when you talk to her, lives in anyone listening with attention and care. It's the quality of the personal when you say: "Oh my God, I really want you to talk to me personally," or you're upset with someone and you say: "Wow, it wasn't personal at all."

You're talking about the quality of the Divine that is personal, that is the alive, awake, aware Love-Intelligence that knows your name.

And the same personal quality in Marc participates in the infinite personalness of the Divine, the personal face of the Cosmos that hears your conversation. That is the revelation of the Eye of the Spirit, practiced by the greatest men and women with the most open hearts and most subtle and spectacular minds for thousands of years, agreed upon by every great tradition that did the great experiment of Spirit, which is now understood as the source of the Love-Intelligence in you that hears. Unless, of course, you think that you're the source by yourself, separate from everyone else, in which case you have an extreme case of narcissism and I recommend many, many incarnations of intense shock therapy.

So first, I invite you to make a commitment, to spend a half hour a day just for the next week, talking to God. Can you imagine if Barack Obama called you and said: "Hey, I'm lonely, would you chat with me once a week? I'm so tired of the politics. Just listen to me and I'll pay for the call." I'd say: "Wow, Barack Obama is talking to me once a week, that's awesome!" Imagine if God says: "I'll talk to you as long as you want every day. I know you're busy, you don't have much time for me, but talking to me is really worthwhile, it really does something wildly beautiful for you. Give me a half hour a day and I'll give you everything I've got." That's what's the Divine is saying at every moment: "Give me a half hour a day and I'm going to give you everything I've got."

Meditation for a Conversation with God

So begin the exercise by taking ten slow, deep breaths to steady your mind. Now take five more breaths, and on the out breaths say the name of God that is 'YAH'.

And now, and I invite everyone to do this out loud, pick a name of God, pick Allah or Jesus, or Adonai, the Hebrew name of God, or Mary, or Buddha if you've got a sense of the divinity of Buddha, any name of God. And now say the name of God and repeat it. This is called the Name of God practice, which brings us inside. Repeat it with love, like you totally love Source, feel the love for Source, because Source is what powers the 50 trillion cells in your body and keeps you alive, caressing you, loving you, holding you in every moment and giving you in grace everything that exists in your life.

And if you think you did it because of your strength: where did you get your strength? If you think you did it because of your skill, where did you get your skill? If you think you did it because of your charm and grace, where did you get your charm and grace? Everything is gifted by Source in every moment.

If you don't want the name Allah or Jesus or Mary or Adonai, you can just say 'Source', and repeat the name out loud, lovingly, fully and rapturously in love with the name, and just repeat it for two, three minutes. And let us feel, and let the Divine feel, that you're falling in love again and again.

At three we begin. Everyone should be talking out loud, talking love talk by saying the name, the same way that you say the name of your beloved when you say: "Oh my God, oh my God." So say the name of God.

[PEOPLE DOING THE PRACTICE]

Now rest, rest in the Presence. And now, in a quiet voice to yourself, so you can hold it privately, we should hear just a gentle whisper of your voice, but not quite the words, beginning quietly and then we'll make it louder, just begin talking to God and saying 'Hi' to God.

[PEOPLE DOING THE PRACTICE]

Now step inside, just step inside in conversation with God, and ask God for a favor. Ask God for a favor, and because God is the personal face of Essence, the Source that knows your name, you say 'thank you' for a minute. So for the next minute, everyone out loud say 'thank you' for everything, wildly ecstatic — say 'thank you' for every need, every part or organ of your body. Go.

[PEOPLE SAYING 'THANK YOU' FOR ONE MINUTE]

As the final part of your conversation with God, you now want to ask God for what you truly need, because you've been talking to God and God is the personal face of Essence that knows your name, sitting in a chair right now, this very second. This is the inner truth of Enlightenment, this is the Enlightenment of Rumi and Shams, the inner truth. Your Beloved is sitting in a chair next to you right now, looking at you, holding you and smiling, filled with gratitude for your 'thank you' and for your recognition, wanting to hear what your deepest need is.

Prayer affirms the dignity of personal need. If you can't ask for your need, you can't ask for the need of your friend, and if you can't recognize your own need, you can't recognize the dignity of the need of your friend. It is to embrace not your want, but your need, your need of what you truly need. I need the energy to give my gifts, I need health in order to take care of my child, I need strength in my body in order to do the job that I do in the world, giving my gifts and supporting my children. I need the ability to open my heart, so I can do the fixing that I need to do in this lifetime. I need to make enough money for a living, so I can do what I really need to do in this world. I need enough wisdom to have a wise conversation with my friends.

Right now, tell God, tell God out loud, so you can feel it moving in your body. Speak directly to God and tell God what you need and ask for it, ask for everything. Don't be stingy with God, ask for everything.

Thank you for letting me pray, thank you for listening to my prayer, thank you, thank you.

This is a cash practice, my friends, no credit-card practice. Just start talking.

Practice asking for what you need

And let me say this really clearly: if you are stuck on the God of the Church that was gay-bashing, homophobic, narrow-minded, bigoted and racist, claiming that only they had the path to salvation, then oh my God, you are an idiot. No nice words for that one. Why would you want to stay seven years old? Why would you want to stay fourteen? Evolve your consciousness, holy brothers and sisters; evolve your love through God, from the petty grip of those who hijacked God for their ethnocentric power drives. Fuck them and love them and let them grow, let their consciousness evolve.

But the second face of God, the personal face of Essence, is not a dogma, it's a realization, it's Enlightenment. Every poem of Rumi shivers with Enlightenment, like every poem of Hafiz, like every movement of Ibn Arabi, every movement of Luria, of Akiva, of Meister Eckhart, of Augustine, of John the Baptist, of Jesus the Christ, every movement of Mary, every movement of my grandmother, who prayed naturally and effortlessly, knowing God was in the room, who recited the words of the songs and found God directly.

My grandmother never meditated a day in her life, she didn't even know what meditation is. If you would say 'dzogchen' she would think your tongue had gargled up. "Dzogchen, what's dzogchen? Theravada Vajrayana? What's that, vaseline?" But she could pray, man. She could pray, she talked directly to God, she was surrounded by God in every second. She opened her mouth and she knew that the Divine, the personal face of Essence, was listening.

This is a cash practice. It's more important than any other single spiritual practice. If you do one practice and no others, do this. Start with the name of God and just let yourself open up. Actually, start first with breath. Let me summarize it for you.

Summary of a Conversation with God, steps 1-5

The first step is the breath. Start with breath. You steady yourself with 10 breaths, sitting in a private place, quietly in your house. Maybe you have an altar, maybe you have a picture of a saint or a beautiful landscape, anything that evokes a sense of wonder in you. You sit and you breathe 10 times.

Second step: You pick a name of God, any name. The names of God have energy. If Jesus works for you, do Jesus, or Allah, or Mary. If none of them works, I recommend to you Adonai. Feel the power of Adonai and say the name Adonai ten or twenty times till you've fallen in love, just like you are saying the name of your beloved as you are making love. Say the name of God in total love, that's the second part.

Third step: Just talk to God and tell God how you are doing. And if it's difficult to start the conversation, tell God: "Hey man, this is hard! Help me out, man, I can't do this, help me out." Talk to God about the difficulties, just talk to God, just say 'hi'. Tell God what is going on in your life, just like you would share with an intimate friend.

The fourth step is gratitude: Thank you, thank you, thank you. Just spend a few minutes saying 'thank you' for very specific things. Get specific with God, God does not like broad thank-yous. You say: "Thank you for all the goodness in the world" and God says: "Fuck off, I don't need that, not interested, you are jerking off. Make love with me, tell me specifically; it's your intimate details I want."

The fifth step is: Ask God for your personal needs, not wants.

On saying 'thank you' for specific things

With a real friend you say: "How are you doing?" "I'm fine." With an intimate, close friend, your friend says: "What happened? Did we lose our relationship?" So God wants intimate details; give God the juicy details of your life in step three and then very specific thank-yous. Whenever you thank a friend, they feel much better when you say: "Wow, thank you for this that you've given me, and thank you for that." When you just say: "Thanks for everything", that's like "Well, great, thanks." Does that work? Really? I just spent last year helping you with that 13-hour thing!

"Thank you for taking the time to fly over and be at the board game, I so appreciate that. Thank you for really working really hard at this internet campaign that we're doing, for the time and attention that it takes every day, and for the pain in the neck that it costs you - thank you for that. I really, really appreciate that." You go on with a list of specific thank-you's and the person goes "Wow!" And their heart opens, and then you open up the channel of grace to you, you open up the channel of goodness in yourself. It's not just a trick to get more: "Well, let me do that, I'll open the channel of grace." You actually open up the channel of goodness in yourself and your goodness opens the grace.

On asking God for your personal needs, not wants

And then finally you ask God for your personal needs, not your wants. Not your wants but your needs. What is a need? "I need not to sleep alone in my bed all the time, it's really important to me." "I need to feel love and I need to feel some pleasure in my life — where shall I find that pleasure? Please help me." And you go through your needs and you list them specifically and you ask for everything.

One of the things that listing your needs does is that it helps you recognize what your needs are. And you know the difference, you distinguish between your needs and your wants, and then you turn to the Universe that's intelligent. Just as the Love-Intelligence in you hears me talking now, just as the Love-Intelligence in me heard you talking, the Love-Intelligence which is Source hears your talking.

How can the Universal Intelligence *not* hear your prayer?

You don't need any theology, you don't need any church. *Of course* the Universe hears your prayer! The universe is infinite, and all that infinite intelligence is the third face of God. All of that mathematical complexity and brilliance, all the hundred billions of light years of infinite intelligence are sitting in a chair in front of you, and you think Source is not intelligent? Really? Do you really think that? If you do, you're an idiot, and I say that intentionally sharply. Really??

You think that just by chance Dostoyevsky's 'The Idiot' was written? Just a bunch of molecules banded together? I don't think so. Oh yeah, a monkey just sat on a typewriter and typed up all the works of Shakespeare. Do you believe that? Then you could believe this has all happened by chance. But there is nothing in the Cosmos that indicates that at all, nothing, and I'm a huge lover of physics, Cosmology and science. Science addresses reality through a completely different lens. So anyone who will believe that a monkey sat on a typewriter and for three hours just typed out all the works of Shakespeare, should believe that it's all non-intelligent, dead matter, by chance. If you believe that, you are an idiot, simple, straight. It's just not true.

It is the Shakti that animates all existence. What George Lucas called 'the Force', in Star Wars, was just a translation of the word Shakti: the divine Love-Energy of Eros that animates all of existence, through the evolutionary process. Is evolution then right? Of course evolution is right! It is an evolutionary process and the evolutionary process is driven by an internal intelligence, called by some physicists 'the fifth force of the Universe', called by Eric Jantsch 'self-organization' or 'self-transcendence', called by Ilja Progogine 'a self-organizing Universe'. It is the unseen hand, the force which moves all towards higher and higher levels of order and complexity. That's the intelligent Universe that hears you, that knows your name. Does the Universe always say 'yes'? The Universe always says 'yes' to your life, but it doesn't always say 'yes' to your request, and that's okay, that's totally okay.

I just want to share with you what I feel right now, and that is that you are all so awesome. So forgive me, forgive me in any way I need forgiveness, and if you think I was talking to you when I said you're an idiot, sorry, but then you are. I still totally love you. You guys are awesome. You women are awesome, you men are awesome. Pauline, thank you for holding this community, Chahat, thank you for holding the center place of spiritual teacher, and all of you at Venwoude, thank you for really moving and unfolding this together. So much blessing and love to you! We'll talk tomorrow, when we'll do the concluding meditation, but just right now

I'm so blown away. I love you all, you're such awesome, gorgeous people.

And I have just one request, if you can just do me one favor? Can everyone in this community just do me one little favor? Please, please, one favor? Here's the favor: just talk to God.

Love you, love you, love you.
Amen.

Sixth Christmas Meditation: Being Love

*T*his is the last morning of this holy, awesome retreat. Let's give a big hand for the retreat, an awesome 'deep bow' and an awesome 'thank you' to Chahat and to everyone holding the space at Venwoude.

We will do two new meditations for our sixth and last session together, now being deeply on the inside of the inside, in the space of the heart.

I'm going to open the space with a chant.

Sit upright if you can, your spine straight, reaching as always up to the heavens, to the crown of your head, and down to the Earth, as the Axis Mundi, the pole that connects heaven and earth. Your shoulders drop, your heart expands, you feel the sincerity of your heart, your jaw drops, the furrows between your eyebrows relax, the tension releases out of your forehead, out of the crown of your head and out of the back of your neck.

From the meditation we will go into silence, and from the silence we will go into two guided meditations that will take you into the last hours of the retreat and into life, sending the deepest love into the world. Oh my God, what an honor to be with you and your sacred community this week. May this be, for many of you, a continuation, and for others a beginning of a worldwide community, developing an evolutionary World Spirituality, committed to profound transformation, committed to the evolution of love, committed to Unique Self Enlightenment. So that's a holy invitation.

Now let's open up the space, holy brothers and sisters. I'm going to ask you to receive the chant, I'm going to do it with lineage words and it's about celebration. Being here, right now, with all of the past and all of the future in this moment, let it enter your heart and open your wings, open our space into silence as we enter into the heart of hearts, the inside of the inside, the deepest of the deep.

Thank you, God.

Introduction to visualization practice

The practice we are about to do is a visualization, and if a visualization doesn't work for you, just follow it in its most basic form. You don't need to conjure up a big picture, just hear the picture that I'm imagining with you and follow its path. If you don't have a capacity for visualization, this is the only visualization we've done in the last six days, just follow and actually visualize it in your mind. We've lost in many ways the power of imagination, of visualization. The power of imagination is one of the powers of Eros, of the erotic, and we've lost our connection to the Erotic.

Sometimes the only place we can find Eros, which is a living power, a burning, aflame aliveness and passion, is within the sexual, and that's tragic. That means that the erotic, Eros, is exiled, exiled into the sexual, and I'll tell you what I mean.

When you go to a spiritual retreat or workshop, usually there are all these visualizations and the teacher tells you to imagine a white light moving through your body; or you are in a field and there's open grass and there's your mother and Pinocchio, right? And they ask you what you saw and you say: "I saw Pinocchio and my mother and white light," but usually nobody really saw much of anything. We have a spiritual inferiority complex, but in the sexual, everyone's very good at visualization.

Just ask the men in the room. If I do one hour of visualization like this: "You see a woman across the room, she has long, brunette hair, her blouse is slightly open, she slowly unbuttons her buttons," and have it going for an hour, I promise you that at least every man in the room could follow it, no problem. All of a sudden, everybody becomes a master of visualization. Unbelievable! That's because the power of imagination has been exiled from the erotic to the sexual.

We need to reclaim the power of imagination to imagine a better world

We need to reclaim the power of fantasy. What would it mean to fantasize about a world in which people didn't brutalize each other through their egos? About a world in which 20 million children didn't die every year of malnutrition? What would it be to fantasize about a world in which millions and millions and millions of people didn't go to sleep alone, broken and crying? That's what fantasy is about, my friends: to imagine, to imagine a better world. Most of the problems in running our institutions, running our spiritual retreat centers, running our organizations and governments is not a crisis of resources, is not a crisis of manpower or womanpower, it's also not a financial crisis; *it's a crisis of imagination.*

We just can't imagine a better world. We're lost in the old structures, we can't re-imagine our reality. And the first key to the portal of transformation is to re-imagine the world, and you begin re-imagining the world through re-imagining yourself, re-imagining your essential identity. That's what we are going to do right now, we're going to re-imagine our very essential identity.

Guided visualization: Becoming a Sacred Figure

I'm going to ask you, with your permission, to imagine yourself as Buddha, as Christ, as any spiritual hero, as the great master that is your Unique Self with its unique gifts to give to the world that are desperately needed by the world. And in giving those gifts, you feel the fullness of Eros and compassion, aflame and alive. Your heart explodes with joy, there's no question about the meaning of your existence, your existence IS the meaning of life.

If you want to imagine what I mean, just imagine eating an awesome piece of pumpkin pie, and as you eat it, you have multiple orgasms at the first bite. Are you at that moment asking: "Oh, what's the meaning of the Universe?" I don't think so. That's what it means to live your Unique Self, to give your unique gifts and to know that you are doing something that's needed by the Cosmos that no one else but you, that ever was, is or will be, can or should do. That's what it means to become the Buddha, or be the Christ.

So that's the meditation, dearest, sweetest, holiest friends, that we are going to do this morning. And I ask you again, like every time we've met: if I say anything that offends you, please forgive me. I apologize insincerely, but I do apologize and I say: "Forgive me, just because." Don't let me get in the way. There's always somebody in the room, or two or three or four people, for whom, somehow, the teacher's voice doesn't work, something he says doesn't sound right, and the truth is, jokes aside, you are probably right! For we are all imperfect vehicles for the light. So if there's something in me that you get stuck on, and I say this now sincerely with all jokes and kidding aside, just completely forgive me, let it go, and enter into the heart of heart, the inside of the inside that teaches so deeply.

So the practice that we're going to do is a guided visualization, summoning an image on which we meditate. What this kind of visualization does is that it harnesses the power of the mind, the mental power that is usually dissipated and lost in casual, uninteresting fantasy, daydreaming and imagining. We'll access the power of daydreaming, of imagination, of fantasy for the holy image. This method was used with particular force in Taoism, in Tibetan Buddhism, in certain forms of Hinduism and in Christian mysticism.

It enables you to evoke and discover the qualities of the imagined being in yourself and as yourself.

Some people have called this practice 'Becoming the Buddha' or 'Becoming the Christ', because these great beings tend to be the archetypes that many people are able to work with. I call it 'Becoming your Unique Self', 'Becoming the Master', that is, the Christ living in you, or it could be 'Becoming the Shekinah', the Feminine, the Divine Goddess, or the Virgin Mary or Kali or Tara.

Breathing into your heart, throat, third eye, crown center

So sit down, shut your eyes, find the right posture and for two or three minutes follow your breath, as I will, together with you, in order to calm your mind and find the inner point beyond and beneath all change, the inner point that is the virgin part of the Heart, which is always eternally alive and present and never cloudy or muddy. We are going to breathe now for three minutes, following the breath in and out, until you can locate an inner place in your heart of calm devotion.

So follow your breath calmly, spaciously, with a smile on the inside of your heart - we often think that spiritual practice needs to be done with a contorted face in agony. Let your heart smile, let your lips smile, gently caress yourself with your mind's eye and spirit. Just gently, lovingly breathe, following the breath, letting all thoughts dissipate until you find the innermost point of your heart, the virgin place in your heart that is never touched and always pure.

And now the visualization begins, brothers and sisters. Love you, love you. Imagine now your heart center, which is located in the middle of your chest, an inch or two to the right of your heart.

Imagine that your heart center has a nose and breathe deeply, in and out, through the nose in your heart center, until this area begins to feel warm and expanded, warm, hot and expanded.

Then rise up to the center in the middle of the throat. Let the warmth, the heat, rise up to the center in the middle of your throat and start to breathe in and out of your throat center until it begins to feel vibrant.

Now take the breath up to the center of spiritual vision, to your third eye between your eyes, and again breathe in and out from here to your third eye until you feel warm, until you feel a slight tingling, until you feel the breath expanding your third eye.

And take the breath up from your third eye to the crown center on the top of your head, and imagine that you are breathing in and out of your head vertically, up and down, in and out at the top of your head.

Now bring your breath back around to your heart center and breathe hot, warm breath into your expanded heart center, into the center of your chest. Now, if you can, feel the living connection between your heart and your head center. Feel the flow of soft, sweet, fiery energy between the heart and head centers.

Visualizing a Sacred Figure in your heart center

Return your awareness to your heart center in the middle of your chest and visualize now the sacred figure, the Buddha, the Christ, the Mother, or any other saint or mystic or holy person alive or dead who you've met or you've read of, and imagine that person, your teacher, any holy person, sitting in your heart center, sitting there, tiny, in your heart center, glowing with erotic, tender compassion, glowing with tenderness and divine light.

Whoever you have chosen radiates now in this very second in your heart center, with intense force, compassion and an all-embracing, eternal love. Whoever you've chosen is now a figure in your heart center, a tiny figure radiating light, and you can see the figure inside your heart center, luminescent, alive, radiating compassion, force, light in all-embracing, eternal love.

And as you breathe quietly and slowly in and out, your stomach rising and falling, imagine with all your power of trust that the sacred figure you have chosen starts to glow brighter and brighter, and follow this amazing, radiant expansion with your breath, with the clarity and flow of your focused attention.

And now feed the sacred figure within you with the power of your own devotion, with the power of your breath, until he or she fills your entire heart center with radiant light and compassion. Feed the sacred figure within you with the power of your devotion, until he or she feeds your entire heart center. Your heart center is now filled with that luminescent, shining, compassionate, aflame, a-love figure glowing inside your heart center.

At this point, pause for a couple of minutes and feel the miracle of this divine presence, alive, palpably vibrant within you. Try and invoke, try and bring to bear now anything you might know about this person, whether it's a living teacher, whether it's the Christ, whether it's the Buddha, any story you heard about his or her power, any intuition you have about his or her heart or greatness or compassion or goodness.

If you are thinking of Jesus, invoke Jesus as fearless courage; if you think of Manjushree, invoke Manjushree's radical devotion to Enlightenment at all costs; if you are thinking of the Buddha, think of his vast poise, the grandeur of his mind, and the quietness and courage of his spirit, and pray to the Divine to fill you with these qualities. Summon into one focus point your full attention and the sacred image we are working with, and saturate your entire spiritual imagination with his or her beauty, truth and power. Feel the luminous alight, aflame, a love-figure inside you. Feel into your entire heart center and imagine his or her goodness, truth and beauty, and pray that that goodness, truth and beauty fills you and permeates your very being.

And then say the mantra: "Oh God, come! Oh God come! Adonai Boh, God come," and invite the Divine into you, inside of your heart, Adonai Boh, God Come, Om Mani Padme Hum.

[Marc reciting mantra]

Breathing the Sacred Figure into your body, and compassion into the world

Keep on breathing slowly, in and out, and as you keep breathing, feel the luminous sacred figure in your heart center with brilliant light and life. Feel as he or she keeps on expanding and expanding slowly, dazzlingly, shimmering, until your sacred, luminous, shining image of Buddha, Christ, teacher or saint has taken over every single part of your body, until it suffuses and spreads with the light and the fire to every single part of your body, from the top of your head to the end of your fingertips, to the very end of your toes.

Imagine this divine expansion as steadily and thoroughly as you can and let the light pour through, through your chest to your tummy, to your legs, to your genitals, to your buttocks, to your back, up your back into your arms, down your legs, through your head, your face, your ankles, the soles of your feet.

And when you completed it, rest now in the absolute certainty that you and the one you have chosen to meditate on, are now one. You have become Source, you have activated the Buddha field, the Christ field within you. Allow yourself to feel in you all of the splendor, the passion, courage, heroism, good, true and beautiful of this oneness and its grandeur, in unshakeable, anchoring solidity.

As you realize this oneness, in full confidence and audacity, begin to breathe into your now divine heart, drawing in light with each breath into your divine heart, and as you breathe in light and oxygen with each breath into your divine heart, transmute it, transform it into pure love in your heart. Transform the light into pure love in your heart, and imagine your heart growing more and more brilliant as you keep breathing in and out. Breathe in light and oxygen and transform it into love, until your heart becomes a blazing diamond, radiating pure, dazzling white light of love.

And now as the God force, now as the Master, now as this unique expression, your Unique Self of Buddha-Christ energy, let that brilliant, diamond light stream from you out into the world, from the third eye between your eyebrows, from your heart center. And as you stream the light into the world as the divine being that you are, keep breathing in more and more light into your always already brilliant, alive, awake, compassionate heart center. As you breathe in the light to your heart center, transmuting it into love, at the same time send out a steady stream of brilliant light and love to your third eye, for your heart and head centers are connected.

Now let this love-light emanate and exit from your third eye out into the world, as you are the Being breathing out Light in this moment, sustaining the world. You are the heart of divine compassion, you are the Master holding the world, breathing in the world, transforming the light of the world into love and then breathing out that love as brilliant light, emanating it out of your third eye and into the world.

Let that stream of light emanating from your third eye become a continuous, dazzling river that pours out from your forehead. And as it does so, it gradually engulfs and dissolves your own body, until you remain a shimmering outpouring of light. And then it engulfs and dissolves the cushions you are sitting on, the floor, the room around you, in ever-widening circles, your house, Venwoude, the town, the country you are in, until the entire Universe is bathed in the light that emanates from your third eye and keeps growing vaster and vaster from the source in your forehead.

Breathe in Light, transmute it by loving it, emanate it out of your forehead, brilliantly into the world as you are the Divine, Buddha and Christ, uniquely beholding a dimension of the Universe held in the power of your breathing out, the out-breath of life and dazzling love-light. And as the light pours out of your third eye, pours and pours and pours, you come to see that all you are now is a diamond heart on fire and a third eye pouring out that fire in all directions.

Now the practice slows down, and slowly, delicately, with awe, with wonder, with reverence, start to draw the light into your heart center, into the sacred image you've chosen. The light begins to recede, you enter into the body of the Christ or the Buddha that lives in your heart, and you feel the burning radiance in your heart center, knowing that this is the true essence of your identity.

And in this moment make a vow never to forget your essential truth: that you are compassion, that you are love, and that this love that you breathe out through your third eye, that expands and consumes your entire body, that unique love that is yours to give, which brilliance no one else in the world can breathe into reality, is the essence of who you are. This unique Love-Intelligence and Love-Beauty, burning brilliantly, aflame and alive, streaming from your third eye into the world, is your breath, your unique personal essence and your love. You are the Buddha, you are the Christ, you are the Master. That is the Enlightenment of your Unique Self.

And you have gifts to give! Sometimes the gifts are private, other times the gifts are public, but your fulfillment, your joy, the organizing principle of your life, the very meaning of your existence, is in the giving of those gifts, and in the giving is the greatest receiving you'll ever have.

Now let's rest in the aftertaste, let's rest in the silence, following the breath in and out, in and out, and feel the radiance of your heart, in and out.

Never marry for love, *be* love

Sometimes you ask a person: "Are you in love?" And they say: "No, I'm not with anyone." What a sad answer! First, it's not true. You are with so many people in so many ways. Let me tell you a holy secret, a really holy secret. Don't tell anyone, it's a big secret: Never marry for love! Never marry for love, because if you marry for love, oh my God, that's so tragic. It's great to love the person you marry, that's awesome, but don't marry for love.

If marriage is the only place you find love, you'll destroy the marriage, because you've got to feel love in so many places. Do you want to have a romantic, sexual love only with your partner? That's a beautiful choice, go for it! That's awesome, that's your life pack, that's the most gorgeous thing in the world, it's beautiful, it's deep, one of the deepest spiritual practices in the world. Monogamous, romantic, sexual love, awesome — but that's just one-time love.

You want to *be* love in the world, you want to be lived as love, I want to be lived as love. I want the world, God, the Universe, reality, to live me as love, to BE love. And that doesn't mean to be weak! Love is not weak, love is strong — love is the strongest force in the Universe. Love is what moves quarks to become atoms and atoms to become molecules and molecules to become cells. Love is the evolutionary love that drives it all, the evolutionary force of the Cosmos, ever driving towards higher and levels of recognition, union and embrace.

Love is not weak, love is strong; it's the strongest force in the Cosmos. Be love, for you are a unique expression of love. That's what we said two days ago: you are a unique set of attractions, of allurements, because the Universe is made up of a field of attractions, electromagnetic and gravitational, the strong and the weak. These are the core fields of attraction, and the unique passions and attractions that make up your life, are the loves of your life, and you are responsible to that love.

In a way, the Christ lives only in you, Buddha lives only in you; only through you can the Buddha be the four Noble Truths of love, only in you can the Buddha live the Eightfold Path of love. Without you, there's a corner of the Universe that is un-love, that is cold, indifferent, scared, filled with fear and therefore with anger, brutality and violence.

Be love! Not weak, sad, New-Age and Hallmark-cards love — how boring — but strong, pulsating, breathtaking, fearsome, awesome love, uniquely expressed as the allurements and attractions and passions that form the unique tapestry of your life, of your Being and Becoming. Be love!

Being Love in practice: give your gifts

We are at the end of our six-day retreat. Wow, what an awesome, special time. Make sure you walk out of the retreat with five new telephone numbers, five addresses of people you are going to love, you are going to walk with in the world. This is part of the meditation, because to be love is not abstract — you give love to the person that's in the room next to you now.

Is there someone in the room you need to love? Is there someone whose love you need? And again, I'm not talking about romantic and sexual love, which is beautiful, it's gorgeous, it's awesome, but I'm talking about something that's so much deeper. Are there five people in the room you didn't know before, that you now can recognize and can see that you have a part of their story and they have a part of yours? Are there people in this room with whom you can weave deep webs of connection, intimacy, support, vision and sacred imagination? I think there are. Are there people in this room for whom you have a unique gift of presence, of wholeness, of yearning? I think there are. Wow!

This is the inside my friends, this is the inside of the inside, it's awesome. This IS reality, you are not going back to reality, this IS reality. This is the way it really is. Wow! When you see Pauline's face shining, you've seen the face of the Mother. When you see Chahat radiant, you are seeing the face of the Mother, the Goddess. You have awesome people holding the community, Chahat holding your retreat. Love each other, support your teachers, support your teacher to rise to your fullest radiance. As Chahat steps into the place as the spiritual teacher, hold her, just as she holds you. As Pauline emerges to her next level of evolutionary transcendence, holding, guiding, training, loving — hold her, just as she'll hold you.

Give your gifts, let the ego settle, kiss the kiss only you can kiss. Kiss so deeply, for your unique kiss is more sweet to me than one of King Solomon. There's only one way to deny God, to deny Spirit, and that is to deny the unique gorgeousness of your face.

Wow, this morning is a gentle morning, my friends, it's the gentle, sweet elixir, sweet nectar of the holy truth. In this moment, as we end our meditation and visualization and you go into the next part of the day, whatever it is, this is the moment to say a holy Yes. Yes, yes, yes — do you believe that you can do it? Yes, I do believe in magic, I do, I do, I do believe in magic, I do, I do! And the magic is the holy Yes of your unique gift and your Unique Self.

I love everyone so much, love you so much, so much, so much, so much...

See you soon!

Loving Your Way to Enlightenment, an invitation to a new spiritual path

W*e have killed* all the gods except for Aphrodite. Aphrodite is the goddess of True Love, and True Love is the altar before which most of us still worship. Our new sacred credo is "I love you". Our true sacred credo is usually revealed when the stakes are the highest - at our moment of death. When the planes hit the World Trade Center and people had a few seconds to live, they called home and recited the credo "I love you".

And yet, somehow, our spiritual world of practice has become separated from our world of love. Our Enlightenment studies often seem to point us beyond personal love, which is then viewed as the realm of attachment and separate self. This contradicts our deepest longing and our deepest knowing about the meaning of personal love.

It is for that reason that we want to invite you to a new spiritual path: the path of Loving Your Way to Enlightenment.

Enlightenment is knowing your true nature. Your true nature, however, is not just one taste, as some are wont to say. It is two tastes. In yoga terms, we might say that your true nature is Shiva and Shakti. Shiva is being, Shakti is becoming. Shiva is your deep sense of being, the deep, impersonal, unchanging essence that lives in and as your deepest identity. Your Shakti nature is more connected to the dynamic dance of becoming. Shakti is the Love Intelligence that lives awake in you and as you.

The impersonal Enlightenment of Shiva may be available sitting in meditation alone, but if you awake to the realization that your true nature is personal Shakti love, then just sitting in meditation will not get you there. This is not the personal before the impersonal, but the personal beyond the impersonal. You will have to awaken to your true nature as personal love, or, said differently, you have to 'love your way to Enlightenment'.

One of the great paths to loving your way to Enlightenment is no less than falling in love. To love your way to Enlightenment is not only more courageous, but as the Zen master Ikkyu wrote, it is also more effective than 'just sterile sitting meditation'. To love your way to Enlightenment is to allow yourself to fall fully in love, and use your relationship as a crucible for spiritual development.

To love your way to Enlightenment is to not bypass your wounds in spacious meditation, but to enter your hurts and transform them into healing, health and heroism. All our wounds happen in relationship, and so they're best healed in relationship. Falling in love, with your True Love, is the most profound and rigorous transformational workshop going on the planet. It's the one place you get reflected back in all your glory and all your darkness. Your lover is your shiniest mirror and your most profound teacher.

The best, sacred shortcut to Enlightenment is falling in love, because it forces you to wake up and take responsibility for all the ways you aren't present to what's so. Suffering, after all, is being in an argument with reality.

True Love

True Love shows up not only in romantic relationship. True Love can also show up in relation to close friends, brothers and sisters, parents, our children, our life partners' varying kinds. We have exiled falling in love to the romantic, but unjustly so.

First, we want to clarify that we are not talking about just any kind of falling in love. We are talking about True Love. You have to believe in True Love before you can know it your life. We've heard about True Love in fairytales, epic sagas, poetry, opera and Shakespeare. It seems fantastical and larger than life, and indeed, it is. John Perry Barlow said to us once: "The difference between love and true love is the difference between a very large number and infinity."

Infinity, as inspiring as it can be, is also terrifying. The vast unknown is hard to wrap your head around. It cannot be controlled or managed. The only true response is awakened surrender.

All our fears, neuroses and shadow issues come up in True Love relationships. No matter how much transformational work you've done, True Love is where the deepest, darkest stuff comes out. Couples in True Love fight the big fights. It is part of the courting dance. It is often called the 'power struggle'. No relationship worth its salt avoids this inevitable initiation and testing ground.

True Love conflict can either be alchemized into intimacy or it alienates you from your partner. What allows conflict to move fluidly into resolution is each partner's willingness to look inside, facing everything and avoiding nothing. Each partner must ask for how and where they participated in the disconnect, the misunderstanding, the heartbreak, which lies at the root of all arguments. This is the stage many couples do not survive. When the agonizing reflections of our defensive self are forced into our attention, everything in us wants to run.

The reason it's important to distinguish True Love from ordinary love is because it is the only force strong enough to keep you in the game. It is True Love that calls you to do the work, roll up your sleeves for whatever it takes to transcend your crazies and find your way back to your lover's heart.

True Love provides the necessary gymnasium or dojo for your emotional training and actualization. Until you've surrendered fully to your relationship -no quitting, no exits, no threats of leaving; you're in for life - you cannot get the evolutionary benefits of deep personal and spiritual transformation.

A quick and dirty test to distinguish True Love: If you're wondering whether or not you're in love, then you're not. It's unmistakable when it happens, there's no confusion; you just know. And once you find it, you'll do whatever it takes to make it work.

In particular, you have to be willing to die for it. Yes, die. When you fall in love, your 'contracted, coiled separate self' dies into an 'us', and that alone can be terrifying. Ironically, however, once you dive off the cliff, you're soon handed back a stronger, more profound sense of self than could ever have been created on your own. We use the word 'us' in two ways. 'Us' is you and me together who form the miracle of We, but we are also using US as an acronym for Unique Self. In a True Love relationship, you do not disappear but rather appear as the most epic version of your Unique Self.

Love is not merely an emotion. Love is a perception that birthes an emotion. Love is a perception of the infinite specialness and radiance that lives in the face of the other. Love is God meeting God. When we fall in love with another person, two beloveds appear in full radiance. We don't only fall in love with the other person, we also fall in love with ourselves. We fall in love with how we're seen by them and with who we get to be in their presence. We fall in love with a possibility, the possibility that inspires us the most. And inspiration is what pulls us in to our highest selves.

When you think about it for a moment, falling in love and spiritual development really start to sound very similar, don't they? Many of the ancient religions and wisdom traditions have one thing in common: they encourage us to be more loving, aware, awake and present. The first core practice is to realize that you are part of something bigger than yourself: you come from an eternal one-ness. This is often called your True Self. In the evolution of this tradition, we teach that You are not only a True Self but a 'Unique Self' that lives beyond space, time and matter. And that 'Unique Self', happening once-and-for-all-and-never-again, is divine; it's one of the many faces of God. And that, of course, is precisely the identity that shows up as You when you fall in love.

A second core practice is what we like to call 'Nowing' - partici-pating in the now – as it stretches endlessly out from this moment across space-time. Of course, that is also the practice of falling in love. When you are in love, just being present with your partner is the greatest bliss and delight.

To practice falling in love over time is no less than simply bring-ing more of your consciousness into the now. You step into the fullness of presence with your romantic partner. The only place an 'US' can live, is in the now. When we are caught up in our neu-roses, in our defensive patterns or are disconnected from our own emotions, then some of our consciousness has left the room. We have left the now.

'Nowing' may be the most powerful spiritual practice there is. Nowing in the context of True Love calls up all our obsolete strat-egies born from historical wounds, but it also forces us into the now. For that is the place from which we can see our patterns and observe how they keep us out of relationship and separate from our partner. When you're in your blind spot issues, you've left your lover, your business partner, your friend, your colleague.

They're alone and afraid and they need you to wake up and come back to the here and now, where True Love lives.

True Love offers a way out of the insidious obsession with our alienated and wounded separate self. Loving your way to Enlightenment is a powerful crucible for self-realization and growth.

Your lover, business partner, friend, colleague, is your ultimate guru and their stand for your greatest self is your access to a whole new kind of Enlightenment, one where you get to be the God you are, while they do the same.

Loving Outrageously

Exercise: Loving a person you feel distant from

At any given moment, everyone has someone whom they feel a little distant from, are upset with or even very angry at, or just feel not connected to. Locate that person in your heart, and hold that person in your mind's eye.

Now put one hand on your heart and one on your stomach: as you breathe in, you feel your stomach expanding, and as you breathe out, your stomach contracts. We are going to breathe in and out five times, very slowly, constantly keeping that person in our mind's eye. Two, allow your shoulders to relax, three, four, five.

Now imagine that person's face and just imagine yourself walking up to him or her and giving a gentle kiss on the forehead and say: "I forgive you, please forgive me." Just say it out loud to yourself.

Because, my dear beloved friends, the holiest teaching in the world is to know that when you shut your heart to one person, you shut your heart to the whole world. You can keep your distance from people, you don't have to be close to or be able to work with everyone, but never put someone out of your heart. When you put someone out of your heart, something closes in the heart of God. You may even decide not to talk to someone for a year, but never put them out of your heart. If you keep them in your heart, then in the end, both hearts open; the heart of God opens in the secret of this Kiss.

The kiss on the forehead will make room for tenderness, gentleness. You don't need to be best friends with everyone; that's wrong, that's not authentic, but you need to hold everyone in your space tenderly in your heart, so that you can never be cruel to them, you never dehumanize them. Feel this deeply, and feel how the room begins to draw together as a community, feel how everyone has a place in everyone else's heart. All the politics of 'who is angry at whom', 'who is on which side', disappear. There are no sides between friends, there is only community. We are all one: all separate, yet together.

Explanation Breathing Meditation

I'm going to name a part of the body and I'm going to ask you on the inhale to breathe your consciousness, your love, into that part of the body, and on the exhale, to release all the tension from that part of the body. Then one or two breaths later, we'll breathe again into that part of the body but on the exhale I will say not 'release' but 'radiate'.

'Radiate' means that the natural radiance, the natural glow, the natural shining of that part of the body comes back on line, because every organ in the body is an organ of the Universe. The great Kabbalah and Sufi teachers say that the human body is actually the figure of the Universe. The arms are the arms of the Universe, the stomach is the stomach of the Universe, the chest is the chest of God, the breasts are the breasts of God, the crown of the head is the crown on God's head and your knees are the knees of God.

We actually left the natural radiance of our bodies behind, so let's re-emerge! Something of the radiance of God will then become stronger too, which is called 'giving power to God'. In ancient Aramaic, the language of Jesus, it is said:" 'Anyone who breathes, breathes in God and breathes out God." The breath itself sustains our planet, as carbon and oxygen are exchanged in the great, sacred, tantric process of photosynthesis.

Guided Breathing Meditation, release and radiance

First breathe into the crown of your head, and release.
When I'm not giving instructions, just breathe naturally.
Crown of the head, release; back of the neck, release.
Cheeks, release; forehead, release; feel the
    tension leave your forehead.
Shoulders, release; let the shoulders drop.
Back of the neck, release.
Now turn your neck slowly, move your head around, slowly
    and clockwise, as you breathe in and out, ever so gently.
Now reverse the motion, even slower.
Breathe back until the shoulders release.

Crown of the head, radiate. On the out-breath let radiance emerge.

Cheeks, radiate; let your jaw drop, radiate.

Shoulders, radiate; shoulders drop again; top of the back, radiate.

Lower back, release; lower back, radiate.

When I mention the lower back, I mean precisely that place where you get cramps when you menstruate.

Breathe in again, and release.

Upper chest, release; upper chest, radiate.

Breasts, release; breasts, radiate.

Nipples, release; nipples, radiate.

Tummy, release; tummy, radiate.

Inner thighs, release; inner thighs, radiate.

Yoni, release; phallus, release; face, release; upper facial lip, release; lower lip, release.

Phallus, yoni, radiate; buttocks, cheeks, release; buttocks, cheeks, radiate.

Anus, open, release; face, open and release.

Shoulders drop; shoulders, open, release.

Forehead, open, release.

Anus, radiate.

Right leg from knee to thigh, release; right leg, knee to thigh, radiate.

Shoulders drop again.

Left leg, knee to thigh, release; left leg knee to thigh, release; left leg, knee to thigh, radiate; right leg, knee to thigh, radiate.

Crown of your head, release; top of your head, radiate.

Pranayama or the shamana shimas, divine breath, radiance.

Feel your knees release, radiate.

Left leg, knee to ankle, release. Right leg, knee to ankle, release.

Left leg, knee to ankle, radiate. Right leg, knee to ankle, radiate.

The back of both legs, knee to ankle, radiate.

Both ankles, release; both ankles, radiate.

Soles of your feet, release; soles of your feet, radiate.

Lower jaw, release; last time: face, release.

Whole body-heart-mind, release; whole body heart-mind, radiate.

Relax in the Silence of Presence, sitting upright; mind, body and heart relaxed. As a thought enters your heart, let the thought release.

Begin to breathe in and out rapidly, into your breast, ten times. Short, fast breaths, in and out; fill your body with oxygen. Let the spaciousness of the Divine Presence fill your heart while you fill your breast and your stomach.

We were all there at the Big Bang, we were all part of the Big Gang and the Big Bang. We were all stardust, awakening into life, awakening into higher and higher levels of consciousness, driven by love.

And once again we breathe in and out fast, ten times, breathing in the love. Then. rest in love. Love is not weak, love is strong, it's the strongest force in the Cosmos. Love is the Eros of Evolution moving through every cell. The universe feels and the Universe feels love!

Loving Outrageously, including your body

We've got to love in a way that's outrageous. The only way we're going to fix the world, is by being outrageous. Enough with holy politeness for politics, enough with trying to be really careful so we make sure we build our brands and make enough money and become famous. No, we need to be outrageous for God, we need to be outrageous in our love. And the way we're going to build together is by being outrageous. We're going to take care of everyone, we're going to be so careful, so tender, so gentle, but in a holy, crazy, outrageous way. It means you've got to love every part of yourself, there's nothing you don't love.

There's a wrinkle on my face and I love it outrageously. There's a little roll of fat on my tummy, I love it outrageously, I love it, I'm so fucking outrageously perfect. And the Universe wants me to be so fucking open to God, and all that part of me that wants to be someone else – no, I'm so happy to be me, I'm so delighted to be me. And you know what? When people feel that delight in me, then they're delighted to be with me. Because who do you want to be with, other than with a person who is totally delighted to be him- or herself? Not in a narcissist, a closing or a contractive way, that is the way of the ego. The ego IS contraction. The ego is not a thing, the ego is contraction. Letting go of the ego is letting go of the contraction. I can tell you how to do it, put the camera on and watch. This is how you do it.

(PUTS SKYPE ON VIDEO MODE,
OWS NAKED STOMACH)

Do you like my black outfit? Okay, I'm just taking my shirt off, nothing else. You see this little fold of fat right there? Do I want to be Tom Cruise, all worked out, the strong man with tight abs? No way, I love this. Be delighted with your body, be delighted with your cheeks, be delighted with your lips — we spend so much time wanting to be someone else, right? You can't be a great lover if you want to be someone else, and being a great lover has nothing to do with tight abs. Being a great lover means that you're madly in love with your body, because that's your body. When you're ecstatic about your body, love pours through it. So be outrageous.

Shut your eyes and just imagine that part of yourself that is your version of Gafni's stomach bouncing up and down. Turn the camera off, for God's sake...J Be outrageous and go inside and find that part of your body that you are unhappy with, breathe in to that part of your body and outrageously love it. Breathe in and laugh about it, gently.

That doesn't mean you shouldn't exercise. Loving all of your body means loving whatever is the body that God gave you, AND do whatever you can to keep it fit and healthy. Loving yourself isn't being lazy, it means doing an enormous amount of physical activity. You eat right, you walk, you run, you exercise, and while you are doing all of that, you love yourself in every minute just how you are. That's what the Bhagavad Gita means when it says: "Live your dharma and don't be attached to the fruits of your labor."

Act passionately, act ecstatically, do all the work you can in the world, and let go at the very same time. Holding those two together is Enlightenment, but you've got to do it outrageously. People may think that you can get it done if you are not outrageous – but you can't!

Outrageous pain needs outrageous love

You can't get enlightened without being outrageous, because the truth is that the world is an outrageously painful place. It's painful to be lonely, to be betrayed, to be unable to live up to everything you want to be. It's painful to move out of your ego and feel 20 million children starving a year, to have a fight with somebody, to hear others fight, to worry about money, to grow older, to watch your friend die of cancer.

And the only way to respond to an outrageously painful world is with outrageous love, with an outrageous refusal to ever shut your heart. No matter what the world does to you, no matter how many times you are betrayed, you say: "I will not shut my heart, I'm going to be outrageously, unreasonably, irrationally, wildly, ecstatically crazy-wise, keep my heart open. And even if you break my heart, we'll find the good time again. There's nothing more whole than a broken heart.

Do you know what it is like to have your heart broken? Oh my God, it's crazy to have your heart broken. And you can't control that, you can't ever control it, and then they tell you that it is your responsibility. Well, maybe; but probably not, though. You always have a piece in the story, but the story is much bigger. There's lots of karma, this life, a previous life, there's lots of egoistic contraction, pettiness, desire to kill the life force. You are going to get killed a thousand times, but don't get insulted, experience it as the wounds of love and keep your heart open. Because every time your heart breaks, it gets callused and stronger.

The practice of Outrageous Love: Keep every boundary, break every boundary

I'm starting a new era of practice, the practice of outrageous love, outrageous joy, outrageous ecstasy. We are going to cross <u>and</u> respect every boundary. We honor every person's individuality, but at the very same time, we are going to cross every boundary of smallness, every boundary of power schemes. We cling to power in order to feel that we exist, making decisions based on narrow self-interest, instead of on the way in which Evolution works, which is holy cooperation.

Let the self expand, let the self become big art, let the self feel the power of the spaciousness as I expand and I include you in my heart. Together we will suffer the wounds of love, together our hearts become more than the sum of parts of the whole, as we love.

To be outrageous, you need discipline; three levels of dancing

And to be outrageous, you need discipline. Isn't that funny? You think that being outrageous is about letting go of discipline, but that is just idiocy. To be outrageous, you need incredible practice, incredible love, incredible discipline, and only after all that discipline, you can let go.

There are three levels of dancing, as we say in Kabbalah. The first level is that you don't know how to dance; you're just kind of moving around on the dance floor, being crazy. The second level is when you learn the dance steps, the choreography; you learn the art of formal dance and you practice. Only then you get to level 3, which is wild, improvisational, ecstatic dance. That is the level of outrageous dancing, and you can see that level 3 and level 1 aren't the same. Being outrageous means that you've got to learn how to dance first, and then you can become outrageous.

And everyone is going to be outrageous in a way that is comfortable to them. Everyone makes their own decision in how much to risk, how much to take care of yourself, because we are really wise, smart, beautiful adults. But the goal is to break the boundaries of small self, to actually taste Enlightenment in your body, and it is going to be the Enlightenment of Love, because what else is it worth living for?

We are going to be outrageous, not just for ourselves, but we *are* going to do it for ourselves first and foremost. For if I am not for myself, who am I for? Yet if I am only for myself, then what am I? And if not now, when?

Let's just rest in that, let's rest in the silence for two minutes and just let our mind go empty. As a thought comes through your mind, let it flow through. Your shoulders drop, your posture is as erect as you can make it, and you relax in the Silence and Sounds of Presence. Know that you are held, right in this moment you are held. I am going to be outrageous now. I am holding you, not as ego-Marc or small-self Marc, because he can't do anything, but as True-Self, Unique-Self, Guru-yoga Marc; I am holding you in total love.

What do I want from you? I do want something from you, you're right about that. I don't want your credit card, I don't want you to be my student; you can be my student if you want to, but that is not what I want. I want you to be wildly, outrageously beautiful as your Unique Self. I want you to melt the fear when you find that painful place of yours, like Marc Gafni's stomach with a slight roll, whether that is a place in your personality, your body, your childhood or your life story. Everybody in your life has that place, the place that didn't work and that you desperately want to be different. Melt the fear around it and then do everything you can to make it different, but at the same time, let it go and love it up.

Turn the fate of your life, do everything you can to transform it, and then let it go and love it. Live outrageously, live in the world as your most gorgeous, outrageous Unique Self, and give the gifts that are only yours to give, knowing that you are held, knowing that any place you fall, you fall into God's hands.

Forgiveness is outrageous - Jesus on the cross

I am going to tell you a secret: forgiveness is outrageous. It was outrageous when Jesus Christ was on the cross and said: "Forgive them, Father, for they know not what they do." That was outrageous, and it's so sad that the Church later became a place of power and ego. The Church became a place of enormous corruption and — I'm going to use a harsh word — of evil. The Church in Europe did both enormous good and enormous evil. Many individual members of the Church, of course, were awesome, but lots of the power structures were corrupt and evil.

But Jesus Christ Superstar fucking rocks, and when Jesus is on the cross, his entire life's work as he knows it is being destroyed, and Jesus is a human being who is loving his God. Then he finds the God inside, he finds the Unique Self of Jesus and says: "Forgive them, Father, for they know not what they do." You know what it means to say that? That's insane, it's completely outrageous.

Dyad exercise: Holding a person as a wounded kitten

Find a dyad partner and sit with him/her. Then think of the people in your life who you love but feel a little distant from, because you hurt them in some way, didn't speak to them lovingly enough, didn't give them enough time or attention or weren't good enough to them. You want to reconnect with them. We are going to do a kind of healing, which doesn't mean that you don't need to talk about things later.

Shut your eyes and imagine that person as a wounded kitten — meow — and just hold that image. Then feel into the deepest wound in your life, the thing that hurts you most, whatever it is. Ask God, ask the Universe, ask Source to embrace you and hold you and hug you and love you and caress you, in that deep wounded place, so you can feel the love of the Universe.

Now the person with the shorter hair is the high priest or high priestess; you are the guru, you are practicing Guru yoga, with your eyes shut. The person with the longer hair is the wounded kitten; let yourself be gathered up by the other person and let them hold you like a kitten and love you with your eyes shut, with all the love of the Universe. So now move towards each other. Be outrageous!

The person with the shorter hair gathers the other person up, maybe a little awkward, but keep your eyes shut until it works. Gather them up and love them completely. You are the high priest or the high priestess, the person should be in your arms, you are holding in your arms a wounded kitten. You don't get angry at a wounded kitten, you are holding the wound and you are pouring your love into the wound. You are the high priest, the high priestess, the guru. Be outrageous – just as Gafni can pour love, or Adi Da can pour love, you can pour love from your enlightened place, as we move towards the democratization of Enlightenment, and pour love into that person.

Keep your eyes shut and you can hug the person with the longer hair, the kitten, back. Feel yourself held, you are totally held, you are totally loved.

Sometimes when we're hurt, we hold on to our wounds because they give us our identity. Sometimes we hold on to our wounds because they're a way to cover up shame. Sometimes we hold on to our wounds because we are convinced we are right, but we don't know how to weigh things properly; we don't know how to give up being right. So I invite you to be outrageous and give up being right!

Now we switch roles and the person with the longer hair imagines the person in front of them as a wounded kitten. You feel your love for that wounded kitten, no ego, no personality, this is a wounded kitten. And the person with the shorter hair feels into that part of your life where you feel most hurt, most wounded, and let it be raw and open and vulnerable. At least for these moments, you don't need protection. Be outrageously open and outrageously vulnerable.

The person with the longer hair, be outrageously loving and begin to move towards the other with eyes shut, and let it be awkward. Slowly embrace them with radical love, as the guru, as the enlightened Master, totally in radical love. You don't need to understand the reason for the embrace, you only need to understand that it is needed. Grace is to go into that place that is impossible to enter, and in that place, to give up being right, to love wildly, ecstatically, outrageously. So be held, wounded kitten, in this total embrace.

Now slowly shift the hug, shift the embrace to loving each other. With eyes shut, shift the embrace to loving each other, in any way that works for you, and give each other a kiss on the forehead. You kiss the kiss that you imagined in the beginning, that little fantasy kiss that we did at the beginning, kissing someone on the forehead. Now make the fantasy real, give and receive the kiss on the forehead, with eyes shut. If you picked a different person in real life to act it out with and you get into your original fantasy, that's fine, that's the way it needed to be.

And in that Silence of Presence, with eyes shut, step apart and relax into your natural place, still in pairs. Now I ask everyone just to relax into it, and imagine that I'm now walking around the room and giving everyone a kiss in the forehead, while receiving a kiss on the forehead in return. This is the Shaktipat of love, the surest thing there is. I totally love every person in the room - what an honor to be in this Holy Sangha.

And so it is. Amen.

Prayer and Communion

Communion: a personal relation
with God or the Divine

*W*e are all desperate for communion; it is what makes our lives worth living. Communion is the movement from loneliness to loving, the experience of being held and received. We are all systematically misrecognized. To be recognized is to be seen, to be seen is to be loved, to be loved is to be in communion. It is only when we are seen, that we are called to the fullness of our glimmering beauty as unique incarnations of the Divine treasure. It is only when we are seen that we feel moved, by the personal evolutionary impulse that lives in us, to give the unique gifts that are only ours to give and that are desperately desired by the All that is. To be in communion is to know that your deed is God's need. It is the realization of communion that gives us joy and calls us to evolutionary responsibility.

'Communion' is the term that Kabbalah scholar Gershom Sholem gave to the experience of God in the second person. This is the inner experience of a human being who is not merged with the Divine but rather stands in relation to God. This state of relatedness to God is the essence of Hebrew, Biblical consciousness, and according to Scholem, it defines Hebrew mystical consciousness as well.

God in the second-person perspective is all about relationship, whether it is the relationship of a servant to his master, a lover to her beloved, a relationship with a partner or even a relationship with a friend. All these models of relationship can be ways of relating to God, of approaching God in the second person, and all of them find expression in Hebrew wisdom teachings. With God in the second person, we meet God and bow; we meet God and partner; we meet God and love; we meet God and pray. The key to experiencing God in the second person is the encounter, the encounter with God in history and in the lived reality of every human being.

Prayer is experience/realization, not dogma/obligation

The most powerful form of God in the second person is almost certainly the prayer experience. It is told that when Hassidic master Levi Yitzchak of Berditchev used to pray, he would begin to say the standard liturgical form of blessing: "Blessed are you, God." Then after some time he would break out of the formal mode of blessing and start crying out in sheer joy, "YOU, YOU, YOU... YOU!" That is the rapture of God in the second person. For Levi Yitzchak, the blessing is what the Buddhists call a 'pointing-out instruction', but the words point not to sunyata or emptiness, but to God as a beloved Other. Nachman of Bratzlav taught the spiritual practice of Hitbodedut, which in one form means: walking alone in the forest "talking to God as you would to your friend."

This is the God of prayer, and the God of prayer is not a concept but a realization. Recently, a well-known Buddhist teacher said to me: "How can a serious teacher like yourself believe in the dogma of prayer?" I asked him: "How can you believe in the dogma of awareness?" He answered: "Awareness is not a dogma, it is a realization." To which I responded: "Yes, of course it is. And so is prayer." He told me later that this simple pointing-out instruction shifted his entire relationship to prayer. Prayer is not a dogma, it is a realization of God in the second person, it is the felt sense that any place you fall, you fall into God's hands. Not the God of the mythic, ethnocentric church or synagogue or mosque or temple; not that God. Not the God that you, as a modern or post-modern skeptic, do not believe in, for remember, the God you don't believe in does not exist.

Rather, God in second person is the personal face of Essence. It is the aspect of personal Essence that knows your name and cares about every detail of your life. You can feel into the quality of the personal Essence that lives in you, as you and through you. Remember, perhaps, a time when you felt alienated in a relationship and you said to your partner: "I feel you are being so impersonal," or when you critiqued some dimension of society as being too impersonal. Inherently, you sensed that Essence has a personal quality, the personal quality of Source. This personal Essence is beyond the grasping of the skin-encapsulated ego, which still believes itself to be separate from All that is.

Levi Isaac of Berdichev in the story above did not faint in ecstasy because he was moved by the dogma of a personal God. Rather, he fainted in ecstasy because of the felt experience, the realization of the lived encounter, in that very moment, with the personal face of God. It is the experience of God in the second person that inspires prayer. True prayer is not a religious obligation, but the ecstatic realization of God in the second person. Prayer is an expression of the radically personal nature of Enlightenment, the place in which the personal Unique Self talks to the personal God. In prayer, the personhood of God meets the personhood of a human being. Prayer is the flight of the lonely one to the Lonely One, or, as Hassidic master Ephraim of Sudykov said: "The meeting of misunderstood man with misunderstood God." Human being and God meet, realizing that they are both strangers in the land. They end up in a friendship in which both are liberated and redeemed from loneliness. The second face of God is an infinity of intimacy, which invites your approach and your prayer. Prayer and intimacy are almost synonymous.

The personal face of Essence, which knows your name, affirms the infinite dignity, value and adequacy of your personhood, even as your prayer affirms the dignity of personal needs. Our praise and our petition, our confessions and even our crying out in need or in anger are all addressed to the second person of God, which is invoked through the sacred art of prayer. Prayer is our way of initiating a conversation with, and thereby invoking, the infinitely gorgeous face of the personal God, God in the second person.

The four interior levels of Essence: pre-self, separate self, True Self, Unique Self

We are used to thinking of Essence or Source in impersonal terms. In the usual thinking of the spiritual world, the human being has a personality or separate self, which is transcended in Enlightenment and melts into the impersonal Essence of All-that-is. However, this is only part of the story. As I have described in depth in my book 'Your Unique Self: The Future of Enlightenment', there is a personal Essence that is beyond the impersonal. To truly understand and embody the interior face of Essence, one needs to move through four core levels of consciousness.

Level One is pre-personal. This occurs before the emergence of an individuated separate self.

Level Two occurs when the pre-personal emerges as the personal self. This is the important level of separate self, ego and personality.

The Third Level is when the personal, in a healthy and non-disassociating process, is transcended and included into the Impersonal. This is the classic state of Enlightenment, which appears in all the great traditions. The personal is trance-ended, you end the trance of the personal self and realize that you are part of the vast, impersonal essence of All-that-is. It is impersonal in the sense that it is beyond the individual personality of any one person; it is the seamless coat of the Universe of which you are a part.

However, that is not the end of the story. The seamless coat of the

Universe is seamless, but not featureless. Some of its features are expressed uniquely as your personal incarnation of Essence. Your irreducible uniqueness is an expression of the personal quality of the Divine, beyond the impersonal.

The Fourth Level: In this stage of development, the impersonal reveals its personal face. You experience the personal face of the vast, impersonal Divine Essence that suffuses, animates and embodies all that is. Here, we are not speaking of a kind of Santa Claus God-in-the-sky. That is merely a reflection of your personality, or perhaps your mother's or father's personhood, written large!

This fourth and most profound level of consciousness is the personal face of All-that-is, the aspect of Universal Essence that knows your name and cares about your life. It is the Divine Mother who holds you in her loving embrace, comforting you, yet challenging you to your greatness at the very same moment.

The Cosmos is intelligent

Think of someone who is very intelligent. Is this person more intelligent than the Cosmos? Of course not. This person was brought forth by the Cosmos, his intelligence partakes of the intelligence of the Cosmos. How could the Cosmos not be intelligent? This person may be intelligent, but surely he is not as intelligent as the Cosmos.

So let me ask you a question. If you can hear me talking, how could it possibly be that the Cosmos can't hear me talking? Wow! That's called 'a pointing-out instruction'. See, we just cut through 2000 years of bullshit theological sophistry with proofs back and forth and up and down; I spent 20 years of my life memorizing all of them. Throw them out, it's the simplest thing in the world — it's gorgeous, it's like boom! If you can hear me, and you're intelligent, it means that it is the quality of intelligence that hears. And whatever your talents and accomplishments, you're not more intelligent than the Cosmos. So if you hear me, then of course the Cosmos hears me. The Cosmos is intelligent!

How do you know the Cosmos is intelligent? Well, let me ask you this: What is intelligence? Intelligence has structure, is organized and sophisticated, is moving in a direction. Just take a look at your immune system, take a look at a little molecular chemistry, just start from physics. Does the Cosmos look random to you? The only chance there's no chance of in the world, is that the Cosmos is random. The notion of a random Cosmos is a statistical insanity.

Now, does that mean that the world was created in six days? Of course not. Clearly the Cosmos evolved, clearly evolution is the principle of the Cosmos, and clearly we're not talking about a God outside in a chair, kind of guiding the Cosmos along: "Do this, do that." No, we're saying that the Cosmos itself is a living intelligence, which is what the people in physics today call the fifth force of the Universe: the evolutionary Eros itself that unfolds reality to higher and higher levels of autopoiesis, according to Nobel-Prize winner Prigogine, through the strange attractor of complexity and consciousness.

So the Cosmos is a living intelligence. That's the quality of the Cosmos, nothing to do with any religion; that's just the nature of the Cosmos. If you can hear me, of course the Cosmos can hear me! It's so simple.

Why not talk to the Cosmos?

Let me ask you just a dumb question. Why wouldn't I say anything to the Cosmos? Do you see how crazy that is? If I know that I have the attention of the Cosmos, why do I keep chatting with everyone else around, but forget to open up a channel directly to the Cosmos that knows my name? Actually, the reason I'm doing that, is because this notion of prayer got hijacked by fundamentalist religions, which we correctly rejected.

I want you to really hear that, it's big. We correctly rejected fundamentalist religion, because it overreached and lied to us about a lot of things. We needed the feminine to emerge, we needed gender to emerge, we needed democracy to emerge and we needed science to emerge, all of which were rejected by a freezing religion. So we correctly rejected a fundamentalist, dominating religion.

But we forgot there were a couple of things they got down the path, that were really good. Their mistake was that they said: "Not only does the Cosmos listen, but the Cosmos talks only to me, the Pope, and it told me what you should do." That's where it gets a little problematic. But the core, second-person realization of Rumi, that I'm in the arms of the Beloved, that the Beloved hears me and knows my name, is the awakened realization of God in the second person. It's why Levi Isaac of Berdichev, when he was beginning to make a blessing, was saying: "You! You!" And he can never make the blessing because he faints in ecstasy. Not because there is a dogma, but it's like: "Oh my! You!"

The Secret of the Kiss

A vision for the future of sex and love

*S*ex and sexuality are a cause of great joy and great pain in the world, both in our individual lives and collectively. It is the source of enormous amounts of violence, depression, brutality, frustration and loneliness. But here I want to talk about sexuality, about love, from the perspective of *what's possible*. Let's talk about the future of sex and love. Even if the world of grasping ego, the world of fear and of samsara, isn't yet ready to live this fully, for all sorts of reasons, it still makes a great difference to us to have a vision of what is possible.

Martin Luther King said the night before he died: "I've been to the mountain top and I've seen the promised land," and he talked about what the promised land looks like, about what is truly possible between human beings, about what it would mean when people generally love and honor each other. The next day he was killed, but the words remain. I hope I will not be assassinated tomorrow, although believe me, you can never tell.

Sexual ethics

So what is the invitation here, what is the vision? There is a lot of talk about sexual ethics, which is unbelievably important. The masculine needs to love the feminine and be good to the feminine, and the feminine needs to love the masculine and be good to the masculine, whether that is two men or two women or a woman and a man or a woman and a goat. However you tell the story, we have to be particularly careful with the goat, because she can't speak up for herself.

Of course we need sexual ethics, that's a given. Of course we have zero tolerance for sexual harassment, and of course we have zero tolerance for false complaints of sexual harassment. Of course we fight with every fiber of our being any form of sexual abuse; that's critical and that's important. Sexual ethics are an unbelievably important evolution of consciousness. Only during the last 25 years have we created laws to protect women against sexual harassment, which is so important and so critical. And we now need to create big laws to protect men from false complaints of sexual harassment, and that's also critical; these are all very important movements of consciousness. But that's just the very beginning. It's necessary, but not the essence, the future vision of it. That's the given, that's the course you have to take before you take the real course.

Sex IS ethics

Let's begin with the end, and then gradually move towards the beginning. The end is the realization that sex IS ethics. There is no split whatsoever between sex and ethics, which I will explain further on. That is why so many great utopian, spiritual movements in history tried to rewrite a higher vision of sexuality. The kibbutz movement in Israel, or utopian movements in Dutch or European history said the same thing: "this is not working, the sexual thing is not working, this great promise isn't realized".

And the amount of destruction that takes place based on the failure of this great promise to deliver, whether in individual lives or in social contexts, is a terrible thing. Individually, there may be one person living in New Jersey who is getting it right, and the rest of us are wildly frustrated and jealous of that person in New Jersey. Collectively, this undelivered promise has been creating havoc in all of human history, past and present. And I'm not just thinking of aids, incest, sexual slavery or child porn.

The great city of Troy falls just because Paris has these several beautiful nights with Helen. Does that make sense? Of course not. But of course, it is not really because of sexuality; sexuality just creates an excuse, because everyone is so confused about it. Agamemnon, the great king, wants to attack King Priam of Troy and he can't convince his brother Menelaus to join the battle. But when Menelaus's wife Helen has an affair with Paris, son of the king of Troy, then Agamemnon can use Menelaus's discomfort about sexuality, his sense of being humiliated in his ego, to convince him to join the battle, which in the end kills thousands of people and destroys the city of Troy.

When the Republicans can't actually unseat Bill Clinton, behind the scenes they spend a lot of dollars to get Linda Tripp close to Monica Lewinsky, Bill Clinton's intern, to record her conversation in order to impeach Clinton. This causes Bill Clinton to be unable to campaign for Al Gore; Al Gore loses the presidency, George Bush is elected, and we have a f*ing Iraq war, because all of America was just buying newspapers tracking exactly where Bill Clinton put his cigar in Monica. That sold more newspapers in the US than anything else happening in the world at the time. Famine, disaster, nobody cared.

These are just two examples to show that we are so confused with the whole thing. We know there is that great vision in us, but it is not realized. And the core of it is that sex IS ethics, meaning that in sexuality itself, in the very understandings that are implicit in the erotic, sexual exchange itself, are all ethical principles to life. If we would just be loyal to the realizations that we have in the Holy of Holies of sexuality, and live our lives based on those insights, we ourselves and the entire world would be transformed. I'm going to be more specific, so go slow with me.

Raiders of the Lost Ark & the Quest for the Holy Grail

Remember Indiana Jones, played by Harrison Ford, in 'Raiders of the Lost Ark'? It was the Ark of the Covenant in Jerusalem that Indiana Jones was looking for, and on top of the Ark, in the Holy of Holies in the temple of Jerusalem, are two Cherubs. And in the mystical tradition, carefully reading the original Biblical text, right there, the Cherubs are engaged sexually, in the middle of making love. These two Cherubs are not the sweet angels that you see on a Christmas Card; these are two fucking Cherubs.

In our modern world, sex has been exiled into pornography, into confusion, into dead monogamy, but the sacred text says: "I will speak to you from between the two Cherubs making love." That is the divine Voice, the voice of prophecy, speaking from between the two Cherubs making love in the Holy of Holies of the Temple! And the Temple isn't just a physical temple; the Temple lives in consciousness, the Temple is a particular space in consciousness, an interior space in our heart and mind and consciousness.

That's why Indiana Jones was looking for the Ark, that's what this cultural symbol means. We have these cultural symbols, but we forget what they mean. As Thucydides said: "When words lose their meaning, people lose their freedom, and culture collapses."

That bestselling book, 'The Da Vinci Code', was also about this, about the sacred Eros in the Temple, about the masculine and feminine merging. You have the Grail Quest, the Quest for the Holy Grail, and a grail is a cup, the shape of the female genitals. In the original Hebrew, the word for grail is 'kos', which means vagina. So the Grail Quest is the quest for the feminine that is making love with the masculine, whether it's two men or two women or a man and a woman. It's the quest for the feminine making love with the masculine, but not trying to get 'over there'. There is a hidden tradition in Christianity that the Grail was Mary Magdalen, the woman who was with Jesus, and that they are the two Cherubs making love on top of the Ark, the Ark of the Covenant.

Now why do we have fucking Cherubs on top of the Ark in the Holy of Holies in the Temple of Jerusalem? Why is the Grail Quest about finding the feminine, which then merges with the masculine? Because, my holy friends, *that* is awakening.

The wisdom of Solomon

Master Aviva wrote in the 1st Century: "If the entire Torah, the entire 24 Biblical books, wouldn't have been given, we could live our entire lives from the Song of Songs." So all wisdom, all ethics, all gnosis is found in the Song of Songs, the Biblical book about love where the details of the erotic, sexual encounter are used as the great metaphor for all of life:

"Kiss me with the kiss of your lips, deep inside, for this is better than wine."

"Plant your flag deep within me, my Love."

"Your breasts are the most beautiful as they merge into my mouth."

There is something in erotic loving itself that tells us everything about everything. That is called the wisdom of Solomon, and it's an erotic, esoteric wisdom. But the Bible attacks Solomon, saying that he was seduced by his wives, that his heart went astray, that he began to serve idols, for the Biblical writers deemed the world not yet ready for this wisdom.

Solomon's wisdom is the wisdom of the living Eros itself. The Song of Songs is not about the Ten Commandments; it's about the Ten Commitments of Love. Just imagine what it would be like if we would be loyal to the vulnerability that we feel in sexuality. Because what is a sexual encounter? It's when two people allow each other to witness their loss of control in vulnerability. Isn't that what sexuality is, when I actually allow someone to witness me in full abandon, in full vulnerability, in full loss of control, as my small self disappears, as in the best moment my dramatic, complex self disappears? What would it be if we were loyal to that felt sense of authenticity, to that sense of meeting one another?

And what a horror it is when we betray that Holy of Holies, when we re-narrate it and we retell the story different from what it was. Because after the vulnerability is over, after the orgasm has exploded and I turn over to smoke my cigarette and the ego rushes back in with all of its defenses and other voices, the grasping starts again. Then I begin to lose my connection to the Holy of Holies, I begin to lose my connection to the authenticity of that vulnerability, and I also begin to lose the connection to the obligation created by that vulnerability.

When we enter into Eros with each other and we make love and allow ourselves to open up in vulnerability, what we are saying is: I promise to take care of you, I promise to hold you, I know that every touch will shiver into you, and I'm responsible for every touch. Even as I overwhelm you, and you overwhelm me, I hold you upright; even when I ravish you, I honor you. And in that place of fully receiving and loving each other, all ethics is born.

The body is more than the temple of the soul - the body IS soul

The Christians say that the body is the temple of the soul, implying that the important thing is the soul, but you should take good care of the body, because the body is its temple. That is the masculine understanding of the body: the body as the temple of the soul.

What feminine mysticism begins to understand is that the body is not merely the temple of the soul; the body IS the soul, there is no separation. The mystical masters used to say something like: "Greater is the source of the vessel than the source of the light in the vessel." Meaning that the vessel may hold light, but actually, the source of the vessel itself is the highest light! According to the mystics, the rocks of the highest place falls to the lowest place, so what appears as a vessel, in its original source, in the pulsating of the Big Bang, actually is the highest light: it's the most clarified, pure spirit.

So we usually understand sex, sexuality, the erotic, as being the vessel that holds the light, which is love, goodness, ethics, an authentic relationship between people. That's true on one level, but on a deeper level, sexuality itself IS the light. It's like an indigenous medicine journey. If you've ever done something like that, you know there is a deep revelation in the journey. The question is: what would it be like if I lived loyal to that revelation, if what I knew in the middle of that journey, I was able to actually live? So that's what the erotic is: an awesome medicine journey, a great state of spiritual experience, and what I need to do is to give voice to that truth, to what that state itself teaches me.

Every thrust, every feeling, whether it is wetness or hardness, whether it is openness for penetration, for conceiving, whether it is the arm or the inner thigh, every dimension of sexuality holds in itself the teaching itself. That is Tantra, what Solomon called the Left Emanation what Kashmir Shaivism calls the left-handed path. One of the meanings of the word tantra, in Sanskrit, is 'to expand', to expand the knowing of the sexual into all of the non-sexual dimensions of my life, to actually *live* in the Holy of Holies.

In the Secret of the Kiss lies everything. The rabbi's and all the mystics said that Solomon is taking sexuality as a metaphor, but they just said that to hide the teaching, or maybe didn't understand it themselves. It is not a metaphor, it is exactly true. The vessel IS the light.

Group exploration: The teachings of the kiss

Any person that has any experience with kissing can give us some teachings about what the Kabbalah calls 'the Secret of the Kiss'. Let's practice with this. Think back to your best kiss ever, that went on and on, and give that kiss a voice, so the kiss itself becomes a sacred text.

Now you will have to resist the urge to come up with funny comments. You'll feel it bubbling up, you'll want to say it, thinking it will relax you into this space, because we've exiled the sexual. We've put the sexual in the bedroom, maybe on the kitchen table on a good day, but basically it is out of our life. But what Solomon was saying was: "No, no, no; sex IS ethics." By listening to what the kiss has to tell us, we are going to realize that every dimension of sensuality holds within itself the entire ethical teaching on how to interact with people, how to run society, how to make decisions - it's all there.

So, what did you learn from your best kisses?

Participant: The teaching of this particular kiss, this very special kiss, is that I didn't do it. It evolved, it was there, it happened, despite of me.

Marc: So there is something in the kiss that takes over and that moves through me and evolves from a place that I don't control. Beautiful.

P: The teaching of the kiss for me is that I knew from that experience that giving and receiving are the same. I felt such an openness, such a complete connection between us two. It made no sense to say that I was giving or I was receiving; it was just one flow, you know.

M: Right, beautiful, thank you so much. So a huge teaching of the Secret of the Kiss is that actually giving and receiving are absolutely the same, but the entire rest of our lives is built on the distinction between who is taking and who is receiving.

Giving is Receiving

You go to your bank and say: "I'd like to take out hundred dollars." So they give you a hundred dollars. Then you say: "Instead of deducting a hundred dollars from my account, please add a hundred dollars." They look at you as if you're crazy; what are you talking about? But if you are a very good client at their bank, they will just laugh. Funny, right? Right.

But then you say it again: "No, no, the truth is that I'm not joking, I really need you to add a hundred dollars to my account." Now they look at you a little funny. Then you say a third time:

"Really, I insist, you must add a hundred dollars to my account." At that point they call the bank manager and at some point the police are called and they throw you out, they lock you up, because that's insane.

You are either putting money into the account, or taking money from it, receiving money. The entire world is based on that distinction. All the politics, the economics, the structures in society are built on the essential distinction between giving and receiving. And along comes this revolutionary, evolutionary force that makes Marx smile and say: "Fucking A!" And all of a sudden you have a subversive force that undermines, in a good way, the whole structure of society and tells us that giving and receiving are one.

So let's go even deeper. I don't know how many of you have a grandmother who speaks Yiddish. If you do, you probably also have a therapist. But if your grandmother speaks Yiddish, you have heard her say: "I got a great deal." You go out shopping and there is this unbelievable deal. How many of us have had this experience? I am a really bad shopper, I never have them. I know, I have had a hard life.

What do we mean when we say that we got a great deal? What we mean is that we gave the least and we took the most. And that is considered to be a skilled person, you are talented, you know how to navigate life, you know how to get along, you feel good, you feel strong and powerful. And what does it mean when we say: "Man, I got ripped off, I've got this horrible deal." It means you got the least and you gave the most, and you feel like a sucker, like an idiot. Don't tell anyone that, it's totally embarrassing.

That is how our psychological selves think. Not our biological selves, but our psychological selves, trained by the grasping ego of separate self which is measuring time all the time, glancing down and checking what is happening in this moment, thinking: "What do I get out of this?" Yet our bodies live from a different principle altogether, for the biological cells of the body are giving and receiving all the time. Each one of us is fifty trillion cells, giving and receiving every single moment. Wow.

The sacredness of kissing

Of course, the Secret of the Kiss is not some guy who keeps pushing his tongue down your throat when you are trying to fucking breathe. The secret of a great kiss is this wonderful place where basically the giver and the receiver disappear and you are lost in this magical place of softness, of wetness, of penetration and receiving, where two sacred openings merge in this larger wholeness of eternity. That is why kisses are so intimate. Having sex in a superficial way is often less intimate than a real kiss, right? We all know that.

There is a Dutch psychologist, Thielcke, who is quoted by Rollo May in his book from the late 60ies, 'Love and will', where he talks about a prostitute who will do everything with anyone or anything, other than kiss. Because the kiss is the holy of holiest, and it is the holy of holiest because a whole wisdom is there, it holds open a vision of a different world.

I would like to hear from any other kisses that want to talk; that is what they call in England 'kiss and tell'.

P: In a great kiss, I want to stay right here and never leave.

Marc: Beautiful. So the kiss reveals the eternity that lives in the moment. The kiss actually says: I want to stay right here and never leave, so it creates a loyalty to a moment, wow. And when I betray that moment, oh my God. There are tears coming to my eyes right now and I get a vision in my mind and in my heart that I never had before. On the Day of Judgment, imagine all of our kisses coming before us and we are asked if we were loyal to those kisses. Can you see that? On the Day of Judgment, it is not this male, patriarchal God asking: "Did you kiss the wrong person?" No, it is this gorgeous, divine, feminine/masculine, androgynous being who is in all of us, which is the kiss itself. The kiss itself asks: "Were you loyal to me, were you faithful to me?" If you want to make that into a kind of B movie, you have these lips all over de screen going 'AAAAA'.

P: For me the kiss is about experiencing totality, oneness, freedom, being.

M: So the kiss teaches me about moving out of my separate self into being, in totality, oneness and freedom. Did everyone hear that? Here we have this great teacher, and it's not Ramakrisna, it's not me nor you; it is the kiss. Sex IS ethics, that is the revolution that everyone is afraid of. If I have had this moment with someone, I can take it with me when I get contracted, when I get angry with that same person, maybe for good reason, but then I could step out of my ego-triggered reactivity, even if I am right, and I don't let my anger become an insult, but let it just become the wounds of love. Then I hold, as I argue with him or her, the kiss that revealed to me totality, oneness and freedom. Even if I have to split from that person, I will do it in a way that holds that totality, oneness, and fucking freedom. Because I'm loyal not to a theology, not to a dogma, not to the picture of a patriarchal, male God in the sky, but to the kiss. Wow, thank you, my teacher.

Chahat: I think about the overwhelming softness in connection.

Marc: Right, softness and connection, the ethics of softness. As it gets hard, to be soft. Soft does not mean that you give up your position, but you soften your position, because you actually know of your connection in the kiss, and the connection is real.

Actually, why would my lips want to touch their lips? What a strange thing, right? I remember my friends in grade school, we were 12 or 13 years old, making jokes about men from Mars who would come and watch human beings kiss each other. It's just weird, these lips looking for each other. You walk along, living your nice little life, and suddenly somebody is trying to put their lips on your lips and then, God forbid, their tongue in your mouth! From the level of ego, you would call the police. And if the person does not have your permission, then they are violating your boundaries, but if it is a place where the heart opens, the ego picture falls aside, and lips look to each other because we are connected, because there are invisible lines of connection between us.

Still, if someone kisses me and they don't stay with me forever, it's okay. Because the desire for the person who kisses me to stay with me forever is the ego that comes back on line, saying: "If I let you into my mouth, I own you. You have to take care of me now." But actually, what if I can hold on to the truth of the kiss, even if we are not supposed to be together? With every person I kiss, my relationship to them changed. We knew something of each other that we did not know before.

Does that mean I should kiss everyone in the world? I don't think so. Of course not. But what would it be like to have all the people in our lives that we ever kissed together with us in a room? Somehow or other, those are our people. They are not all of our people, for I'm also close to people that I have never kissed, but the people that I have kissed are definitely in my tribe.

Exercise: write down all people you ever kissed

We can do an exercise, I am making this up as we talk, of writing down all the people in your life that you kissed, and then write down what your relationship with them is right now. What would you like your relationship to be, what did you think your relationship was going to be at the time when you kissed? And maybe we could heal those kisses. Maybe we could write a letter to each person we kissed, to create a healing. And you will actually find, I think, that some of the most difficult people in your life today, who may be suing you, are people you kissed. My heart breaks for all the betrayed kisses in the world.

Let's hear some more secrets of the kiss.

P: The kiss means: I surrender and I want to drink you.
Marc: Wow, I surrender and I want to drink you, which are two

different moments. I surrender, I have made all the moves I can make, and now I surrender. Hafiz says at the end of this poem: "The difference between you and a saint is that you still think you have a thousand moves to make, and the saint knows that God has just made some incredible move - all he says is 'I surrender'."

That's another teaching of the kiss: just to surrender to your lips. If you don't surrender to the kiss and try to control it, it loses its sacredness. And I want to drink you, I want to drink your Unique Self. Not just anybody, I want to drink you! The kiss is: I want to drink your shimmering, dazzling, unique, gorgeous essence that tastes unlike anything in the world. And sometimes, when persons kiss deeply and they can't hold it, they just say: "My bad," and that's how it goes. But to be able to hold the kiss in all of it and stay loyal to the kiss, that's really huge.

So our teacher today has been the kiss, feeling into the longing of the kiss. Great kisses are few and far between, and when they come, they have great teachings. We need to make them less few and less far between. If we were developing this and trying to share it with the world, we would do exercises about our first, our best and our most disastrous kiss, all three of them.

The Evolution of Love

I thought about these things for many years, until about six years ago I spent maybe two, three, four years trying to feel into this subject, to teach a little bit about it, and then I stopped. I stopped because I said: There is so much energy around this stuff. I wrote this book about Unique Self, I started this Centre for Integral World Spirituality, and I'm going to continue with that. But in some sense, I feel I turned my back on the Goddess and said to her: "You know what, this kiss stuff is becoming too complicated, and I don't want to be the lightning rod that has to teach it. Integral World Spirituality is much safer for me. And sometimes the Goddess says: 'You have no choice.'

And so I want to invite you, together with your awesome Venwoude community, over the next years, to really take responsibility together for creating a private container for the Evolution of Love. There we can enter deeply into the secrets of all the kisses, into the secrets of the Holy of Holies, the secrets of Eros. What does Eros actually tell us? What is the revolutionary, evolutionary, subversive voice of Eros that we give our voice to? And we study it, not from books, but from the contexts of our lives, and we write it and record it and develop it together. Because there is no one person, man or woman, who owns the kiss. It is only a sacred community that owns the kiss, that IS the kiss, together.

The strength of Venwoude is to create a vision in this world, that a sacred community is possible, where people hold each other in their hearts even as they work through all the difficult issues in life. And maybe, just maybe, we have something to share with the world that is absolutely vital in the source code of the Evolution of Love.

We may begin developing a training based on the principles of pleasure, which I talked about a couple of years back. It's a very exciting thing to do and it's a huge step in a world organized on fear: can we organize a world based on understanding what our deepest pleasure is?

The level-line fallacy in monogamy versus polyamory

The other day, I said to someone: "You should check out Ven-woude, a fantastic place, man, really cool, awesome. You've got to go there." And this person looked at me and said: "Are you kidding? I hear those guys are into polyamory." I said: "Well, let me ask you a question. Why is that a bad thing?" And he said: "Are you kidding? My grandmother and grandfather had the most beautiful, monogamous marriage, they were married for fifty years. And I went out with this guy seven years ago, whom I loved and he loved me, and he said he was polyamorous. But really, he would not make a commitment, and he lied to me, he cheated six times, and he said that was all cool because he was polyamorous. So polyamory is just a bad thing in the world and monogamy is beautiful."

I said: "Really? Why don't we talk to the millions of couples who went through thirty years of monogamous marriage that was dead from day two? They lived the 'perfect life' but have been in pain for thirty years, without any moment of openness, of beauty, of divinity, because they married the wrong person and did not know how to get out of it. Let's talk about all these abusive family systems that cause their kids to be devastated, that raise teenager suicides to astronomical proportions, all born from these perfect, monogamous families. Why don't we compare that to a beautiful polyamorous couple who works through everything, who love each other, who respect each other, who honor each other, holding this very high level of living? Then tell me: which one is higher?"

That is a level-line-fallacy again, meaning you compare the

highest form of monogamy with the lowest form of polyamory and say "monogamy rocks". Or you compare polyamory to celibacy. Celibacy can be really holy, in the sense of just being dedicated to God, unless I am a Catholic priest fucking altar pages. So it is not about whether you are doing monogamy or polyamory or celibacy, that is not the issue. The issue is *how* you are doing it. What consciousness you are bringing to it, what forgiveness, what healing? Are you willing to say: "I made a mistake"? Are you willing to grow, to be authentic, to be called to your highest integrity?

The new vision of sexuality is not about monogamy or *polyamory,* which is basically a stupid conversation, uninteresting, kind of 'yawn, boring.' The issue is sacred, ethical Eros or non-sacred, non-ethical Eros. There's ethical, gorgeous, beautiful monogamy and there's destructive, debilitating, demeaning, life-killing monogamy. There are beautiful, gorgeous, holy ways to love more than one person, and there are silly, degrading, unethical ways to do that. So it's not about the particular style of loving, it's not about on top or bottom, gay or straight. It's about the intention of the heart in loving, the loyalty to what was created right from the sacred start, and the commitment to that.

A Prayer for Haiti

omeone once asked me: "How can you believe in a God who cries?"

And I said to them: "How can you believe in a God who doesn't cry?"

God in second person as the infinity
of caring and compassion

When we think and feel about God in an Integral evolutionary framework, we think and feel into how God feels. The second-person realization of the Divine is not merely to feel Tat Tvam Asi, 'Thou art that', as I feel the 'I AM' arising in me; it's not merely the awestruck wonder as I behold the infinite, vast complexity and gorgeousness of the systems of Cosmos and psyche, all the way up and all the way down. God in the second person is the experience of all of that infinity and gorgeousness as a second-person Being-Intelligence, which animates and infuses All-that-is.

God in second person is the God before whom I bow, before whom I prostrate, the Christ before whom I cross myself, the altar at which I kneel, the place at which Rumi and Hafiz fall in radical devotion, wanting only to be held in the arms of the Beloved. It's the God who cares so much that we cannot even imagine that level of caring. The Divine is not only the infinity of power, but the infinity of compassion and of caring, the Divine who knows my name, who knows your name.

How could God allow for Haiti?

How do we bow before the Divine who is compassion, who is love, who holds us with infinite tenderness, in a world of Haiti, in a world where we witness terrible levels of destruction, of pain, of violence? Children in hospitals, amputees crushed under rocks, no help available; slow, painful torture of death even as we were eating our chopped-liver sandwich last week, in our comfortable, air-conditioned, middle and upper middle-class, landed-gentry places of the world, where we read Integral Theory to amuse ourselves, which gives us some sense of intellectual stimulation, looking for meaning in our too comfortable lives.

How do we talk to God in the second person, the great realization of the Divine Lover that inspires all the great traditions, from Sufism to Hebraism to esoteric Christianity and the Aboriginal traditions, when this Divine in the second person seems to allow for such pain and for such suffering? How could God allow for Haiti? And I offer this question to you in prayer. The question is not impudent, the question is not arrogant, the question itself is a prayer. I want to try and pray with you, and I want to pray an

answer with you in several different ways, each holding a different, sacred spark of the Integral Divine that needs and waits to be
redeemed by us.

How do human beings allow for Haiti?

First, the most direct and clear way is to turn the question around.
The question is not, 'How does God allow for Haiti?', it is: 'How
do human beings allow for Haiti?' The Divine supplied the world
with all that is necessary to handle effectively, even prevent, natural national disasters, like that which took place in Haiti: properly
structured earthquake-resistant housing, appropriate road and
aid systems put in place well in advance, for the disasters that will,
nonetheless, happen, which will allow for quick and efficient de-
livery of relief and medical services.

All of it was completely possible, could have been put into place
a thousand times over by all the global UN and other relief agen-
cies. And weren't, despite the full and clear knowledge that such
a disaster would happen. Why? Because we were locked in our
collective separate-self ego, because we were concerned with egocentricity and ethnocentricity, because human strife and tension
and pettiness prevented us from coming together and realize that
what unites us is so much greater than anything that might di-
vide us. We did not put into place what was completely within our
reach and ability to put into place. And the Divine waited for us
to act.

Mystical Hassidic thinker Nachman of Breslov writes that the very
existence of atheism in the world is in and of itself an expression

of the Divine. Can you feel the radical, non-dual, intuitive realization in that? The Divine is All-that-is, and All-that-is is included in the Divine, therefore, even the atheistic impulse is included in the Divine.

Nachman of Breslov is then asked: "What is the divinity in the atheistic impulse?" He says: "When confronted with the world suffering, behave as if there was no God. For you are that God, you are the one who is responsible in every possible way to assure that the hungry will be fed, that the disaster will be averted, that the pain will be healed, that the shattered hearts will be mended."

So in our first understanding, 'How did God allow for Haiti?', it is actually not what the human being asks God, but what God, turning to the human being, asks: "How did you, divine miniatures, with all the gifts and resources that I gave you, how did *you* allow for Haiti?" That's our first understanding. Let us breathe into it, breathing in the pain and breathing out the light in the holy, sacred technology of Tonglen, the Buddhist meditation in which we take in the pain and transmute it into light.

What is God doing as God waits for us to act?

We now turn to our second understanding in our prayer to at least approach the quest we're on, the quest to understand: How do we live and love the universe of Haiti? Clearly, it must be an approach in which we understand that we need to do everything possible to prevent and to act. So, my dear friends, how does God feel in a world of Haiti? What is God doing when Haiti is happening?

Waiting for us to act, waiting for us to be God verbs, Gods adjectives, Gods dangling modifiers, to act, to heal and to transform. And what is God doing as God waits? That is the second teaching. What God is doing, is just crying. God is crying so deeply, so powerfully, so passionately that we can't even begin to imagine or to touch God's tears.

I want to share with you a holy teaching, the teaching of Kalonymus Kalman Shapira, of Piaseczno, a master who died in Treblinka, outside of the Warsaw ghetto. He cited an ancient Aramaic text from the fourth century, which asks: "What is God doing on the inside?" That is the way of esoteric masters: to try and feel into the Divine, to actually touch the Divine in the Divine's innermost feeling, and in that way to hold the Divinity, even as the Divinity holds us. And they hide this mystical, esoteric, radical activity by asking simple questions, just as the text questions our own, encoded esoteric teachings.

So the text's question is: How does God feel on the inside? The question is asked of Jeremia, who lived the time of Lao Tzu, in the 6th century BC, and Jeremia has two answers to this question. One is: XX(HEBREW): "In the divine place on the inside, God is filled with audacity and laughter." And Jeremiah's second answer is: XX (HEBREW) "God is crying, on the inside."

Is God crying or is God laughing on the inside?

This is what the Aramaic teachers tell us in the 4th century BC, and they seem to be two different realizations, two different meditative graspings of what is happening on the inside of divinity. One is that the God on the inside is somehow crying, and the other is that the God on the inside is somehow laughing. So which is it?

The masters tell us, in Aramaic, that the first text, the first realization, refers to the inside house, and the other refers to the outside house. That is to say, in the inside house, God is doing one thing, and in the outside house, God is doing something else. If you are a Buddhist, you might say: in the absolute and in the relative. In the relative, there is one expression, one realization of All-that-is, of Divinity, but in the absolute, it is a different realization. But which is which? That is the question that the masters then go on to ask, and this is the mystical process.

Which is which? Is God laughing on the inside and crying on the outside? Or is God crying on the inside and laughing on the outside? Many masters take the classical Buddhist way. In the absolute, of course, all is audacity, all is laughter, meaning all is beyond change; there is no pain. On the inside, as it were, in the absolute, all is beyond tears, because how could there be tears in the absolute? The absolute is a manifestation of the divine in the relative, the changing world, it's God's relationship to world. Beautiful teaching.

But that is not our prayer for Haiti today. Our prayer for Haiti today is the second teaching, the radical teaching offered in Treblinka 1942 by master Kalonymus Kalman, the last great master of the Kabalistic lineage of Poland. He says it so deeply when he says: "No, what I realized in Treblinka is that we always read this text wrongly. If you actually enter and understand the deepest truth, you will know that on the inside of the inside, God is crying, and only on the outside does God laugh. And the reason why God cries on the inside and not on the outside is because God's pain is so infinite, God's tears are so infinitely painful, that if but one tear of the Divine were to fall on the outside, the world would be instantly destroyed."

Human beings as God's partner in healing and transformation

Master Kalman teaches us and reminds us that if we speak of God in the second person as all-powerful, the infinity of divine power, we forget the infinity of divine pain. God's power is infinite in that God stepped back and turned to us and said: "You be my partner in completing the creation of the world, you be my partner in the healing and transformation, you be my partner and take responsibility to heal the shattered hearts."

And so God waits for us to become miniature divines, to step up to exercise the radical capacity of choice, to act as gods in the world. And when we don't, then we suffer, and when we suffer, the Divine suffers infinitely, for we are literally part of God - that's what non-dual realization is.

The infinity of divine pain

You know, you and I only suffer the pain of our limited bodies, our skin-encapsulated egos, as long as we remain in our separate selves. But the Divine, who is ultimate realization, who is ultimate, non-dual embrace and incarnation of All-that-is, the Divine suffers all of the pain instantly - the infinity of divine pain, the infinity of divine tears. Can you imagine that pain? Can you imagine the infinity of divine pain as Haiti takes place?

Christ, in all her distressing disguises, is nailed to the cross, in perpetual crucifixion. And the only way that we can take Christ down from the cross, the only way that we can heal the pain, is our willingness to step out of the narrow confines of our woundedness and our egocentricity, the narrow confines of 'business as usual', the narrow confines of grasping for security and egoic fulfillment, to prove to ourselves that we exist. And then to begin to practice, and to realize that the heart of the Cosmos lives in my heart and in your heart, and act from that heart, to make life choices from that heart. It may be to adopt another child from that heart, to find the person in the world whose tears can only be healed uniquely by you, to find the place – not in Haiti, because you might not able to get to Haiti today – in your local community that awaits healing, which you have full, absolute, radical power to heal, but you are too fucking busy.

Can you hear that, sweethearts? I am saying that to myself just like I am saying it to you. When does business as usual stop? When do we actually let go of the egocentricity of the skin-encapsulated, separate self and begin to feel the Bodhisattva heart of the Cosmos beating in us, as us and through us?

God's heart loved us so much, that God chose to incarnate in us, as us and through us. In us beats the Bodhisattva heart of compassion, and through the prayer we offer, we bow before the God who is beyond the form, God in the second person, the God who is in us and lives as us. Tat Tvam Asi, "Thou art that" – we are God whose compassion needs to be aroused, and whose action needs to be manifested. And we bow to God in the third person, who manifests in love, and animates all the great systems.

Let there be healing, let us be the healing.
And so it is.
Amen.

Being a Home, Receiving a Home

The second year is not a repetition of the first year

*T*his is the first Circle meeting of this year, which is our second year. The second year is not like doing the first year again; you are not doing the same year twice. In the great mystical schools, they used to say that when you study for two years, it's not like studying one year twice. The second year of a relationship is not like doing the first year again, thank God. Actually, the second year you go really deep, because in the second year, if you're doing it right, you're really taking off, you're blasting off from all of the depth that you established together.

And so we, as a holy community, as a holy gang of wild outlaws, as a sacred coming together, a sacred fellowship, we have gone some distance together. We've been together, and we know each other, and we have the beginning of a deep trust, of a love that can only deepen, because trust is infinite, and love is infinite.

If you love someone and you've know them for a year, you really love them. And then you love someone for five years, and you look back and say: "I didn't even know you that first year." And then ten years, it's insane. Today, if I talk to the people in my inner circle and I say 'in ten years', people get scared. O my God, ten years, what's that? Because we live in a world in which it's all sound bites, it goes viral on the web in a day, it all happens really fast. We have lost the idea of deepening, of getting cooked.

Slowing down: sending letters versus emails

Does anyone here remember sending letters? Writing letters was a great thing. How many of you know what a bungalow colony is? How many people saw the movie Dirty dancing? In Dirty Dancing, there was this Catskill Mountains hotel with a bungalow colony next to it, in which people would come for the summer. If you go to a bungalow colony and you are 8 or 9 or 10 years old, there is this very exciting moment when you meet your first romantic interest, your first love.

I remember I was 10 years old when I met Debby Weinbach, also 10 years old, and we went skating at Funfair, the local skating ring. The big excitement was that you would go to your Debby Weinbach and ask her to skate together, to skate doubles. That was like a mayor, life-changing event, and then we went back to Columbus, Ohio, where we lived, and Debbie and I decided to write each other letters.

And it was a big deal, first off, what kind of stationary you would pick, and then: Would the stationary have perfume or not have perfume? Then, how would you sign the letter? With a heart, or 'love', or: 'I love you'? Or 'love you and miss you'? These were all major things, but here is the big one: Would you write 'SWAK', 'Sealed With A Kiss'? For a ten-year-old, at a summer holiday in the Catskill Mountains in New York in 1970, that was the greatest plateau of liberation and enlightenment.

Now what happened is that we have lost that art of letter-writing. When I was 15 or 16, they started sending - now watch this word - faxes. All of a sudden you have to give good fax - will you fax me? Fax is a whole new world, for faxes were much faster than letters. So people were all excited: "Wow, this is really fast." But the problem was that you lost something, didn't you? You lost the art of writing a letter. Nobody is now going to take three weeks to get to the mail system, choosing every word carefully, choosing the paper, the stationary.

And then, about 10 or 15 years later, they started what they call 'email'. With email, you send it and in one second it's there. I get about a 150 new ones every day, right? It's just overwhelming. You write it really quickly - the whole point of email is that it's quick, down-and-dirty, fast.

I tell you, love letters are not doing well on email. Thomas Jefferson and John Adams were the second and third president of the USA, they pledged allegiance to the flag, born in the USA, Bruce Springsteen, thank you very much. The second and the third president hated each other, they were major political foes, and they both lived long lives. And at the end of their lives, they began to write each other letters. We have their correspondence, and these are some of the most beautiful, profound, gorgeous letters ever written.

What have we lost in moving so fast? This is my teacher today and tomorrow we're going to have another teacher. Let me try that seminar, let me go to this six-day tantric retreat where they teach seven ways to find an orgasm 15.000 times, and that will break my heart. Then I go sit with Isaac and then with Abraham and then we will be going to Marc and then to Jack, right? We're moving around, we are kind of trying to fill up our Enlightenment basket with this person and that person, this teacher and that teacher, (SPEAKING FASTER AND FASTER) and we can't keep up, he's talking so fast, oh my God, oh my God, oh my God.
(SINGING) *Slow down, you move too fast, you've got to make the morning last, just kickin' down the cobble-stones...*
We've got to go slower.

Changing the source code of love

And so, as we begin this second year together, that is a big deal.
I started these first ten minutes just to hang out with you, just to say: "Hey, this is a big deal." I want to invite my dearest friends at Venwoude, where I am just delighted to be, in deep partnership, where I love the people, where we're building something gorgeous together, to go and build something that changes the source code. And not only of you and me, not only of World Spirituality and Venwoude, for we are going to change something in the very source code of love in the Universe. We are going to evolve love together.

But we've got to do it by slowing down, we've got to breathe in together. Here we are, we're building a love, we are building a trust. And that is a very beautiful, tender, fragile, gorgeous container. We've got to move through steps sometimes, we are going to be careful not to be caught in all the fast-pace things that are happening in the world. It's a big deal. And sometimes we are going into a session and wonder: "Did I get anything yet? Did it change me?" You know, as the Talmud, the old Jewish text says: "Fuck that!" Yo, let's just breathe in, let's find our place, let's locate.

How many people in the room have taken the sacred practice of cuddling? Did all of you cuddle? Good. There is a moment in cuddling where you have to locate yourself, right? You are not quite in the right position, it is not exactly working, you are not sure why, but you have to move the pillow, change your leg, or your arm, something. You know what I mean? You've got your arm stuck in that wrong place behind her or his neck, you don't know what to do with it, you cannot locate yourself, right?

That's what we have to do together. Here's our relationship: our relationship, our spiritual relationship, is that we are going to blow open the world with love. We're going to challenge, we're going to comfort the afflicted and afflict the comfortable. We're going to make love with God, with Source, we're going to open each other's hearts, we're going to cuddle. That is our spiritual relationship. We've got to locate, to find ourselves, find that spot where it's kind of perfect: I am home. And then from that place, you can do all sorts of gymnastics, but first you've got to find that place, that home.

And as we're going into the second year of our Mystery School of Love, I really want to invite everyone and invite myself and invite God: "Hey God, we weren't just doing this for a few months, we are really together." God is Source, the power of all being and healing that exists and lives in every cell, the Eros of the Cosmos, the gorgeous, shimmering energy of All-that-is-and-lives. "Hey, that's you, God. We are really here to stay, we're really going to do this together, you can trust us, so come on with us."

There is room for everybody

Let's find our place, right? This is home. The temple in Jerusalem was called: 'the home which is holy.' We're home, in this place, this Circle we're in together. We're inside the circle, and when you are really inside the circle, you don't need to demonize anyone. Because then we'd only place people outside the circle and we don't really feel inside. We talked about it in summer: do we have to put somebody outside in order to give us the illusion of being inside? Are we then really inside? Wow, no, there is room for everybody. Isn't that wild?

I will tell you a wildly beautiful, mystical teaching that appears in a third century Hebrew-Aramaic text called Masechet Midot, which is about the measurements of the temple in Jerusalem.

We talked about the Raiders of the last Ark, Indiana Jones, the Ark of the Covenant, the Templers, the Masons, The Da Vinci code - all this stuff is about the Temple in Jerusalem, the mystery temple which is really alive and is called 'the home which is holy'. So it says in this ancient text that on the holiest day of the Hebrew mystical calendar, called Yom Kippur, there were thousands of people in the courtyard of the Temple and they were all completely smashed, crammed in, all standing with barely room to move. And then, at one point in the ritual service, there was a moment of deep ecstasy, when everybody was totally loving each other.

I'd like you to open your heart now, in a deep Silence of Presence. At that point, they would all do a prostration, fully bowing out the whole body flat on the ground, every one of those thousands and thousands of people. And there was room for everybody. There was room for everything. It was a miracle of love, because when you are really in love, there is room for everything. That's what it means.

When ego is at play, you can have the biggest house in the world, you can have a mansion. Like Cat Stevens said 25 years ago, you got 'a mansion with too many lonely rooms'. But if you are really in love, you can be in one room in a two-room flat and hang out with someone you love and you feel like you're in the biggest mansion in the whole world. Right? So when we really love each other, we are not smashed any more, there is all the space in the world, it's spacious.

This Mystery School of Love, which meets in this Circle every month, is about loving each other. For when we love each other, we are at home. And at home, sometimes there are challenges, and there is deep work that has to happen. It's not always easy, but we are home.

My family are the people I walk the Path with

I want to invite everyone to shut your eyes now — I'll shut mine —
too, and just feel the experience of home. Oh my God, I'm home.
The internet is not my home, nor is email. My biological family,
I love them, they're totally awesome, maybe, but they're not quite
my home. My home is the people I decided to walk the path with.
Do you hear that? That's my home.

My lineage master, my teacher Isaac Luria, says it so deeply: "In
the age of the coming liberation — what the astrologists sometimes call the Age of Aquarius, the New Age — my biological
family is really important, and I want to honor them and respect
them and love them the best I can. But my deepest family are the
brothers and sisters that I choose." So sometimes I say: "Hey holy
brother, holy sister," and people look at me and say: "He's weird.
Why does he call me brother? He's not my brother." But he is, she
is, my holy brother and sister. This is home, and it's only home
where I can locate myself, where I feel fully held and honored. And
it's only from that place that I can transform.

Home as the Divine Feminine

I'll tell you something really wild, really deep. People talk about
the divine Feminine, everybody's talking about the divine Feminine. But actually, most people don't know what it means. What
and where *is* the divine Feminine? Is it a soft breast? Well, not exactly. That can be an expression of it, just as beautiful arms hold-

ing me, but it's not what it is. What is the divine Feminine in its core, the difference between the feminine Face of God, the female, the woman face of God, and the man face of God, or Source? Because God means Source, the Dao, the way, reality. We say that reality and God are the same thing.

So what is the difference between the feminine face of reality and the male, man, masculine face of reality? We need both. The man, the masculine, looks at us and says: "Hey buddy, you gotta get in shape man, you are all over the fucking map. Get your life together, pull yourself together, let's get some rules here, follow yourself, find some will, find some discipline, make it happen, rock it out, now." That is the masculine. Is that an important voice? For sure. And you know what? It's not enough to transform. That masculine voice can be a spiritual teacher, it can be your own inner voice, it can be a God voice, a religion voice, a friend's voice, a therapist's voice. It's a good voice, we need that voice. But it's not enough.

To really transform, you need the divine Feminine. What the divine Feminine says is: "You know what? I love you so much, you are so beautiful, gorgeous, wondrous, so uniquely special, unlike anyone else. I am madly in love with you, and I know how good you are. And because of that, I know what you can be and I want to be proud of you. Make me proud of you, I love you so much, be everything that you can be. Please."

The divine Feminine holds you and knows that you are already good. And when you know that you are already good, then you can transform.

When someone criticizes you, how do you respond? "Thank you for the feedback, I really appreciate that." Maybe. But actually we don't. When someone criticizes us, the first thing we do — for our mind is like a computer — is find all the things they have done wrong over the last 70 years. We remember every possible thing they've done wrong, and we basically say, either to ourselves or to them: "Who do they think they are? That guy killed someone, shot his mother, why is he criticizing me?" And secondly, we think of the 70 reasons why they are wrong, right?

We experience being criticized as an attack. If someone criticizes us, what we hear is: "You are bad", and we can't bear to be displeasing to ourselves. But the biggest shift we can make to Enlightenment is to know: "If someone is giving us feedback, they totally love us. And even if they don't really know how much they love us, we receive it as love. You care so much about me, you believe in me so much, that you want me to be even better. That's so awesome." That's the divine Feminine. The divine Feminine holds us in radical love. That's the Beauty and the Beast. The great legend is always the same: the beauty will stay with the beast, the spell will be broken, and he will turn into a prince. What's that? That's the divine Feminine, expressed in that fairytale. If the beauty stays with the beast, the beast becomes a prince.

The home of our community

So that's what our community is, that's what our holy game is, right? We are in the second year, and we are saying: "We are going to stay." This wasn't a flash in the pan, it wasn't just a moment, it wasn't just an incredible high of Enlightenment, like a deep enlightened experience for eight days. We really held that enlightened space for a couple of weeks. That's awesome, that's not just a deep transmission of Enlightenment experience this summer, it's deeper than that.

We're staying, we're here, we're committed to create an evolutionary 'We' space, in which we, together, as a Sangha, change the source code and participate directly in the evolution of love, by being at home with each other, by comforting the afflicted and afflicting the comfortable, by being committed to stay and create a sacred miracle of love in each other's eyes. That is a big deal. So, holy brothers and sisters, spiritual friends, teachers and students — because we are all of it to each other — the teacher transmits, the teacher receives, and we love each other outrageously. That's what we said last year, five months ago, that we would love outrageously.

Staying and being a home for each other

So our second year is not like our first year, it's a whole different game, potential, possibility. In loving your way to Enlightenment, the second year is the opposite of how the world usually works. Usually a person meets someone, and it's so awesome because they're excited by the newness. Then when the newness wears off, when the novelty wears off, people usually say, "Well, let me get something else, let me have the newness again. I've touched that body, let me go for a new body."

If you are really loving each other, and you get to the second level, when the excitement of a new body isn't there, then it can go deeper. There's a location, there's a home, and the body actually becomes more erotic and more lovely, because at the core of it, there's love. When you really love, somebody else's body becomes your home, and your body becomes somebody else's home, not because of the newness but because of the depth of the lover. Has everybody felt that? So the second year is not like the first year. So deep, right? We're often like "Oh my God, man, he fucked you open with a new idea, wow, that was awesome. Well, there must be others with a bunch of new ideas, let me move on."

But for creating a home together, for living, what I'm inviting you to do in this Circle - I cannot say it to the world, but in the inner circle I am saying, "I'm inviting you to make me your home. I'm willing to be your home, you can live here. I will be an imperfect vessel for the light, but I can be your home, I can hold you." That's huge. That is not like "I'm going to hit you with a great idea, to dazzle you with my charisma, to give you a brilliant talk." That's fun, but kind of boring. Now I'm saying, "Hey guys, you can live in me, and you know what, if you sign up, you say: 'Hey Marc, we can be your home, too.'" Wow. Can you feel that? Does that move your heart? It opens mine.

We don't need just great ideas, although great ideas are so important, but they've got to be filled with love. A new book came out, just a couple of days ago, at Amazon.com, called 'Your Unique Self, the Radical Path to Personal Enlightenment'. Great book, I like it. Chahat got some of them, you can get them at Amazon. com. That's really important, but that's just the outside. The inside of it is, can you feel at home with each other? Can you be a home for each other? That's my invitation for the second year, different from the first year. And in the inner circle, the Holy of Holies, that's what we do. It's about being a home for each other. I like that.

So let's chant. We know how chant works on Skype, it's always a little bit awkward, God knows who's doing what when. Don't worry, it's totally part of it.

CHANTING

To the seven types of sexing, I recently added type eight. And type eight is what I call home sexing. Home sexing does not mean you do it at home, as opposed to in a parking lot. Parking lots have their advantages, but home sexing is really something else. It's about sexing as a way of coming home. That's very, very deep. Our whole conversation today is about really coming home, it's about the second year, it's about staying.

Exercise: Sentence Completion

We are going to do a sentence completion exercise, about what it means to come home. So I ask people to hold the Silence of Presence and split up into groups of four or five people and make a circle. I give you a sentence and each person in turn is going to complete the sentence, and then I'll give you another one, and so on. Sentence completion exercises are a great practice in developmental spirituality, for really making the teaching mine, coming from my own first person speaking.

The first sentence is: "When I feel at home, I feel..."

PEOPLE PRACTICING

The second sentence is: "From the safety of home, I have the power to..."

PEOPLE PRACTICING

Third sentence: "in order for me to be a home for the people who need me, I need to..."

PEOPLE PRACTICING

Okay, let's take it to the next step. In order to be a home for someone, there is no greater joy, no greater privilege, no greater delight than to be a home for someone. In order to be a home for someone, I have to move beyond the early images of home that I might have, that weren't a home for me. Everybody's got some snapshots, some early pictures of what home looked like, and what we do is something that is called 're-enactment'.

Re-enactment is a term in psychology and also in mystical teaching. We naturally, unconsciously, re-enact the home that we grew up in, that we were raised in. And so, although we want to be home for someone, and we want to know how to be in the home that someone's offering us, it is often extremely difficult, if not impossible, for us to do, because there are hidden patterns of home within us, that determine the way we are in the world. Unless we make those hidden patterns of home obvious, open them up, can see them, we can't actually retract, we can't reweave.

Exercise: Sharing about childhood homes

We are going to go one more step, and I really want you to hold the container, hold the space, hold the love, hold the honor. We are going to do another round, but this time we give each person two minutes to speak, and while that person is speaking, the other people are holding the space of the Holy of Holies. In those two minutes, the person is going to share either the wonderful ways that they were held as home in their early years of childhood, or they might share some of the ways that they didn't feel held as home, some of the really painful facts, or they might share both. And then when you finish the sharing, just by making it conscious, you then say: "And these ways of home, that were not home for me, I let go, I liberate, I send them away from me, and I embrace my power to be a home."

So you go around: each person gets two minutes, in which you share both the ways in which your early childhood was a home, you felt held, you felt like it was a home in a deep way. And you also have the audacity and the courage to share the ways in which it wasn't a home, in which you didn't feel held, or perhaps you even felt violated in some core right. So you share both. By sharing it, the hidden pattern of negative home becomes conscious and you bring it into the light. By bringing it into the light it melts, dispels, disappears.

And then, at the end of your sharing of two minutes, what you say is: "In this moment I release from me the patterns of negative home. And I affirm in myself the power to be a home, and to receive a home." So that is the conclusion, the way you finish. You won't get shot if you haven't got the words exactly right.

Thank you, dear friends, holy brothers and sisters. We really hold the space so preciously.

PEOPLE PRACTICING, FOLLOWED BY CHANTING

God is looking for a home in us

So we are in our second year, and we are becoming a home. I'm going to leave you with a holy, awesome story, a short story, about Afa Mendel of Futz. It's about some students who were sitting with him, his holy students, and he shouts to them: "Where is God, where is God?" He is going crazy, like a holy crazy wisdom master: "Where is God? Where is God?" So the students say: "Holy master, the holy books say: The heaven to the heavens of God, God's in the heavens." He says: "Nisch, nei, no!"

Then another student says (and this student is more of a mystic), "There is no place without God." And the master says: "Nisch, nei, no!" Wow! And every student tries to say something, and each one cites a verse or a text or a holy source, and every time the master goes: "Nisch, nei, no." He is getting sadder and sadder, so finally the students do what students should do and they say: "Nu, Rabbi, holy rabbi, you tell us where is God?" And the master says: "God is where you let Him in."

God is where you let Him in, God is looking for a home, God is knocking on the door. And how do we respond? Salomon says in the Song of Songs: "And as the lover knocks on the door, the beloved inside says: "I've already taken off my clothes and in bed I am warm. How can I get out of bed to go and open the door to the knock?" And so the beloved sleeps, and then she realizes, oh my God, what I am doing, I am sleeping, God's knocking at the door. And she gets up, three-four minutes later, and runs to the door and opens the door, and in the Song of Songs, Salomon writes: "And my lover was no longer there."

The voice of my beloved is knocking. Where is Source? Where is liberation, where is God? Will you let it in? God is looking for a home. Are you willing to be God's home? That's the only question of life. Am I willing to be God's home? There is no other question, and it is a question that only has one answer. Let's be God's home.

Our second year. Total, total love.
Deep bow to the God in the center of the Circle.
Amen.

Love before and after creation

The love before and the love after creation

here are always two kinds of love. There's what we call 'love before creation' and 'love after creation'. What does it mean to love someone after creation? It means that if you meet someone, you say: "Wow, they are a good person, they are so beautiful, so good in the world!" That's love after creation: you meet someone, you love them. You love their personality, you love how you hang out with them, or you love their body, their funniness, but you love them, you think they are awesome, right? That's love after creation and that's good. But there's also love before creation and that's totally different.

The love from before creation is not meeting someone and loving them, but desperately searching to meet everybody and loving them. It's not that something appears in front of you and you say: "Wow, I really love it!" It's that you yourself are love before creation. So you are looking, seeking, searching everywhere to love everything you can see, seek and find. If there's no one around, you go crazy, you've got to go find anyone, in order to love more people. You see the difference? It's huge. Go deep with me here, let's totally open our hearts and go deeper.

Sometimes someone gives you a gift with the love after creation. Let's say they give you $ 5,000, and you say: "Wow, thank you so much, I really need that $ 5,000, you know. Wow, that's so good." Or they give you $ 50,000. "Wow, thank you so much!" You're so appreciative, right? Of course we are all very appreciative of a gift like that. But I want to tell you a holy secret. Open your hearts, holy brothers and sisters, open your hearts. Sometimes someone gives you a gift of the love before creation and they can be giving you just $5 and it blows your heart open in a way that nothing does in the whole world. Wow!

Sometimes someone gives you a hug after creation. It's so warm and nice in there, since they are doing a great hug, I love that hug. But wow, open your hearts all ye brothers and sisters, sometimes somebody loves you with the love before creation and it goes right through you and you're home, good, blown open, it's like nothing you've ever felt before. Sometimes somebody tells you "I love you" with the love after creation. That still feels so good, but do you know what it feels like when someone says "I love you" with love before creation? Oh my God.

So when you love someone with the love after creation and they agree to meet your friends, sometimes you're a little embarrassed, right? "Yeah, this is really good, but you know, I guess he doesn't have a job." "Yeah, she is such a good girl, yeah, she was a murder-er once but we're working on it." It's as if you want your friends to think: "Wow, you are so great, you are with this great person." But sometimes it doesn't work out and we are a little embarrassed. But when you love someone with the love before creation, you bring them to your friends and you are so proud of them, which is awesome. They are so beautiful, you are so filled with "Oh my God, look, my beautiful friend," and your friends look at them and they can only say: "Oh my God, wow, it's so beautiful," because they see them with your eyes.

The love after creation is to see someone with your deepest perception, as deep as a human being can see, and that's so holy, that's so great. If you clear away your false self, your shadow, and you work out your stuff and you throw mummy and daddy out of bed, you did all your psychological work and then you love them, that's beautiful. But when you love someone with the love before creation, you see them with God's eyes. The love before creation is to be a lover who sees through God's eyes, who IS God's eyes.

And you say to yourself: "I'm a body that wants to look with eyes to see, aflame with fierce tenderness. I want to look into the eyes of all I meet and sprinkle shimmering delight into every cellular contraction in the very fabric of their being. I want to kiss every bare shoulder of every man, woman and child whose vessel seems to have shattered so long ago that they forgot."

Love Before Creation: you were there at the Big Bang

The love before creation is when you remember that you were there at the Big Bang. It was you! Who else could it have been? It was you who started it all. That singular point of energy, which exploded into love, who could it have been other than you? Where else could you have been? It was you; it was you who did it all. *That's True Self.* You see, separate self loves with the love after creation, while True Self loves with the love before creation. It was you, it's the love that moves the Sun and the stars, it's the love that is the initiating energy of the Cosmos itself, it's the love that creates Creation, it's the love that searches for people to love. It's not about "I wish I was in love and I'm not in love. I remember I was in love once, but now I'm not in love." That's love after creation. But to be a real lover, to love outrageously, really means to love with the love before creation.

The Love Before Creation breathes life into matter

The love before creation is the love that causes quarks to come together in a union and become atoms, atoms to come together, a single boundary drops around them and voilà, they become molecules. When atoms love each other and make love to each other, they become molecules. It makes no sense, you can't explain it in any way. When molecules come together, they form a multi-complex molecule, like strands of molecules together. And they are so moved by their togetherness, it's like a holy secret, and all of science says: "Well, we don't know how this came about."

Let me tell you what it is right now. You think that that is chutzpah, a form of audacity? It sure is. I'm telling you, and I know this is true, this is holy audacity from 'the inside of the inside'. How did molecules wake up to become life? Science is still like: "How did that happen?"

Now I am telling you the holiest secret in the world, the holy secret of the Love Before Creation. It's not really true that there are two parts of reality, like inanimate matter awakening at some point to become living cells. Science can't address this, but actually quarks and atoms and molecules are already alive, even when still asleep. When the atoms were drawn together to form molecules, that was love, and it was actually awake, but it was hidden. And then when these complex molecules came together in a particular way and formed the first cell, it's like the princess that opens her eyes, kissed awake by the prince. It is the divine kiss of love which awakens matter into life.

Actually, there is no split: every rock, every tree is alive, every blade of grass sings a song, every river teaches its Torah, every mammal says its dharma. It's all right there, in the split between life and not-life, we just can't see it so clearly when we look at it with the love after creation. With the love after creation, we make a split between what's alive and what's not alive, between what we see and what we don't see.

A couple of years ago I stopped eating meat, because I realized: Wow, I'm only loving animals with the love after creation. I don't see how they are raised and hurt and brutalized and killed. And we could deal with the killing, but they are tortured along the way. As long as I don't see it, I could just eat my great hamburger, which is the love after creation. Or I say: I really need this meat to support me to live longer. Well, I'd rather die younger than eat the meat of an animal that was brutalized and tortured. If you need meat, eat free-range meat, man, raised beautifully.

Okay, let's chant.

Sit straight, in a comfortable posture. Feel your head, the crown of your head lift up to the heavens, your shoulders drop, and your beautiful, holy spine becomes the pole that connects Heaven and Earth, as the Sufis say. You become the Enlightened One, the Axis Mundi, the connector of the higher and the lower. And you hold the chant forever, yes, *you*, you and everyone else, just you and me, just you. And we chant with generosity, we chant to the Enlightenment of fullness in which no voice contradicts any other voice, no body contradicts any other body.

CHANTING

The value of chanting the same chant: neuro-dharma

The key to chanting is that it's like making love: do try to do it more than once. It is about doing it again and again, like eating. I eat because I am hungry, I chant because I am hungry for contact, I want to make contact. You don't say: "But I have already drunk water, why would I drink water again? Let me drink something else." No, you keep going deeper and deeper, sometimes for 50 years, and in the 50th year you finally get the chant in the deepest place, for doing the same chant over and over makes a neural pattern in your brain. It's neuroscience and it's also dharma teaching; it's neuro-dharma, the dharma of the body-mind-heart.

So in neuro-dharma, we know that when you keep chanting the same chant, it will open you up, just like a particular song will arouse a particular response in your heart. Often a song carries a memory: a couple will say: "That is our song, that's the song we first danced to in Paris in 1926." So the song carries the memory, holds the memory, and every time you hear the song, it brings back that experience of love. Remember Marcel Proust's 'Remembering Things Past', when he is at his grandmother's house and she gives him the marmalade cookie and he remembers fully the taste of the same cookie that he used to get when he was a child; it brings back all the warmth and love that he felt as a child.

So when we do a chant during which we one day have broken through, in which we have tasted God, in which we touched True Self, then every time we do this chant, it carries the memory of all the times we have chanted it before. When I am teaching in new places, I do lots of different chants, but in my inner circle I always use just three or four, I don't switch them, even though I grew up with some 500 chants. Sometimes we do new ones, because it's also delightful to make love to new people, but the real depth is in the person who holds the memory with you.

Dyad Practice: chanting Om Namah Shivaya to each other

Now you find a partner and sit in dyads, in pairs of two, to be ready for the next chant, which will be Om Namah Shivaya. And we keep Silence of Presence, meaning we move around without talking, without making any sound.

The person with the longer hair is going to chant first. They are going to worship the Goddess of Devotion, and the person with the short hair is going to be the Goddess. The key to this practice is to reclaim the holy art of giving and receiving devotion. We always think that if we're devoted to someone, they must be taking advantage of me: "Oh my God, maybe I am co-dependent." We are so confused; of course there is something called co-dependency, but it is much overstated.

Devotion is a big deal, devotion is about "I am totally devoted to you. It's not just that I love you, but I am so devoted to your emergence, to your goodness, that I want you to feel good." Devotion is in the details, it is when someone takes care of you, makes sure you have food, that things are okay and you got a shaver, your clothes are okay. That is devotion, it is not being taken advantage of. To serve with devotion is so awesome, it's to send a little text to make sure somebody is okay; it's the great, wild desire to serve. The Force, the Source of all existence serves existence with devotion, feeding existence in every moment, making a billion billion moments of delight in service to a billion billion beings, available in every second — that is devotion.

To be devoted to each other is such a big deal. We have lost the art of devotion, and we've also lost the art of receiving devotion, when we are actually sitting back and say: "Wow, my friend is like totally devoted to me, wow." We don't think we are worthy to have anyone be devoted to us, we don't think someone is going to come for two weeks just to turn our world around, to make it work so that it will be good for us. That is devotion.

So we are going to chant 'Om Namah Shivaya', and then at some point you replace the name Shivaya, Lord Shiva, the God of the All, with the name of the person you are doing the exercise with, because you realize that this person is a total incarnation of Shiva and Shakti.

And you think that the easy part is when you are being chanted to — no problem, just sit back and hang out and it's done. But it's not so easy. If you receive the devotion from the place of ego, it has no effect. You have to receive devotion from the place of your God/Goddess. When I tell someone to write me an email every day, I am saying: "I am going to read your email every day, because I'm devoted to you." Whether you are giving devotion or receiving devotion, it's the same thing; it's both utter devotion.

Rumi was not a philosopher, though he was a philosopher also, and Rumi was not a meditator, though he meditated as well; Rumi was not doing Satsang, though maybe he did a little, but that's not what he was about. Rumi was about utter devotion to the Beloved.

Introducing a colleague dharma teacher (Coleman Barks)

I'll tell you guys a little story. There's a man named Coleman Barks who translates Rumi. I invited him to come and hang out with us at the Integral Spiritual Experience, which doesn't exist anymore, but had a couple of beautiful years. We'd never met and Coleman thought: "Well, I'm coming to do a gig and give a little talk." And Coleman is total devotion. He's really wise, he's discerning, he's smart, and he is really all about devotion. So before introducing him, I spoke to him backstage. And the reason I did the introductions was because I felt that when teachers introduce other teachers, they are often afraid to really love them, because their ego is so often in the way. They think: "If I introduce this person who is so great, then maybe I'm a little less," but that's not the way to introduce someone.

When you introduce someone who is about to give a Dharma talk, you've got to give them total devotion, you've got to totally love them, by introducing them with the most beautiful and accurate words. You open their heart because they receive your devotion, like the Goddess who receives our devotion and so becomes more powerful, more alive and more Goddess, because of our devotion. So I pulled him backstage for maybe five minutes and said: "Tell me about yourself." And I felt I totally opened my heart and received them both, for he was there with David Darling, a great cellist, and when I introduced them I did it with total love and they knew it.

After this gorgeous, beautiful evening was over, I said: "Hey Coleman, let's go to the holy taverns and drink wine," and of course at the place where we were gathered there was no holy tavern, there was no wine, but it didn't matter. We all went into the lobby of one of the guest houses with Coleman and a bunch of other people, and for some hours we drank wine and all of us told holy stories with total devotion to each other. That's devotion, that's love before creation, which is just awesome, so awesome.

The mystery of Tzimtzum: the secret of contraction

There's a mystery in Kabbalah called the Mystery of Tzimtzum, meaning 'contraction'. The mystery is: "If God is the source of Essence and God is everywhere and Essence is all, then where is there room for me?" Do you understand the question? If Essence is everything and it's everywhere and it's totally real, more real than real, more solid than a concrete block, more physical than the physical, not less, the most real, substantial thing that could ever be — if Essence is All in everything and infinite, then where is there room for me? I am fragile, an imperfect vessel for the light and I make mistakes, so where do I exist? Does everybody understand the question? It's the question the mystics ask. It isn't a logical question, it's a mystical question. I can taste the infinite, divinity, Source, Essence, everywhere, totally, but then, how can I exist? Where am I?

The holy mystics of Kaballah call this 'Sod Ha Tzimtzum', the secret of contraction. The secret is that when you love someone so very much, with the love before creation, then even if you take up all the space, there's always space for them, too. Even if there are 50.000 people in the room, there's room for everybody to bow down in full prostration on the floor, which is what is said about the Temple of Jerusalem, which was only so big. But it was the Holy of Holies, a place of the love before creation, so in the courtyard of the temple, where pilgrims would come on the Day of Atonement, at some point they would bow down in ecstatic prostration, stretched out on the ground, and there'd be room for every single person. They say it was a miracle, but really it was just the love before creation. The love after creation says: "Is there room for both of us? How can we both get our needs met? Am I in the board, am I not in the board? I'm a busy man, what's my work, what's my status, what's my position?" That's the love after creation.

And the love before creation comes through for everybody. Everybody has their exact right place, everybody can stretch out, everybody can do what they do and there is room for everyone. Because when I love you with the love before creation, I take up all my space and you give me all mine, and at the very same moment,

I step back and give it all to you and there is no contradiction, you see that? At the level of separate self, there is conflict between two people, but at the level of True Self, there is no contradiction. It's love before creation, and that's where devotion comes from.

Love after creation doesn't understand devotion. Modern psychology says: "Co-dependence is terrible," and sometimes it can be that and of course that's not so good. The love after creation says: "Well, I'll be devoted if I find someone I fall in love with. Why would I be devoted if I am not in love?" But making love before creation is: "Things are good, I'm so filled with devotion, give me someone to be devoted to." Of course I know that you need the love before creation AND the love after creation; I know that. But you can't do without the love before creation.

About Ted Wilson, founder of Venwoude

I'm going to tell you guys a little secret about Ted*, okay? You think you know Ted because you were with him, right? But sometimes I think that today, people love Ted with the love after creation. You know what I mean? "Ted who? Oh yeah, right, actually he's great, he's the founder and he brought me here, but things are so complicated, right?"

And I'll tell you a secret: I love Ted with the love before creation. I am madly in love with him and he is madly in love with me and we talk to each other, and he said to me: "Marc, go work on Venwoude. They are great, beautiful, awesome people, and I want you to love them with the love before creation." I saw the look on his face when he was talking to me and I could cry now. He said to me: "Now sometimes it's as if they love me only with the love after creation." And I said to him: "No Ted, they really have it in their hearts, they didn't forget," and then I promised that if I can, I'll remind my friends: Let's love Ted with the love before creation. It doesn't matter if the public position is here or there. Remember? Remember when you were with him? Was he perfect? No, we are all imperfect vessels, but he loved with the love before creation. He was my tall brother.

So I'm going to dedicate this next practice to Ted, my holy brother. I totally, totally love you with the love before creation, totally love your holy manifestation, your wild, crazy, ecstatic manifestation, your refusal to compromise, your refusal to love only with love after creation. Om Namah Ted! We don't talk about that so much these days, right? We have these other teachers, like Marc Gafni. Marc is awesome, I love Marc, he is fucking awesome. Then Miranda (McPherson) comes, that was great, and Diane (Hamilton) comes sometimes, and JunPo, who is totally beautiful. And Ted was the guy who founded the place, you know, Ted is with us. We don't want to be a place where we are just worshipping the teacher who died, that's not our style, but we want to love Ted with love before creation.

I'll tell you another little secret, okay? It will blow your heart open. Ted is trying to go on a journey, he is trying to get to the next place; he's been doing it for a few years. And he can only go to that level if we love him with love before creation. It's the love that breaks all the vessels. Is it dangerous? Of course it is. Why wouldn't it be?

Here is the crazy thing, right? Ted and I are soul-root brothers, we know each other through the soul's world. I never met him, but three weeks ago, when I came to Venwoude, I made a decision, I said: "I've got to meet Ted!" And so I went to meet him and we talked to each other, just for like five minutes and we totally knew each other. And we are talking now, it's a new thing, it's a new conversation. We totally fell in love with each other, it was awesome. He likes to try everything. I told him I wouldn't sleep with him, but he's still trying. J

We've totally got to love Ted with the love before creation, because that's how he loved you, that's how he loved me, that's devotion, whatever his human shortcomings may have been. Now, I'm going to do this practice with Ted, who is going to be my partner.

Can I tell you a secret? You think I'm kidding, you think this teacher is being metaphorical, this teacher's thing is a metaphor. But here is the secret: I'm not kidding. See, in the love after creation, there are boundaries. With the love before creation, as I said before, there's no split between atoms and cells; cells are alive and atoms are alive also, so the split between life and not-life disappears. This is the same thing: if I am loving Ted with the love after creation, then when he dies and I am alive, I can't find him. So when I said that I am going to do this with Ted, you say: "Ha ha, that's funny." That's because you are listening with ears of the love after creation, but if you listen with the ears of the love before creation, you will realize that I probably mean it, it's not a joke, a metaphor, or a symbol. It's simply true that there is no split. From the love before creation, I'm inviting Ted, right now in this moment, to do this chant with me. And he just said yes. If he'd said no, I'd feel the no, but he said yes.

CHANT

Let's come together again and go around the circle. How many people in the room actually met Ted, were with Ted at some point? And how many never met Ted? Okay, good. I just want to say something about it now for a second.

Group exploration: The Three Stations of Love in families

You're in a family, we all come from a family. Now, you have three levels of relationships to your family. The first level is that you're identified with your family. 'Me and my family', that's who I am. You're five years old, you may know your name but you don't exist independently from your family. Let's illustrate this.

(ADDRESSING A PARTICIPANT)

Marc: Who is in your family?
Participant: My mother and my father, and my brother.

Marc: So there's three besides you, right? So you're six years old and this is your family. When you're six years old you can't think about yourself independently of your family, because in terms of developmental consciousness, you're completely identified with your family. Now at some point in your life - and you're going to tell us when, okay? – you were able for the first time to think about yourself, independently of your family. So try and find when that happened, just think about it and wait till you find it. Can you find it?

P: No.

Marc: It's like the first memory you have of yourself independently of your family. Oh my God, maybe it was the day that you shot your mother.

P: I think it's when I was seven or so. I've got this memory of when my parents separated and my father left the house.

Marc: Did that touch everyone's heart like it just got right into mine? So at seven years old, all of a sudden the thing that was called a family didn't exist the same way any longer. This was something that you thought was forever, and all of sudden it's not there, so for the first time something in you experiences itself as separate from that womb that holds you.

And all of us have a moment where we dis-identify with our family. The first level is identification, I'm part of the family system, and the second level is dis-identification, not being part of it anymore, and the dis-identification can take a long time. I can be living in Venwoude and my family is saying: "What are you doing there?" and I'm saying: "Well, I love you a lot, but actually, this is what I'm doing and I'm not identified with you any more, I've dis-identified, so I can make this decision even if you don't agree with it."

Now every healthy child has to dis-identify with the family system, but at some point, inside your heart and soul, you have to re-identify with the family. This does not mean that you go back to being six years old, it doesn't mean that you follow your parents' instructions, it doesn't mean that you don't hold on to your own individual identity, but at some point you have to go back and actually realize: "This is where I came from," and have gratitude for that, be deeply grateful for any gifts that I received, and actually locate myself in that family. So for some people that means they'll really get involved in the family again and for other people it means: "I'm not going to be really involved, but you're totally in my heart. I relocated myself in the family, I'm no longer in the war." That's level 3, reintegration.

So in the Three Stations of Love, station 1 is submission: I have submitted to being part of the family system, I'm not separate at all. Level 2 is separation, dis-identification: "Mom and dad are separated, what does that mean? I've got to dis-identify, in order to survive." Then at some point, whenever it is, I get to level 3: in my heart there is something that integrates, I re-identify. I don't go back to level 1, for this is something else, a higher level.

The Three Stations of Love in teacher-student relationships

And it's the same when being with a strong teacher. On level 1, you give them your heart, just as when so many of you went to Ven-woude even before it existed. You said: "I need someone, I'm going to give you everything. I'll be with this strong teacher and I'll give you my total heart." And I can tell you a secret: you should! You don't want to NOT fall in love; of course you want to fall in love. And then at some point, even when the teacher's alive, or sometimes when the teacher dies, you separate. There's issues coming up, it's complicated, it's not easy; I've got to claim myself, I'm going to find my own voice, and so I separate.

So ten years ago, Venwoude is Ted, Ted is strong, and there are some great people rallying him. Then Ted dies, you separate and all this stuff comes up. Whenever you would talk to Ted about it, he would somehow push it aside, but now it all comes up, because he's not there to push it aside anymore. So that's separation. Is that holy? Of course it is. Is that part of love? Of course it is. It's the level-2 love of separation, dis-identification: I'm independent, I'm strong.

But in order to be a holy lover, I also have to go to level 3. And level 3 is called 'hamtaka', or sweetness. I don't go back to level 1, I'm not in submission, but I fall in love again from a different place. I fall in love knowing all the imperfections, all the limitations, I fall in love not by losing myself, but by finding myself.

So when you fall in love with the teacher for the first time, you fall in love after creation; that's the funny thing. Because you need the teacher, he is giving you something, an anchor, direction, guidance, it's fantastic, beautiful. But then, at some point, you have got to fall out of love, to see that he or she is flawed, imperfect, a little bit broken, what can you do, right?

Well, there's actually two things you can do. You either get rid of your teacher, or you fall in love again with the love before creation.

You receive everything, you are a total student, and at the same time you're with your teacher and you're receiving your teacher in his greatness AND his brokenness. That's so deep. You totally love someone and you can't believe they just smashed you on the head. So you can walk away or you can keep loving them, no matter what. Love after the creation walks away, love before creation practices patience and works it out.

So for Venwoude, I want to say something with holy audacity. We have to love Ted with the love before creation. I realized this when I left Venwoude last time - it just all of a sudden hit me. Other than at the dining room table or here and there once in a while, basically I don't hear Ted's name here very often. So I asked Chahat: "Will you introduce me to Ted?" And she said: "Sure," and she just introduced me. I didn't know what to tell him and we went for a walk in the woods and I just saw how sad he was and we talked about it.

He doesn't want the love after creation, he doesn't need big pictures of Ted in the hall in worship of the dead guru. That's kind of boring, we are not about that. We are about economy, strength, taking control, we are in this new era, finding our voice. That's what we should be doing, but in a healthy way, in a way that is holy. You've got to find Ted again and love him in your heart with the love before creation.

Practice: Holding hands with the love before creation

When we're living from True Self, we're living in the love before creation, and when we're identified with separate self, our love is the love after creation. Feel into what it feels like when you hold hands with someone with the love after creation. It's nice, it feels good. But when you hold hands with someone with the love before creation, oh my God, there is nothing like it, right? It's so beyond anything else.

So now, hold hands with the love before creation. No one is outside of the circle, and bring it to a place where the only thing you hear talking is the hands, and let Ted join hands with us with the love before creation.

I'm going to invite anyone in the room to bring in someone in your life that you haven't been able to find lately. Maybe they died, maybe they passed away, maybe it is a parent, maybe it's a lover, and in this moment, as our hands are held with the love before creation, you can find them and feel their hand in yours and your hand in theirs. Feel your hand so totally, wholly alive. The Temple is created with the hands of God, with the hands before creation. Actually feel it in your hands — my hands are aflame, burning up as the love before creation.

When we clap after someone speaks, we can clap with hands after creation and we can clap with hands before creation. It is the same when we shake hands with someone, or are singing a song or chanting. And sometimes, when a parent sees a child crying and the mother puts her hand against the child's head, sometimes the child keeps crying because they are hands after creation. When the child feels, it is the hand before creation, the child gets all sweet and serene and quiet; such is the difference.

The World is a Waiting Lover

Loving our way to Enlightenment

W*e are going* to Love our way to Enlightenment. People think they can meditate their way to Enlightenment, but I will tell you a secret: it doesn't work. You can be the best meditator in the world, but you will never wind up enlightened. The only way you can get to Enlightenment, is by Loving your way to Enlightenment. We are going to talk about that today, because it is the holiday of Passover, of Easter, both of which are big love holidays.

So we are going to go to the 'lineage' – do you know what I mean by the lineage? The lineage is the deep, inner source code of Spirit that is passed down by the great masters in a tradition, who enter into the inside of the Cosmos and reveal something of its true nature, and then pass down that revelation as an esoteric, sacred teaching, from generation to generation. In every generation it is practiced by the inner-circle students, who create a field which people like Sheldrake call 'morphic resonance', meaning a field of alive, awake loving, which has enacted and lived that secret teaching that is revealed.

When you go into this awake, alive, love legacy of the lineage, you step into the authority of Spirit, you step into the inner eye of Spirit, and you speak and you transmit, as I am transmitting and speaking and sharing with all of you beloveds now, not from the place of superficial self or of the conceptual mind, but from the inner, alive, awake, holy integrity place of the lineage. That's what I mean by the lineage.

So we will talk about love today, the love and lineage of Jesus, of Moses, of the shamans, of all the great traditions that are alive today in the world of spirituality, and World Spirituality is the new lineage that we are creating together.

Let's begin with chanting, because chanting is the way we live into love. Awake and stretch your bodies, and let's sit in silence for a moment, and then we chant.

[CHANT]

How do we love God, and how does God love us open?

What does it mean to know that the world is a waiting lover? What does it mean to know that the whole world, in its essence, is a lover, waiting to be loved open, and waiting to love you open? What does it mean at all? What does it mean to be a lover? In Aramaic it is said: "The small gathering of three beloveds gathered together and opened up the Cosmos, and it all depends on love." So what does that mean?

We have talked about love in different ways, and we are going to enact and be love in so many ways this summer, during our Summer Festival of Love. Now I just want to touch on one holy part of it, a big part, a huge, wild, incredible part. It is the teaching of how you make love to God, and how God makes love to you. That teaching is the essential teaching of Rumi, of Ibn Arabi, of the Chassidic masters, of the lineage of my master, the Baal Shem Tov, the Great Master of the Good Name, but all of these teachings have been lost.

Nowadays, you can read a poem by Rumi, but you don't really know how to do it. You can read a poem that points to it, but you don't really know what it means. It speaks to your heart, it sounds so awesome, but then, what do I do? They are like hints, directions, but we don't really know what it means, or how to do it.

The erotic merger with the Divine: *What the fuck?*

So I want to do a prayer today with you, a dharma, going into how you do it, what does it really mean? In Kabbalah, we call it 'Zivug', the erotic merger or the erotic fuck with the Divine. That's what Zivug means, and if you say it in Aramaic, it sounds a bit more relaxed, but we really don't know what it means, right? We don't know how to love God, how God loves us open, what it means to be fucked open by God.

We don't even know what the word 'fuck' means any more, we use it in so many crazy ways. You say: "Fuck you." What does that mean? "Go and have sex"? "Go and have sex and it should be bad, I curse you"? Or when we say to someone: "Go fuck off," what does that mean? "Go away and fuck with someone whose name is Off"? Or is it that we are fucking and I tell you to go off me because I don't like you?

We also make it into curse words: "You're a motherfucker." What does that mean? Is it that your mother fucks? Or do you fuck your mother? Or is it that you think your mother should never fuck again after she fucked and got you? It's so confusing. Or when we're really upset about something, we say: "Oh, fuck!" What does that mean?

Sometimes we use 'fuck' as a question: "What the fuck?" What does that mean? How I fuck, as in "What is my style of fucking?" Or maybe I need a sex education course? When we really get ecstatic, we say: "Fucking A!" What does that mean? "I'm so ecstatic that I'm going to have an orgasm"? Or "This idea is so good that it reminds me of that", or "I want to fuck my friend A"?

We're very confused about it all, and the reason we are so confused, is that it reflects the confusion we have over the whole sex thing. We technically know how to do it, but we don't know what it means, and that makes us uncomfortable, because we do know that it is really significant. We know that it is really important, we know that it is the place where we touch this world that is beyond our world. In sex, we touch something of essence, something that is ultimately important, and we are afraid that if we do it wrong, we're getting it all wrong. So we make it into a curse word, and use the word in ways that we don't even understand ourselves. If you sit and talk about it, you realize that it is a mystery.

God is fuck: opening up in sweet surrender, in three steps

So here is the teaching, a three-word teaching: "God is fuck." You could reverse it: "Fuck is God," but that's not it – it actually is "God is fuck." So what does that mean? Let's feel into it. What may it mean?

Not only is it true that God is fuck, but actually, in every moment that you live, you can either fuck the moment open to God, or die - die in the deadness of your daily life. So it means that there is a way to open up, a way to open up in sweet surrender. Let me give you three steps for this.

Step 1: Take it all in
The first step is: I take it all in, everything. No matter what it is, I don't deaden, anaesthetize, hide, deny or meditate it, I don't fall asleep to it. I take it all in and stay awake to it, as my major practice. I refuse to fall asleep, I take it all in. As I take it all in, I don't explain it, I don't write a book about it — well, maybe I will, I don't know — but you don't give a dharma talk about it, you just take it all in, and then, step 2, you sit with it.

So step 1 is: I take it all in, as love. I actually understand that everything that is happening, no matter what, is actually a love particle — a particle of living, awake Shakti, of living, awake Goodness, of living, awake raindrops, snowflake essences, real subatomic particles of love. No matter what is happening, it has a thousand billion skies, but underneath it all, I know it's the Beloved in the tavern, drunk with wine, wanting to pour himself into me. No matter what happens, I take it in, I take it all in, and I say: "Love, give me everything you have. Give it to me, everything. Bring it on, whatever you've got. All the beauty, ecstasy, goodness, limitation, brokenness, sweetness, chocolate and pain, I am going to take it in."

Step 2: Sit with it

Step 2 is that you sit with it. You sit in the joy of it and you sit in the hole of it, in love, and after you sit with it for 15-20 minutes, half an hour, you get to step 3, which is that you begin to fill up, with the natural, unique quality of your essence. You just sit in it, and then the natural, unique quality of your essence begins to fill up the hole, the unique expression of Love-Intelligence that is the unique quality of your being and becoming that holds it all.

Step 3: Coming home

And you begin to realize that everything you take in is exactly how it needed to be, that every rebellion, every rejection and every acceptance is how it needed to be, and that you are living your life exactly as it needed to be: fully awake, in spaciousness, and fully urgent at the same time. And you realize that you're home, that this is your story, this is your life, there's no place to go, and no place to get to.

As we said three meetings ago, it's not there, it's right here, right now. And you begin to awaken as love, you begin to be love in the world, you begin to experience what it means to be lived as love. And you get wet, you get hard, you get open, you get soft and you get excited, and you begin to engage each moment of life, and each moment of life begins to occur to you (occurring is a word from phenomenology), and it occurs to you as something awesome. Whatever it is, it's yours, and you engage it.

The brain is a repetition machine

Your old ways of being, your old thoughts and your old patterns live in your brain, and we know from neuroscience that your brain is a repetition machine. Your brain almost never had a new emotion, your brain almost never had a new thought. We know from neuroscience that your brain is already beginning to react to something before you are consciously aware of what its reaction is. Do you get that?

According to neuroscience experiments, you already totally get into action when something has happened, *before* you are even aware of what your brain has decided to do. That is because the brain just scans all the previous times that you had a similar encounter, and it decides, without you, how it will respond. Your brain actually collects snapshots of every situation that looks like other situations that you've ever encountered. It does a split-second, immediate gathering and integration of all the information, it compares this new situation with the old situation, and then it has you react in the exact same way.

So when something happens to you and you have to make a decision on how to react, the decision is made in your brain *before* you become aware of it. The decision is actually made about half a second or even a second before. And your brain is already making the moves to act out the decision before you're even aware that the decision has been made. So your awake, conscious mind isn't making the decision, but your brain, which is a repetition machine: it repeats exactly what you did the last time you encountered this particular situation.

Safe relationships and challenging relationships

Isn't that wild? You think you're awake, you think you're free, but you're actually asleep. Sometimes you see it really clearly in the world, when someone calls you and says: "I'm going out with this new guy," and starts to tell you about the new guy and it sounds really close to the old guy they've gone out with four times.

Usually, people go out with only two people in their whole life, or different versions of them: one is the person who totally challenges them and pushes their buttons. They're erotically attracted to them and want to fuck them open badly, they make them crazy and it's painful and they can't really work it out; that's Person 1. Then the other person is the person you're not really attracted to but they kind of feel safe, you feel safe with them: "I am not going to get hurt here." It's a little bit boring, he doesn't excite you, but it's kind of safe; that's Person 2.

So people spend most of their lives going out with new versions of Person 1 and Person 2. They keep doing the same thing, because they keep repeating the same pattern, unless they are willing to say that they recognize that yesterday is the biggest slave driver. The only idolatry is the idolatry of yesterday.

Awaken as love, breaking the patterns of the past

Basically you are a huge repetition machine, unless… unless you awaken as love, and then take each moment as your unique way of lovemaking that never was before. When you make the decision to live as love, then all is totally fresh and new. You actually begin to create your future, instead of reliving your past. You create your future by being a lover who is opening up to a new future and is not a slave of yesterday. Thanks to neuroplasticity, you create new neural patterns in your brain, which open you up to new possibilities for the future that you are creating in love, that never could have existed before.

If I'm willing to say that I'm going to step in and have life 'occur' to me differently, meaning I'm going to show up differently because I have decided to show up differently, then I create a new pattern in my mind and I break the neural patterns of yesterday. Thanks to the neuroplasticity of our brain, if I decide that I'm going to show up differently, I can stop living from the past, I can step out of the box of the past and create a new possibility. Then I can create a new future, a future that's not a repetition of yesterday.

I can actually awaken as love, willing to open myself up to the full possibility of love in this moment, to be a lover and to take in everything that's living in this moment. I'm going to take in what is, for real. I'm going to be completely penetrated by this moment and I'm going to penetrate this moment fully. I'm going to be the female and be fucked open by the moment and I'm also going to be the master and fuck the moment open in a way that I never did before.

If I access that quality of loving, that's the quality of a lover. "Why do you make love a second time? You already did it once. Do we really need to do this again? Come on, we do the same thing every time. You say this, I say that, then you do this and I do this, I mean, really!" No, it's not like that, is it? When we are really making love, it's totally new every time.

And I am going to awaken into this as a lover. I'm going to realize the infinite invitation and possibility that live in the eternity of this moment, awake and alive as love. It's love that opens the moment from the prison of yesterday; it's the only thing that does it. As long as you go into the world not awake as a lover, you are in the neurological mind prison of yesterday. We knew this from Rumi and Shams, and now we know it from neuroscience as well.

Love creates new reality

It's wild: literally 99.99 per cent of what you do is repeating yesterday. You keep doing it again, for as my master says: "It's all the rules that define your life," until you say: "Oh my God, I am going to awaken as love." Then I am becoming a particular expression of the awakened Love-Intelligence that was brought into being in this moment, which actually did not exist before. But love does exist, and I want you to hear this and bring this to heart: *Love creates new reality!*

That's what we mean in the mystical traditions when we say that the coming together of Shiva and Shakti, of the upper waters and the lower waters, in that moment of love, creates a new world. Love creates a baby, fuck creates a baby, and love and fuck are actually the same, meaning that on the inside of fuck, there is always love. It could be distorted love, it could be unconscious love, but fuck is always saying: "I am not alone, I am not by myself."

That's why fucking is not masturbation, because to fuck, you always need somebody else, something else, some other reality. Sometimes it's distorted, sometimes it's brutal, sometimes I'm so dead and unconscious that it becomes rape and that's horrible. Then you either sit in prison because you fucked up and have to atone for it - not okay!

But fuck always means: "I am connected to you." There is this meeting that's going to happen, and in this meeting, something new is going to be born, a new baby, a new creation. Every time people come together and they fuck, something new is created. It may not always be a physical baby, but something new is created in the world.

So if we want to break the existing patterns and we want to create a new future, a new possibility, you can only do it through fucking the moment open and letting the moment fuck you open, as lovers. There's no other way to do it. Fuck/love creates new reality, it creates new worlds. So the divine force makes love to the world every single moment and therefore breathes the world anew, afresh into existence. Nothing else does it. Everything else is repetition, everything else is being 'the living dead'.

You can be at Venwoude, in a spiritual setting, and you can still be the living dead in a spiritual community: you go through the same conversation, the same vulnerability, the same medicinal journey all the time, you keep doing the same things. But you are not really in love, you are just trying to program it. You go through the business or the spiritual journey, it's the same thing, it's not alive.

Daring to fall in love

The only thing that makes it come alive is to say: "I am going to fall in love." Then your ego says: "Don't fall in love. I'm going to lose myself, I won't be safe," and the brain goes back to the patterns of yesterday and says: "I've got to stay safe." Safe is about survival. The mid-brain is our old frame for survival, and survival means: "I can't do anything new, I have to stay safe. This is how I survived yesterday and this is how I'll survive today." This is the process of adaption, an apt response to evolution: to repeat the patters of yesterday.

But you realize that in order to create a new response, you've got to create a new moment. Because we are living in a new world where the old responses won't keep us safe, where the old traditions won't comfort us. The only thing that will comfort us is to fully open up, take everything in and give everything back, as a radically awake and alive lover. It's the only way to look. Don't look back, it's love or die. So you've got to be willing to fall in love!

I'm going to fall in love with everybody in the room, and I want you to fall in love with me. "Did he really say that?" Of course I want you to fall in love with me! Oh my God, that's the only way we can meet each other. But that doesn't give me authority over you — you are always going to be self-authoring. If you lose your own self-authority and you disappear, I can't love you. You've got to be you and I've got to be me for us to love each other.

But we do want to influence each other. What we normally do is: we stop, we don't allow ourselves to influence each other. "I'm not being influenced, no, not me. No, I've done that for a long time. I'll just take what I can, I'm not going to let him in, no way!" So let me make it really clear here: I want in! That's always what I am talking to you about: I want you in, I want to let you in. God is where you let her in.

My master, Mordechai Leiner of Izbica, asked his students: "Where is God?" And one student said: "God is in the vast spaciousness." He said: "No, no!" He asks another student: "Where is God?" And he said: "God is in the Holy Commandments." He said: "No, no. Where is God?" And one student said: "God is in Gaia, in the Earth, alive and awake." But he said: "No, no. God is where you let Him in."

You hear that, my friends? So I want in! You want to study with a teacher who doesn't want in? Don't hang out with me, man - I want in. Open up, I want to let you in. I don't want to stay the nice teacher, giving the Dharma from a closed place, to support my wounded ego because my mother did this or that to me. Which she did, and I love her. She is awesome, oh my God, my mother was awesome. She would walk in and I let her in.

We've got to let each other in. To let each other in is to open up to the infinity of this moment and feel the integrity of it, the authenticity of it, and to let the moment fuck me open, even as I fuck the moment open. God is fuck.

Fucking out of an impasse

I want to give you an image for it, an image from being in a relationship. If you have never been in a relationship, you can do it just as well - just imagine it.

You know how sometimes you are in an argument and you are in an impasse. It's been going on for a few weeks, you can't crack through, you are just on a level of consciousness where you can't find your truth. It's too stubborn, it's too sticky, it's too broken, there's too much at stake here. And you are afraid that if you compromise, or if you forgive or confess, you are going to lose yourself. And you just can't, you don't want to, you just can't do it. And your partner is in the exact same position. It's too sticky, too stuck, too complicated, too crazy. You just can't do it.

And then you find each other, and you kind of completely, insanely, wildly, roughly, softly make love, fuck each other open, and you do it in a way that is not escaping the problem. God is fuck, fuck is not God. You do it in such a way that in your love-making, in your awakening, you bring it all in, you bring everything inside, you are totally open, unguarded.

And when it's over, something shifted, something is softer, something is open. You find a way for the first couple of issues and you begin to talk to each other, because something has moved. You created a new reality, because you have broken the pattern of yesterday. Through neuroplasticity, you opened a new neural path of Love-Intelligence in your heart-body-mind, which charts a new path into the new future, to the new possibility of the relationship.

God is the possibility of possibility

I'm going to tell you a secret about me and Mukti. He asked me: "What's God?" Mukti used to be one of those religious, orthodox church-going guys, living the dogma, and I am just a freewheeling spiritual teacher. So here is what God is, in six words: *God is the possibility of possibility.*

God is the possibility of possibility, and the only thing that creates possibilities is love. When you're not in love, man, you just can't do it, it's just yesterday — all yesterday's patterns, programming, tapes and ego-defense mechanisms, all of yesterday's traps. In the labyrinth of yesterday, you can't find your way out. The only thing that allows you to find your way out of the labyrinth, after you fought to slay all the dragons, is Ariadne's thread, and then you'll be free from death. Ariadne leaves a thread for the hero, a thread of love, and if he follows that love, it opens the labyrinth, he can find the doorway. It means that you need to get out of the old patters.

The games of ego

Everybody is running a game, and that game is called ego. It's running the game of being really smart, funny, spiritual, or the broken one: of getting some sympathy. So I'm in the game of being the depressed one; that's my game, it's my racket. Now how do I let go of the game? How do I step out of the game and create new possibilities?

Put a mouse in a maze, put cheese at the end of the maze and put electric shocks in all the places where the mouse shouldn't go. It will take the mouse a couple of hours and a few shocks, but eventually the mouse will find the cheese. Human beings often keep going for the electric shocks. But we also like cheese, and that's love. Love is openness, love is to be open, love opens new possibilities. To be a lover is to be open. To stop being a lover is to be closed.

The Crucifixion at Easter, or
Tonglen: taking in the pain

That's what we are going to practice today: to be open. That's Easter. Easter means that I can be crucified — I am completely crucified, the nails have been driven into my body. "Jesus Christ Superstar, who are you and what is your sacrifice?" I am on the cross, and I am crying out: "Eli, Eli, lama sabachthani." Those are the words of the New Testament: "My God, my God, why have you forsaken me?" I am crucified and I'm taking it all in, all of the pain. I've done the Buddhist practice of Tonglen, taking in all of the pain, and I let the world fuck me — that's the practice in Tibetan Buddhism. Tonglen is getting fucked like a woman; that's the practice, the practice of crucifixion.

And then I move from Good Friday to Holy Saturday, and why do I know this as a rabbi? God knows — it's a funny world, okay? So, I move from Good Friday to Holy Saturday. Now Holy Saturday is to wait, it's the waiting, and the waiting is the teaching of staying in the hole. That's what Holy Saturday is: it's yesterday, staying in the hole, sitting there.

The first step is get fucked — God is fuck, let the world in, Tonglen, take it all in. Whatever you've got to give, give it to me, bring it on. Give me the beauty, the poignancy, the laughter and the pain, give me the betrayal. I am holding it, I'm not explaining it, I'm not rationalizing it, I'm not meditating on it, I'm not denying it, I'm not hiding from it, I'm not wallowing in it, I'm just taking it in. Step 1: Take it in.

Then step 2, Holy Saturday: It's just staying in the hole and waiting, waiting. And if you wait in it, what happens is that the natural, unique expression of your Love-Intelligence will awaken in you. The quality of the Unique Divine that is you, the unique Love-Intelligence that lives in you, as you and through you as love, will awaken in you. And love will open up the possibility into step 3, Easter Sunday: resurrection. You know, after some waiting, your life always looks different, and you embrace that new possibility through love.

Radical integrity: love as the opposite of power

I am delighted to be with you. It is happening. I am happy to be here and to fall in love with you. And if you don't want to fall in love with me, don't play with me. I want to fall in love with every single person the room, and let's dance! For me the only reason to be alive is to be Krishna and to dance with the milk maidens, make love in the unique way we want to make love, with every single person in the room. Maybe not in the physical realm, but to make love with every person in the room in that unique, special way we love to make love, and to receive from you that unique love that you have to give, which is different than any other. It opens up new possibilities of audacity, new possibilities of healing.

And to be in love, you've got to be in integrity, my friends - you can't be playing politics. If you're playing politics and you've got this explanation, then I'd feel betrayed and I couldn't bear it. People create such elaborate stories on why they are not really a lover. "We give a course of 10 weeks on the heart," how interesting. You write 10 books on love, how awesome. But to be a lover means not worrying about what they're going to say, how it's going to look. To be a lover is to have radical integrity.

Love and power are opposites. To be in love is to give up power over someone, and to give them their power back. To be a lover is to bracket the grasping ego and to serve, with radical and utter devotion, the emergence of someone, for real. To delight in her power absolutely, without thinking: "Oh my God, I am playing second fiddle here." No, you delight in each other's power, in each other's audacity. It is to listen deeply, to always hear both sides, and then to act in utter integrity and not to hide behind a level of psychodynamic babble, the betrayals of love.

To be in love is to feel in your toenails. When you are really a lover, your cock and your cunt are the same as your toe nails, no difference, same thing. It's all the same, you're open and you want to radically give. When you give to the moment and you want to receive everything that is to be received, you want to just stay in it, be in it, live in it.

Chant: "I Am Opening Up in Sweet Surrender"

So here is the chant. The words are:

"I am opening up in sweet surrender
to the luminous love light of the One."

Then the refrain is: *"I am opening, I am opening,"* four times.
Then part two: *"I am rising up like a phoenix from the fire."*

How do you rise up like a Phoenix from the fire? You take the possibility, and you've got to burn yesterday. Because as a lover, open, aflame, you are creating new realities; you are not being the repetition machine that repeats itself unconsciously all the time. You're creating a new reality, because you are a modality of the love that brings the Universe into existence in every moment. That is the great revelation of quantum mechanics, the great revelation of neuroplasticity, which is the revelation of love.

For me, that's what it is to a rise up like a Phoenix from the fire. The ashes themselves become the fertilizer that creates the new plant.

I am opening up in sweet surrender
to the luminous love light of the One
I am opening, I am opening
I am rising up like a Phoenix from the fire,
brothers and sisters, spread your wings and fly higher
I am rising up, I am rising up

This is the year of loving outrageously, because we are set in a world that's outrageously broken, and the only way to heal a world that is outrageously broken is to love outrageously, to open up as sweet surrender to the luminous love light of the One, to rise like a Phoenix from the fire towards the new possibility created by love, which creates the neuroplasticity that opens up to new plasticity, which creates a new reality, which in turn creates radical, wild, ecstatic openness.

God is lonely

I am going to tell you a holy crazy secret, which is: The Universe is lonely, which means that God is lonely and that God feels like a stranger in the land. Imagine going to a party where nobody says hello. Do you know how it is, to walk into a party and nobody says hello? You feel kind of strange and all of your insecurities of summer camp come online, and all of the stuff from your family system when you were embarrassed in public. You feel like a stranger.

I'm going to tell you a holy secret from the holy tradition, which says: "I am a stranger with you in the land." The holy mystics say that the Divine voice asks: "Won't you be a stranger with me?" If you will be a stranger with me together, then we'll be two weird people together and we won't be lonely anymore. We will create a new place for all the strange people, for God is a little bit of a nerd.

God says: "I write all these books and all this poetry; you can't even imagine what an awesome design person I am." God is waiting for that beautiful woman, who is a software engineer, and says to her: "My God, you are so beautiful, you are so fucking beautiful." Or maybe it was a beautiful man. So God is waiting for us to say: "Oh my God, I know you are a nerd, but you are really awesome. You are a stranger with me in the land."

To live is to move loneliness to loving. To be lonely is to be trapped in a skin-encapsulated ego, trapped into my limitation, my limiting beliefs, my old patterns. Then I open up and step into the full gorgeous possibility, not of where I was, but of what I may become, which is already here, in the present now.

And that's the whole story, that's what it means to fuck God open, to let God fuck you open, two strangers in a strange land together, who are creating a holy reunion of radical love and radical friendship. That's what Rumi and Shams were all about, that's what you and me are all about together, at least on this Sunday. We are talking not just to all of us in this room, but to the unseen choir. That's our audience: the unseen, nerd God, who is lonely, trapped in a Church that is distorted, wrapped in pain, misinterpreted, misunderstood, stolen, hijacked, fucked over in the worst way. And God says: "Please fuck me open, recognize me, kiss me, kiss this God frog and turn me into a prince. I stand behind all the detractions and distortions and false narratives of the skin-encapsulated ego, now make me open up through wild, ecstatic love."

Participant: Amen.

The meanings of 'Amen'

Now they will think we are fundamentalists, because of that 'amen', but we're not daft, we're cool. Oh my God, how ecstatic is that? We are going to say 'amen' to the things we really want to say amen to. We say amen to being open as love, to being holy, crazy, wild lovers, to loving outrageously. We are going to say amen to create new possibilities, to transform fundamentalism into a higher and real love.

"When the worst are full of passion and intensity, and the best lack all conviction, surely some revelation is at hand. Amen." And that is the revelation to be willing to stand up and say amen to new possibilities, amen to Venwoude, amen to new ways of love, amen to getting beyond the old limitations that shut down relationships because the ego is so afraid. Amen to love that wins over fear.

We don't even know what it means. Amen, in Hebrew, means 'omen', which is the nursing mother who offers her breast and says: "Suck my breast and know that I will never drop you." Wherever I fall, I fall into God's hands. I am sucking at the divine breast, I am sucking at the divine God, I'm sucking at the divine yoni, I'm sucking at the divine toe nail, it doesn't matter. The point is that I'm so inside, I'm so nourished, I'm so held, I'm so penetrated, I'm so open, and so I say amen, for amen is the experience of knowing that I'm not going drop you.

Amen, in Hebrew, means three things. It means 'sucking at the nursing breast', and it means 'practice' — 'imun' means practicing all the time, practicing opening every moment in sweet surrender, all the time. Because in that very moment, I make the decision if I'm going to close or open. It's the only decision you ever make in life: whether you close or open, and you've got to practice that decision time and again; that's the second meaning of 'amen'. The third meaning of amen is to trust: I trust that I will be all right, that it is going to be okay. I trust that you are not going to drop me, I trust that even though you see me in my narrowness, my brokenness, still you are not going away. Just know that I'm never going to abandon you, I'm never going to go away, amen.

Tonglen practice: breathing the particles of love

Here is a practice: sit up straight, back to back with your neighbor. Try to do it in holy silence. Feel that you are being supported by the other person. Find just the right balance between you. Sit up as straight as you can, back to back, and we will do the inner tantra practice of Tonglen.

First breathe in every particle of Shakti, every particle of love that's all around you, the quarks of love, which the inner eye of Spirit reveals and which no one believed existed, until they discovered subatomic particles. And these subatomic particles are moved by an inner Eros to join together, quarks joining together to form an atom. Because the quark itself is love, and it's allured, it is attracted, it comes together in higher embraces of recognition and union.

The ancient tradition said that there are particles of love that your eyes can't see, and you thought: What does that mean? And now you actually realize it's true: subatomic particles that are lured to each other, that are attracted by Eros to other particles of love, of which all of reality is made.

Now breathe and on the in-breath, breathe them in, and breathe them in again. Breathe the love particles, the subatomic particles of Eros, into your heart. Breathe them into your forehead, and breathe them into your cheeks, and breathe them into the cheeks of your butt, and bring them into your stomach. It is almost a way of dealing with an ulcer — bring the particles of love into your stomach, let them relax your stomach muscles.

Bring them into the back of your neck and let the shoulders drop, and bring them into the crown of your head and let you shoulders drop again. Bring them into your eyebrows, and bring them into your neck, your whole neck, and bring them into your upper chest, all those particles of love which are reality. Bring them into your upper back, and bring them into your lower back. Bring them into your yoni and your phallus, and bring them into your inner thighs. Bring them into your anus and let it slightly open, and bring them into your perineum. Bring them into your left leg, from the thigh to the knee, and then to your right leg from the thigh to the knee, and then to your left leg from the knee to the ankle, and into your right leg from the knee to the ankle. Open up to these subatomic particles of love, take it in, take everything in, into your ankles, into the soles of your feet.

And this time, as you breathe in, when you breathe out, breathe out your unique quality of Love-Intelligence which is your Unique Self, which takes in everything at the moment, all of the love particles, which is all of the joy and all of the pain, all of the broken heart and all of the heartache, all of the ache and all of the comfort, all of the ecstasy and all of the depression, because in the love particles is everything. Each one will be perfectly scooping up the new possibility, if you've created your future, which is occurring in the world as a new possibility.

So as you breathe in, breathe it in, and breathe it out, the you who encounters the world unlike anyone else, who encounters the world afresh and anew in every moment, for your Unique Self today is different than your Unique Self yesterday – that's the essence of your Unique Self. Yesterday's Unique Self is not your Unique Self, your Unique Self is only unique today. Let go of your past way of being, step into your current way of being as you're surprising God, who is

surprising the Universe in the radical delight of radical possibility,
and breathe it in and breathe it out.

Let the tantra of Tonglen cut your heart open. Take it in and fully
open, open your breast, open your thighs, open your phallus, open
your yoni, open your ass, open your eyebrows, open your toes, open
your hands, open your stomach, open your back. Take the world in
and feel the yearning you have to be venturing, the yearning you have
to be totally penetrated and fucked open by God, for God is fuck.

You take it in and don't solve, explain, hide or deny it, don't make
it up, spiritualize or rationalize it, just sit in it, with it, as it. Bring it
on, God, I'm here, take me, take me now.

Here I am, I am yours, do with me what you will

[SINGING]

Here I am, take me now, do with what you will. Here I am, I am
yours, do with me what you will. I am open, I surrender, my heart
is in your hands. Even if all is taken from me, in my voice your
heart is heard. Through the pain, you are with me, do with me
what you will. Here I am, I am yours, do with me what you will.
Rip me open, take me now, my heart is in your hands. Even if all
is taken from me, in my heart your voice is heard. Through the
pain, you will reach me, holding me in your love. Here I am, I am
yours, do with me what you will. Spread me open, take me now,
my heart is in your hands. Even if all is taken from me, in my heart
your voice is heard. From the pain, you will raise me, holding me
as your love.

And that is what I say to the Divine and All-that-is: Here I am, I'm yours, do with me what you will. Break me open, take me now, my heart is in your hands, and I sit in it, I sit in the hole. I sit in the hole and I let the hole fill up, as it always does, and then I realize that wherever I fall, I fall into God's hands. And I realize that even though everything is taken from me, in my heart your voice is heard. From the pain you will raise me, holding me as your love.

So take God in, take in the full infinity of the moment, breathe it in. Breathe in, and breathe out the unique receiving of your Unique Self.

The story of Krishna

We're going to finish with a holy story that I will read from my heart, from the mirror of the heart. It's the great story of the goddess Radah.

You know that many mortal women make love to Krishna, and Krishna is the sensuous God, the child, the lover. He was often caught stealing butter. He would walk among the villages in the hot, moist, Indian land, and he called the women to join him for an afternoon of lovemaking. Age didn't matter, the rolls of the stomach didn't matter, gray hair or black hair didn't matter, curve of the breast didn't matter, marital status didn't matter. Krishna loved all women and all men, and Krishna wanted to be loved in turn.

And any lover if they had any erotic curiosity at all, would answer the call. How could you possibly choose not to? And Krishna's alluring invitation to open up as love, would interrupt whatever their task happened to be at the moment: the mother might have been in the middle of preparing dinner for her children, the husband in the middle of his work, the young daughter in the middle of doing her school work, the old men sitting and reading, the old women writing some new chapter. Whoever they were, lawyers, gardeners, doctors, spiritual teachers, cooks, bottle washers, truck drivers, traders, they all felt Krishna's alluring invitation. (And this year we're going to love outrageously, we're going to bring the invitation of Krishna and we are going to be Krishna).

They felt the invitation of possibility, and they awoke. They smelled perfumed skin and fresh mangos. They heard bells tinkle, and felt long grasses tickle their legs. They experienced, maybe for the first time, the dark touch of the sun lighting up their dark, hidden places, that they had forgotten themselves. And suddenly, something that had once burned in them, something precious and bright, began to call them again. They remembered that it had been quite a while since they had thought about this elusive thing, and maybe even longer still since they tended to it, since they experienced that small shiver lightening up their spine.

They began to feel regret: How could I have forgotten that, and allowed it to fade? And they began to awaken, to answer the call of Krishna. The Gopi, the cowherd girl, left her animals browsing the hillside, and the obedient daughter paused and came to listen, and she stood and left the loom, turned and melting in the doorway, the servants set their spoons in their cooking pots, the mother walked past her children playing under the jasmine bush, the elder withdrew her thoughts and gathered up the hammock, all of them went off to the green slope, with flapping robes, where Krishna awaited them.

And there, my friends, and the only way that I want to come to you is as Krishna, and there the dance began. And the women raised their eyes, the men raised their eyes, and the sky twirled and laced their arms together and moved as winemakers, pressing out the luscious juices of the Cosmos. They danced with a band and Krishna danced among them, and at some point, they scarcely knew how to distinguish when it began, the God made love with each of them. With each and every one of them in the way they liked best. So intoxicating Krishna's touch, so attentive this presence, that each woman felt herself to be the full recipient of his passion, as did each man. Each woman, each man that he loved in that moment. Beloved of the Holy One and no jealousy existed.

And then it ended, after all, no one can remain for long in the embrace of a God. Waves of orgasm smoothed into ripples of contentment. Each woman and each man fluttered down from their ecstasy and recalled their humanness, and the God, lighthearted and lightfooted as ever, moved on. The women stood up, the men stood up, arranged sari's and trousers, and went back to their houses, their looms and work and duty. But they were not the same! They were transformed! From that day, from that moment forth, they listened with their whole being for the call of Krishna to summon them back into his Grace. And their yearning, their longing became a source of an exquisite, delightful torment, formed in them a hole, shaped like the Divine one himself, and able to be filled only by him, when they would sit in the hole long enough, the unique quality, configuration, texture and taste of their unique, gorgeous incandescent shimmering self, receiving everything the moment had to give, filled them up. And their yearning was fulfilled, even as they long.

The yearning, the lovemaking, had broken them open so utterly, that they found they remained open expectantly, like a clay urn just before it's dipped into a rushing stream. Every experience of prayer, every gesture, every piece of business, of relationship that passed through them, molded to the longing that shaped the unique quality of their embrace by Krishna. Every act they undertook became a beauty and readied them for the next encounter with Krishna.

And thus they began to walk in the world as one walks into the arms of a waiting lover.

Walk in the world as if walking into the arms of a waiting lover

This is the year of loving outrageously. So gently, I finish by asking your forgiveness, because I'm sure that something I said, or maybe the tone of my voice in a particular moment, wasn't clear enough for you or wasn't pure enough for you. I ask forgiveness for that. I do my best, and I'm sure I fail a thousand times, I'm sure I make mistakes. But I promise you, with all my heart and soul, that I am trying to make mistakes in the right direction, and to give you the transmission in the most pure and clear way I can.

And I love you, every single person in the room, whether or not we know each other's name, or have met. I know who you are, and you know who I am. I look forward to meet all of you in person and embrace you in person; some I will see again, maybe one or two people for the first time.

Do you think you are going back into reality, when we finish in a minute? This is reality. Take it with you. Walk into the world knowing that in every minute, you walk into the arms of the waiting lover. Let every moment fuck you open to God, fuck every moment open to God. God is a stranger in the land, you're a stranger in the land, I'm a stranger in the land. Together, we liberate each other from loneliness to loving, and we create a new possibility and a new future of evolutionary consciousness that we, and the world that is us, desperately yearn for.

And it's already here, it's already so, as we loved each other today.

Amen.

Woundology: Ten Steps to Approach Your Wounds

Our wounds as obstacles to love and Enlightenment

I think it's so important that we talk about wounds, for what's in the way of my love is always my wounds, my unique hurt. What do we do with that? How do we work around that, walk through that? Because everybody is wounded, there's nobody in the world that's not. We've all been hurt, and we've probably all hurt others, too. In some way we all have been betrayed by life, or by a person who did the unexpected. Maybe my body betrayed me, maybe my finance has betrayed me, maybe my friends, maybe I betrayed myself. And that leaves a scar, leaves a wound. So what do we do with the wounds?

I will share with you the Ten Wisdoms of Woundology. Now each one of these is a big practice, you could do an entire retreat working through people's wounds and letting them go, doing practices for each step. So this is a cash dharma talk, we go very quickly, but all of these steps live together, and you've got to have them in your heart, in your cells, otherwise you can never get to Enlightenment because you always get lost in your wounds.

And anybody who works with people, teachers, counselors, coaches, therapists: use these wisdoms with your students, your clients.

The Ten Wisdoms of Woundology

Step 1: Working with your wounds directly

The first approach is that we actually work with our wounds directly. That's really important to say. Here in Venwoude, we have Emotional Bodywork, which you all do so well, which Ted thought was so important, and it is. It means that you actually recognize the wound, dramatize the wound and start excavating, like in archeology. You go inside and you feel it, and you feel it again, you tell the story and you work on releasing it, which can be done in many ways. That's always the first step, and that's important. In this way, you do the work, and that's awesome. You can't skip this step, you can never skip it.

Yet the problem is that most people spend their entire life (are you ready for this?) addicted to this level. They play a very clever game, and I'm sure you all know what I'm talking about. You can actually really be doing the work, or you can have an addiction to working with your wounds. It's a new form of addiction, you just love telling the story and would love to do some more work on it. "Let me just tell it to you one more time, and in case you get bored, I'll just tell the story again. Did I ever tell you the story of what really happened?" And then you look for new friends, new people to tell the story to. You keep your therapist for 6 months, and then you switch therapists because you get a new person to tell the story to.

So you need to do the work, but you have to be careful not to get addicted to this step. We've basically got lost in Woundology, you can earn doctorates in Woundology. This is Dr. Marc; "What are you doctor in, sir?" "Woundology." "Whose wounds?" "My own, I love them."

Wounds are very seductive, for a lot of reasons:
they are about your favorite subject: YOU!
when you really go into them, you *feel*.
because you earn everybody's sympathy and attention.

You get a lot of attention and energy telling about your wounds and being a victim. You actually get a sense of power from it. So beware of the shadow of step one, which is getting addicted. You've got to do it, and you've got to do it more than once, but you don't have to do it a thousand times.

Step 2: Hurt is a passing state

A state, in psychology, means that something happens to me that lasts for a while, gets very intense, and then goes away. So an orgasm is a state, being high is a state, being drunk is state, grief is a state, and for most people, a glimpse of enlightened consciousness is a state. So a state happens, it gets intense, it fades and it goes away, and then what people usually call their 'normal consciousness' comes back in. Now here's what's unbelievably, insanely important about a state: *all states require interpretation*. We give them meaning, we make meaning out of the state, but we don't know that we're making meaning out of the state; we think the state has meaning by itself. And our interpretation depends directly on who we are, on our own level of consciousness, on our own psychological interiority inside us.

For example: the way you experience your sexuality has very little to do with what happens objectively and has everything to do with your interpretation. Except for rape or sex with very young minors, all other sex is interpretation. It's how you interpret it, how you read it, how you understand it; it's the meaning you make out of it. So the intensity of a sexual encounter is a state, but how you interpret what happened, that's yours, that's your freedom, that's your responsibility, that's your joy, that's your delight, and it depends in a very large measure on your stage or level of consciousness.

Here's another way to say it: hurt is just what it is, a state, and our life is what we do with our hurt. Now we have to interpret that state, and if I interpret it to mean that I'm brutalized, destroyed and abused, and for the rest of my life I've got to work with that abuse, well, that's my interpretation. You got that? That's not what happened, that's my interpretation. I'm going to tell you something really radical, kind of provocative, but it's really helpful to hear.

I have a well-known friend, a teacher in America, a very deep man, who was telling me this a few years ago: "When I was 11 years old, maybe 12, my teacher really liked me and started fooling around with me sexually." And my friend Diane said: "Oh my God, that's terrible. That must have been terrible." And this guy looks at Diane and says: "No, it was awesome!" That's a crazy story. Now, let me be very clear, teachers should not be fooling around with their 12-year-old students, that's obviously wrong, and that's not the point. The point is that he chose to interpret it in a particular way. He could have chosen, ten years later, to say: "Oh my God, this terrible thing happened to me, I've got to work with it for the next 50 years, and maybe sue some people on the way. I'll just stay stuck in the hurt of that moment."

And you know, for many people, a moment like that is legitimately hurtful, that's real, but the way you interpret the story changes everything, and the power of interpretation lies with you. And here's the deal: however you interpreted it yesterday, you get to interpret it in a new way today. The power of interpretation never leaves you. Today, right now, you can interpret the story differently.

Step 3: Don't cry more than it hurts

Once upon a time there was a King whose son was crying, crying, crying, and then crying some more. The King got all the master therapists and Gestalt workers and Emotional-Bodywork people and wizards and doctors and psychiatrists and pharmacologists plus sixteen spiritual teachers, and each one of them came to work with the son of the King to try and help him to stop this crazy, all-the-time bitter crying. And every one of them failed. None of them could quite do it, and the King was beside himself, he was just devastated. This is his son, the heir of his throne, his successor, and he is literally a cry-baby. He can't stop crying, ever.

Then a great master, an old woman, wandered to the King's court and said to the guards: "Tell the King I'm an old woman and I heard his son is crying, and I think I can help him." And the guards said: "Who are you, you have no credentials, you haven't written any books, how can you possibly work with the King's son? Everybody else tried, everybody else failed. He's done every training in the world." The woman said: "I understand, but please, tell the King I'm here and I'd like to help." So they told the King, and the King said: "You don't have any credentials, you seem to have no training, no degrees, you've written no books, but I'm desperate. I give you half an hour with my son." "I don't need half an hour," said the old woman, "I just need five minutes."

So she went in and sat for about four minutes with the son, who was crying. Then she whispered something in the son's ear, got up and walked out. And about a half hour later, the crying got a little less intense. Another half hour later, it got a little bit lower, and another half hour later it was much quieter. Within three hours, the King's son had stopped crying. And everyone wanted to know what the old woman said to the King's son, but she's disappeared. So they gathered round the King's son and asked him: "What did she say, what did she say?" The King's son looked at them and said: "She said to me: 'Don't cry more than it hurts.'"

And we all know what that means. We use our tears, we use our wounds to give us identity, to gain attention. They give us fullness, we use our wounds in a thousand ways. Don't cry more than it hurts. Cry in the right proportion. Don't dance after the music's gone.

Step 4: Stop it

You saw it in the Bob Newhart video that you sometimes play at Venwoude, where he says: "Get off it," which means: just stop it, it's enough. Now remember, you've done the deep work already; this is not to skip the deep work, you need all of that. So the order of these steps is important, and this is step 4: Get off it! And the way you can do that, is to ask some questions, satsang questions. A teacher friend of mine, a lovely woman named Byron Katie, came up with these questions, which are really simple: Is it true? Can you really be sure that it's true? Who would you be without that thought? And then you turn it around.

And the way I'm going to say it is: Is it true that it hurts that much? Is it really true that it hurts that much? Who would you be if you gave up that hurt? And then you turn it around: Where's the place, not where you were hurt, but where you were the person hurting. Wow.

Now, my friend Byron Katie goes really far. She actually asks these questions of people who come before her and tell her: "I was raped by my uncle five times, and I'm like dead inside, it's horrible, I can't do anything, I'm just in trauma, it's so painful." So Byron Katie looks at the woman that's raped, or the man, and says: "Is it true? Is it really true that it hurts so much? Who would you be if you gave up that hurt?" That takes a lot of chutzpah, to talk to a person who really got brutalized and then say: "Is it true? Is it true that it hurts that much, is it really true?" Now, here's the deal: it might have hurt that much then, but does it really hurt that much now? Or is it a way of filling yourself up with the hurt, because you haven't actually found something else to fill yourself up with and so you fill yourself up with pseudo-Eros, pretend-Eros, because you can't find real Eros.

Step 5: Bring it to the Mother

Bring it to the altar, bring it to God. Image a woman carrying a heavy suitcase. She gets on the train and keeps carrying her heavy suitcase, she won't put it down. And the conductor of the train says: "Don't you understand, you can put it down." And she says: "I can't put it down, who's going to carry it?" And the conductor says: "Just put it down, it's going to be okay," and she says: "No, I can't put it down. If I put it down, it'll get lost! Something is going to happen." And she doesn't understand that she can just put it down and the train is going to carry it.

That's a famous story, everyone's heard that story, just like the famous story of the man walking on the beach, leaving footprints in the sand. When he looks back, he sees a second pair of footprints next to his, and he knows they are God's footprints, for he hears God's voice and God is walking right next to him. But then a crisis happens, a tragedy strikes, something goes really bad and he looks for God's help, but suddenly there's no second set of footprints on the beach, only one. So he's devastated. "God, how could you abandon me, how could you leave me at this time, when I needed you so much? I don't see your footprints next to mine, you're gone." And God says: "My dear son, you see only one set of footprints, because I'm carrying you on my shoulders; those footprints are mine."

Wow, that's to bring it to the Mother. She can carry it, let the suit-case go, and she carries *you* as well.

[SINGING]

The river is flowing, flowing and flowing
The river is flowing, back to the sea
Mother, Mother, carry me, your child I will always be
Mother, Mother, carry me, back to the sea.

Let go of your wounds, put them in the arms of the Mother. That's what Rumi is all about, that's what the great Sufi mystics are all about: bringing your wounds into the arms of the Mother.

Step 6: The barroom view of love

Step 6 is to apply the barroom view of love. 'Barroom' meaning a pub, not a fancy bar, just a simple bar with a pool table and tough guys hanging out. I'm going to read you a poem by Hafiz, called 'A Barroom View of Love'.

I would not want all my words
To parade around this world
In pretty costumes,

So I will tell you something
Of the Barroom view of Love.

Love is grabbing hold of the Great Lion's mane
And wrestling and rolling deep into Existence

While the Beloved gets rough
And begins to maul you alive.

True Love, my dear,
Is putting an ironclad grip upon

The soft, swollen balls
Of a Divine Rogue Elephant

And
Not having the good fortune to Die!

So what is this about? Love is not like all those sweet, candy-phrase love songs, for love is not simple. Love and pain always come together, there IS no love without wounding. And that's written by Hafiz, the love poet. He's saying: "My friend, don't worry so much about the wounds." Actually, love and pain are always together, just like love and joy, and love and ecstasy, but love is also painful. And you've got to be willing to hold the pain, if you want to get the love. Remember Simon and Garfunkel in the late sixties: "I am a rock, I am an island, 'cause a rock feels no pain, and an island never cries."

Love and pain come together, and to know that, just knowing that deeply, that's the way of the world, then you know that it's okay. As if you're in a relationship, and it's painful, and you say: "Man, it shouldn't be that painful," but actually it should be. It's painful sometimes. And you have got to be able to walk through the pain and hold the pain, and not run away when it gets painful.

There's a man in the Bible named Noah, who built an ark, remember him? Mr Noah, right, married to Mrs Noah, and they have great sex. Now here's the deal: the word 'noach' in Hebrew means 'comfort'. That's what the word means, so Noah is Mr Comfort. God says: "I'm going to destroy the world," and Noah says: "Okay, I'll build an ark." He forgets about the world, and he even imagines that he hears God commanding him to build an ark. But really, what he should do is crying out loud: "God, how can you destroy the world, you motherfucker?! I'm not going to let you do that, I love the world, I'm going to stand for the world." Instead, he builds a paper airplane, a big model ark and saves his own immediate world.

That's not good, it's not a good story. To actually be a lover, you have to be willing to let go of the comfort in order to get the pleasure, for pleasure always involves pain. So the 6th approach to wounds is to know that it's okay if it's painful sometimes. It's okay, it's actually part of being alive and feeling alive. When you're hurt, you know you're alive, and there's something glorious in being alive.

Step 7: The wounds of love

Step 7 we call 'the wounds of love', and it's really simple. Someone hurts you and you're insulted that they didn't take you seriously, that they don't think you're powerful enough, so they think they can hurt you. So you experience the hurt as an insult. "Oh my God, you insulted me!" And when someone insults me, I feel like they're saying that I don't exist and I don't matter. So how do people respond to an insult? They insult back, they hurt back, they hurt back in order to hear the other person scream, which reminds them that they're still alive, that they still exist. What a terrible way to be.

So usually, when a person is hurt, they feel that as an insult and it activates the cycle of rejection. You rejected me, and I'm going to reject you. "Really, you don't want to go out with me? You bitch, I never wanted to go out with you." And that's what we do. We might not do it that explicitly, but we do it all the time. We're going to make sure that we're never hurt and never rejected, because that's an insult, and that undermines my very feeling that I exist. So that's a tragedy, and that creates a circle of un-love.

We have to break the circle of un-love and re-invest it with love. And how do we do that? By experiencing the hurt not as an insult, but as the wounds of love: "I've been wounded in the great battle for love." And just like when you are in an army, you get an award for being in the battle for the right cause, the battle for the good. So I've been wounded in my great quest towards love, and that's okay, that's beautiful, that's good.

Take the hurt and don't let it devolve into insult, which activates the cycle of rejection; let it evolve into the wounds of love. I wear the wounds of love that are won so hardly in my journey and my battle for love, and I wear them proudly.

Step 8: Laughter

Laughter holds wounds. Hahaha, just cut my arm off, haha, cut my legs off. When you laugh, you hold it all, right? Laughter lets you hold it in a different way, laughter takes away some of the sting from the hurt, it nullifies the reality that's too difficult to deal with, and it lets you hold paradox, it lets you hold the strangeness of life.

Now we get to steps 9 and 10, which are the most important, but you need all of them to know how to melt your wounds.

Step 9: The magnet of Unique Self

Unique Self is what we call in physics a strange attractor, meaning that Unique Self is a magnet that pulls you to the Eros of your story, to the aliveness of your life, to the ecstasy of your particular dharma in the world, it invites you to the glory of your story. AND it demands that you respond to your unique response-ability, it demands that you take the unique risk of your life that's yours to take.

And when that is happening, when you're being pulled magnetically forward by the Eros of your Unique Self, your wounds take on much, much less significance. They just don't matter that much anymore, they're not that important, they're actually not that exciting to revisit time after time and again and again.

So your Unique Self pulls you magnetically out of your wounds. It's kind of awesome. Without Unique Self, you don't have the erotic Eros of your story, so you look for fake Eros, pseudo-Eros, and you find the pseudo-Eros in your woundology and your wounds. So to move beyond your wounds, you've got to actually live the Eros of your Unique Self, for your Unique Self draws you directly beyond your wounds.

Step 10: The context of the Great Story

Step 10 corresponds to the Fifth Awakening. It is to live life and feel yourself in an evolutionary context. It is to actually widen your lens to feel the 13,7 billion years that it took to bring us to this moment of time, to feel the wideness of the evolutionary context happening all over the world, and to feel your unique gifts that you have to give to this evolution. It is to widen your lens from the egocentric and ethnocentric to world-centric, to kosmoscentric. And kosmoscentric means that you feel evolution itself awakening and living, evolving through you. You see yourself in a larger framework, in the story of the great unfolding of the evolutionary revolution. When the story gets that big, your wounds, again, matter so much less. By creating and evoking a larger evolutionary context, you begin to play a larger game, and the wounds just don't matter that much.

None of these approaches is the whole story

Now is number 10 the right approach to wounds? No. Is number 9 the right approach? No. And of course it's all 'yes' as well: they're true, but partially so. They are all partially true. Everyone tries to take one of these and make it the whole story, but you actually have to use them all. And you have to teach yourself this and put it in your hart, and teach it to all the people you teach. These are the Ten Unique-Self Wisdoms of Woundology. They're not published any place yet, we'll publish them together. It's a big deal, for if you leave any one of these out, it doesn't work. If you bring them all together, you're awesome.

Writing Outrageous Love Letters

The Song of Songs, the Holy of Holies

*I*n *one* of our earlier Circle meetings, we said that the only response to a world of outrageous pain is outrageous love. In that Skype session we created the Society of Outrageous Lovers, so we are outrageous lovers, and we talked about what that means. And today, with your permission, I want to add a whole new dimension. For we're going to practice this, the practice of writing outrageous love letters.

I just want to share with you how this practice was born, what the practice really is. I think this is the first time that this esoteric teaching has ever really been shared in public, so I want to do it very gently, very slowly, very carefully. I offer a deep and profound prayer to the Goddess, to the Divine, to Source, that this should be clear and powerful, and should open up worlds.

There is a great sacred text called the Song of Songs, which is a collection of love letters. It happens to also be one of the 24 books of the Bible, but the people who put those books together really wanted to throw this one out, for it is not actually a story; it's a collection of love letters between a lover and a beloved.

"Let me be kissed by the kiss of your lips, for your secret garden, your love place, is more sweet to me than wine."
"Plant your flag in me, my love."
"The fragrance and the beauty of your breasts intoxicate my mind."

And it goes back and forth.

These love songs are written by King Solomon, the great lover of the Queen of Sheba, who takes a thousand wives, who brings images of the Goddess into the Temple in Jerusalem, and who is attacked in the Bible by the Biblical writers - "The feminine made corrupt his heart" — because the Bible wasn't yet ready for the fullness of Solomon's teaching.

The famous teacher Akiva, who was living in the time of Jesus, said: "All the books of the Bible are holy, but the Song of Songs is the holy of holies." More holy, more sacred even than the Ten Commandments. The holy of holies is the inside of the inside, the deepest of the deep, and if you want to find that place in consciousness where love is alive and aflame, the sacred centre of all existence, then you can find it in love letters. What a teaching!

Writing love letters wakes you up as love

You remember when we still used to write love letters? Some of us have never written love letters, others have written love letters maybe for a month. Remember that month, when you were 17 or

27, in the first heat, in the first flush of sexual love, writing wonderful bad poetry to someone? That awesome time?

How tragic it is that we have lost the awakened, enlightened capacity to write love letters, because the love letter is not so much even about the person receiving it. The person receiving it may be imperfect, but you are actually able to see that person through the eyes of God, and it opens up your eyes, it opens up your Eros and it opens your heart. When you become a writer of love letters, you awaken, aflame as Source, in powerful, audacious, sensual, radically alive, radically true, outrageous love.

So think what it means to be a writer of outrageous love letters, to do the spiritual practice of writing outrageous love letters. I began this practice about 20 years ago with a group of students, and then, truth be told, I forgot about it, but about a year ago I was reminded again of this practice, life brought it back to me, and I realized: "Oh my God, we've got to be writing outrageous love letters."

The world as God's outrageous love letter

Because what is the world if not God's outrageous love letter? What is the world itself, what is the Cosmos itself? The Cosmos itself IS a divine love letter. In an old sacred text, in Aramaic, the language of Jesus, it is said that God looked in his letter and created the world. And remember, the God you don't believe in, doesn't exist. We must always remind ourselves and each other that we are not talking about the God of the Church; we are talking about the God-Source initiating the Cosmos, the Love that gives birth to reality, the Evolutionary Love moving from simple to complex, to ever higher levels of consciousness in mutuality, recognition, embrace. The world is initiated, says John in the New Testament, by Logos, the word, and what is the word if not an outrageous love letter? God, Source, the Dao, Torah, the Word, is the outrageous love letter that initiates reality.

The Divine has fallen in love

The Divine Source is infinite and has no needs, for it is the absolute nature of perfection. Then why does this perfection reach out to someone else? Because it fell in love. You know what happens when you fall in love. Last week, you didn't know that person existed, you didn't even know their name. Then you meet them and you start talking and then, whenever it happens, sometimes after 10 years and sometimes after 10 minutes, you fall in love. And when you fall in love, all of a sudden your self-definition expands. It used to be just about me, but now I am 'me and you', my circle of identity has widened, my circle of care and compassion has expanded. There is no longer just I, there is WE, and you are part of me, you and me make we, and the miracle of We-space is created, by falling in love.

So when you fall in love, you say: I'm willing to limit my power to make room for you, I am willing to step back and allow you to choose, because I love you. I'm willing to bracket my own internal ego to support your evolution in growth, because I am madly in love with you. So the Divine, in the mystery of manifestation, in the mystery of the Big Bang, in the mystery of creation over billions of years, the Divine Source falls in love. And that falling in love is Logos, says John in the New Testament, it is the Word; it is

God who looked into the love letter and created the world. It is the Dao, it is the love letter that cannot be spoken, and that love letter creates the world.

An ancient, secret text in Kabbalah and in Christian hermeneutics, out of which the Da Vinci Code emerged, says that the entire world, all of Reality, are divine letters. And we know that is true. All of our knowledge attained in physics is encoded information of wisdom, love letters from God to us: dancing superstrings, quarks and particles, neurons — they are all dancing love letters initiating reality. All of reality is a love letter from God to us.

Every human being is a unique letter in the cosmic scroll

Let's go even further. In one sacred text it is written that every human being is a unique letter in the cosmic scroll, the cosmic story, the cosmic text. That means that every human being is a love letter, meaning that to live your Unique Self is to write God's love letter that can only be written through you. To awaken to your Unique Self is to realize that you ARE the letter, you ARE the message. And we are messengers who forgot the message, because the great esoteric secret is that the message is *us*. *We* are the letter. There is a place in the world of non-love, of un-love, and by being the unique love-intelligence and love-beauty of our own Unique Self, which is the unique letter in the cosmic scroll, we are God's love letter into that reality.

To awaken to Unique Self is to remember, to recover memory; it is to know that who I am is a love letter, that I am a messenger who forgot my message, and that the message is *me*. Oh my God.

How do we love our way to Enlightenment?

So how do we realize, how do we love our way to Enlightenment? How do we become like God? You can't meditate your way to Enlightenment. You can be the best meditator in the world, and you know what you are going to be? A great meditator. Wonderful, it is a good skill. Car mechanics doesn't hurt either; skills are good. You might realize the Spacious One, but that's not why you and I are on this planet. Meditation opens the door, and then, when I meditate, and I meditate on the One and we have to awaken as love letter.

That's not impersonal, it's totally personal. Everything is personal. The whole world, all of reality is personal, it's all a personal love letter, written as you to reality. And you are the only person who can be and deliver that love letter. And so the way we become like God, the way we imitate God and the way we become Divinity itself, Source itself, is to write love letters, writing outrageous love letters.

Guru yoga: its shadow and its transmission of radical love

In India, there is a tradition called guru yoga. Osho, whom Ted was close to, came out of this tradition, which has some shadows in the modern world in that the guru often claimed authority over people. The guru kind of said, or was perceived to say: "You know, I'm perfect, I know how to live, I am going to tell you how to live, listen to me."

So that part of guru yoga we can do without. Because actually every human being is a Unique Self and every human being has authority over the path of their own life and responsibility to be its self-author. I am self-authoring my own life, I am writing my own story. The teacher can guide, the teacher can open a space, the teacher can give transmission of Enlightenment, but ultimately, only every Unique Self has authority over their own life. So the part of guru yoga that claimed more authority than it should, we can do without.

But there is a second dimension of guru yoga that I want to share with you, and that is a very beautiful, holy dimension that exists in the great traditions of India. It is the tradition of the guru, the teacher, embodying radical love, embodying the radical love of the Cosmos that knows your name.

Every minute you are being showered with particles of divine love, Shakti, sustaining the 75 trillions of cells elegantly moving within you in infinite wisdom, in this very moment — 75 trillion cells, each with unique properties, uniquely interacting in a gorgeous overarching, stunning symphony of dancing wholes and parts. Love is not hard to find, love is impossible to avoid. And that love, that insane, wild, ecstatic, crazy love that initiates the Cosmos lives in you as an outrageous love letter.

Writing love letters is seeing with God's eyes

For this practice, find a person — a teacher or a friend, but not a friend that you are naturally in love with, or your partner, or you write love letters to Source, which is a later stage. The good news about the teacher is that if you create the relationship properly, in a way that is pure and clean and totally personal, then it is also totally beyond personal.

The idea is that you practice writing outrageous love letters, wild, ecstatic love letters, and in doing so you say: I am going to open my eyes, I am going to see with the eyes of God. When you do this, it actually enlightens you, it actually changes your entire life, it is outrageous. You actually awaken into the divine force of Love itself, and it changes everything. So the way to be like God is to write outrageous love letters. The way we incarnate God, to actually feel God living and acting as you, is to do what God does. And what does God do? God writes outrageous love letters.

I will tell you something completely wild. That same famous master Akiva said two more things about the Torah, the great book of Hebrew wisdom; the Torah is like the Dao, 'the Way'. He said: "If we had no Ten Commandments, if we had no laws of the Torah, no ethical guidance, if the Torah would never have been given, you could have learned all ethics, all wisdom in the Torah from the Song of Songs."

So if there would be no law, no spiritual philosophy, no meditation dharma, you could learn everything from the Song of Songs, meaning you could learn everything by writing outrageous love letters. You find yourself, find your truth, find your love, find your integrity when you write a love letter, because when you write a love letter, you begin to really see. You begin to see what you really believe, what is really important, what you value, where your commitment is, where your sacrifice is. Writing outrageous love letters, you make the decision to see with the eyes of God.

The blank spaces in love letters

And Akiva said one more thing. Akiva used to read the parchment of the Torah scroll, and the letters of the Torah are written in black ink on a white papyrus parchment, and above every letter there is very fancy calligraphy. Akiva was said to be such a mystical master that he would pour over the Torah, which is one version of God's love letter to humanity, and read and give interpretation of every flourish of calligraphy in every letter, and even of the white space between the letters. Because a love letter is not only what is says, but also what it doesn't say. A love letter is not only the black ink, it is the white space between the black letters, and sometimes the white spaces in a letter are holier than the letter itself. There were two famous masters who would write each other letters and the letters were blank, just a white space, which is even higher than the letter itself.

And sometimes the love letter gets destroyed and things get distorted. Remember that rock group in the mid 80ies, Crosby Stills Nash and Young? They had a song that said: 'So many people died in the name of Christ that I can't believe it all.' Love letters get distorted, then jealousy happens, then it becomes not love but ownership, and love gets twisted and crimes of passion and hatred happen.

So we have to reclaim the original intention of the love letter. We have to reclaim not just the black letters, but the white spaces of pure, radical love in between. We have to be writing love letters to each other.

Dyad practice: speaking in the language of love letters

Write or speak to each other in the language of a love letter, of love poetry. Speak as the lover and write the Song of Songs, as Romeo and Juliet at the balcony, saying: "Oh my God, my beloved, I love you so much, you are so beautiful. I can't bear to be without you. You arouse me, the very sense of your finger sends me into a shivering of bliss. I yearn for a moment in which I might embrace you. I yearn for us to walk together in the meadow, singing songs of God."

Let's find that voice in us, the voice of Solomon who writes outrageous love letters to a thousand wives, who is the voice of the poly-amorous God who writes billions of love letters. You find the voice of the love letter by realizing: I AM the love letter, I have the unique capacity of love-intelligence to see the world with the eyes of love, uniquely, specially, unlike any other.

Find a partner, and first sit together for a while, holding the silence, gently, lovingly. Because if we lose that silence, we lose that voice. When you start, you'll find yourself a little giggling, you want to make a funny joke, because, yo, it is threatening! For to find the voice of the lover, I've got to leave my small self behind. My small self is not a lover; the lover is ecstatic. Now speak a love letter to the Unique Self of your partner, who is a unique expression of love-intelligence and love-beauty. Let each person do the love letter for three minutes, and if the person stops, the other person says: "Is there anything else you might want to say to me?"

This practice is not a psychological practice. This is a mystical, non-dual, enlightened practice of loving your way to Enlightenment, the practice of the Song of Songs, of the mystery of the Cherubs making love above the Ark, from between whom the Divine Voice speaks: the practice of outrageous love letters.

Chahat about Venwoude and its founder Ted Wilson

*V*enwoude has been my home since its foundation, some 25 years ago. Like so many others, I have lived and worked, laughed and cried, played and practiced in this magical community, often described by visitors as 'a warm embrace' - a place where you are welcomed, acknowledged for who you are, and supported in all the ups and downs of your journey of personal and spiritual growth.

There are two things that until today I say from the bottom of my heart:
- Venwoude is the best thing 'that has ever happened to me';
- Venwoude gave me everything I could ever want.

It has supported and held me all the way in realizing the Radiating, Beautiful, Unique Self Mystery that I am.

Over the years Venwoude has become a conduit for liberating, inspiring, evolutionary, cutting-edge insights in the human condition put to the test in our community and translated into hands-on practices to be shared with others through our workshops and trainings.

The combination of an intentional community and a retreat/training center has been such a fruitful, joyous experience.

I have seen people shake off layers and layers of limiting conditioning, emerging as more radiant versions of themselves with a new zest for life. I have seen participants in our programs get inspired and empowered to transform their relationships to deeper levels of commitment, openness and vulnerability. I have seen people come to Venwoude with a yearning for deeper meaning and fulfillment in their life and work, ready to be challenged to play a larger game, learning to contribute their gifts to the world through our leadership trainings. I have seen people find in Venwoude the perfect place for self-inquiry and spiritual awakening, supported by great teachers and the peace and beauty of its human and natural surroundings.

But most of all, and certainly for me personally, I see Venwoude as the ultimate pressure cooker for human relationships and growing consciousness.

Ted Wilson, Venwoude's founder and leader until his death in 2007, my teacher and life-partner of many years, used to say: *'Always make sure to be part of a community where you are truly known, where you can't hide when things get difficult.'*

I want to express once more my deep gratitude to Ted Wilson, for the way he has realized his dream, the formation of this amazing, ongoing community of daring spirits. In some way, now that he is no longer physically with us, I am starting to appreciate even more the full scope of his achievement. Ted's dream was born of his great love and concern for people, with all their vulnerabilities and possibilities. One of the ways this love expressed itself was in his unquenchable thirst for ever-deeper insight in the human condition and the evolution of society.

Ted's focus was always on the unfolding of people's highest potential without shying away from challenging their shadow sides. He honored the unique inner world of every individual, while always emphasizing our relationships with others and our roles within the greater whole. He was just as interested in the dynamics of tribal community living as in ancient and modern spiritual approaches or the latest findings of (neuro)science.

After Ted's death in 2007, interesting and challenging years of reorientation and reshuffling followed. We managed to evolve from a one-teacher/leader community to a Uniquely evolving WE-space held by a dedicated group of core-teachers. We all realize that none of us can or want to do this alone. We need the Unique Expression and Greatness of each one of its' members to make it the wondrous whole that is it.

I had the opportunity of an intense, 20 year long committed partnership on many levels with my teacher, inspiring friend and life-partner Ted Wilson. I made a sacred vow to him to stay with him until death do us part. The journey of Ted leaving his body has been one of the most beautiful, profound and Holy Gifts that was ever given to me.

In all its wondrous ways it opened up numerous new layers and possibilities for me. So many beautiful beings have supported and helped me to deepen my level of understanding, through this whole process. I felt held by many. Next to my dear, dear friends at Venwoude, I experienced Isaac Shapiro & Meike Schuett, Miranda Macpherson and in a later stage JunPo Denis Kelly, lovingly holding my back as I started walking the path without Ted next to me, in this realm. The fact that they were somewhere on this earth, helped me trust myself and gave me courage to experiment in finding my own way!

About Venwoude

*V*enwoude is a long-standing experimental community as well as a training & retreat center in the Netherlands. The Venwoude Training Company offers workshops and trainings for personal growth and leadership, based on Integral principles, grounded in embodiment practices. Founded in 1988 by Ted Wilson and friends, Venwoude has been internationally acknowledged by trainers and modern spiritual teachers from all over the globe as a truly Integral center:

> *"an amazing place where hearts and spirits are*
> *renewed, new visions are born, and humans*
> *become fully the best they can become."*
> DON BECK, AUTHOR OF 'SPIRAL DYNAMICS'

Since Ted Wilson's death in 2007, Venwoude is run by a core group of Venwoude teachers including Chahat Corten.
www.venwoude.nl - http://mysteryschooloflove.com

About the Center for Integral Wisdom

The Center for Integral Wisdom is an Activist Think-Tank dedicated to partnering with leading thinkers and change agents to formulate and articulate a global ethics for a global civilization. We are committed to evolving the source code of human existence based on Integral principles.

Our vehicle is our Activist Think-Tank. At this time we are working on a series of landmark projects in the areas of Conscious Capitalism & Entrepreneurship, Medicine, Climate Restoration, Conscious Society, Eros & Relationship, and Education. We believe that these projects will provide important frameworks for implementing integral strategies on imperative social issues – and will powerfully impact public culture in a significant way. When taken together, these will unfold–for the first time in the modern era–a genuine shared narrative of spirit and a genuine framework for a world spirituality or world philosophy based on Integral principles.

http://www.ievolve.org/ - http://www.marcgafni.com/

Acknowledgement

Gisella Gouverne is a long time dear friend of many of us here at Venwoude. She is a deep Lover of Truth and a true spiritual practitioner in her own right, living at the beautiful island of Lanzarote. Without her depth, dedicated editing skills and enthusiasm this book never would have been born!

Angelica de Bruin, as the fine artist she is, got what I wanted to express and made this awesome piece of art for the cover. Thanks for total support!

And a special 'thank you' to my Sister-Friend Claire Molinard.

Made in the USA
Coppell, TX
04 June 2021